FULLY
HUMAN,
FULLY
DIVINE

FULLY HUMAN, FULLY DIVINE

AN INTERACTIVE CHRISTOLOGY

MICHAEL CASEY
MONK OF TARRAWARRA

Liguori/Triumph
LIGUORI, MISSOURI

Imprimi Potest:
Richard Thibodeau, C.Ss.R.
Provincial, Denver Province
The Redemptorists

Published by Liguori/Triumph
An imprint of Liguori Publications
Liguori, Missouri
www.liguori.org

Library of Congress Cataloging-in-Publication Data

Casey, Michael.
   Fully human, fully divine : an interactive christology / Michael Casey.—1st ed.
      p. cm.
   Includes bibliographical references indexes
   ISBN 978-0-7648-1149-4
   1. Jesus Christ—Person and offices. 2. Catholic Church—Doctrines. I. Title.

BT203.C37   2004
232—dc22   2004044141

Printed in the United States of America
11 10 09 08   6 5 4 3

Contents

Preface

For the past ten years I have been interested in the theme of divinization.[1] According to the teaching of many Church Fathers, particularly those of the East, Christian life consists not so much in being good as in becoming God. The Holy Spirit's work in us goes beyond the reformation of our morals. It is a matter of forming us so that we become sharers in the divine nature and, because of this, capable of fulfilling the impossible demands that the New Testament imposes upon us. We can begin acting as Jesus taught, not because of some titanic effort of will on our part, but because we have become different beings. We have been reborn into a different sphere of existence. We are the products of God's new act of creation. Divinization is God's work and not the result of human striving.

For many of us, this is a bit much to swallow. Morality we can understand and the divine mercy is not beyond our comprehension. It is much harder for us to understand the call and the gift to be as God is. The reason for this, as I explain in the first chapter, is our profound dissatisfaction with the nonperfectibility of our human nature. To be convinced otherwise we have to ponder the central mystery of our faith which is the incarnation of God. What this central mystery of the incarnation means for us is that human nature of itself is of such dignity that it is possible for God to live and act through it. We are not outcasts from the court of heaven, but "noble creatures" created by God for communion with God, not as outsiders but as persons raised to participate intimately in the divine being.

By pondering the humanity of Jesus, we can learn to accept ourselves as human and to admit that by God's grace it is possible for us to live and act as he did—to be perfect, as God our Father is perfect. By going more deeply into the mystery of Jesus, we begin to experience our own inner mystery more intensely.

This book walks on two legs. Half of the chapters are about Jesus, the rest are about us. I call it an interactive Christology, because we have to walk on both legs if we are to make any progress. We grow in understanding Jesus through owning and reflecting upon our own experience, and it is in the light of our deeper awareness of the dynamics of Christ's life that our own life becomes meaningful.

This book needs to be read slowly. I would not consider it excessive if a reading of it stretched out over most of a year. Reading it will probably invite you, as writing it compelled me, to expand your horizons and to look deeper into your own heart. It may be a difficult book for some because I have tried to prevent rapid reading by various means, including the footnotes. Do not be afraid! Sometimes I am trying to surprise you, or wake you up, or pose a puzzle for you. Usually I explain what may seem initially obscure, and often I return to an important point several times in the course of the book, viewing it from different angles. I am aware that what I have written will be a challenge for some readers, but I have made it deliberately so because most of us need deeper and sharper concepts if we are to pass beyond the tepid oversimplifications of our faith that so many today find unsatisfying.

It will quickly become obvious to the reader that the source of much of this book is my personal reading. I have not directly researched my topic but rather summoned forth from memory elements that have been deposited there during several decades. Inevitably, there are overlaps with what I have written elsewhere. Some of these I have been aware of, and others, probably, have slipped in unnoticed by me. The result is a little chaotic, but I hope that it is, at least, a coherent chaos.

The dominant influence on this book have been Bernard of Clairvaux and the other Cistercian Fathers of the twelfth century, their sources, especially Augustine and Gregory, and the early monastic writers such as Evagrius and John Cassian and Benedict. For those unfamiliar with this area, I have included a short introductory note on Cistercian spirituality. I have identified my quotations carefully, to facilitate the task of those who might enjoy chasing up the references. For better or worse, I have translated nearly everything myself, partly to ensure readability and partly to have some consistency of vocabulary. This strategy also enabled me to avoid the bother of seeking permissions for large blocks of material under copyright.

I hope that the struggle to come to grips with the message of this book is of some assistance to each of you as you continue your journey to become fully human and fully divine. At this point, I would like to thank all those who, in the past decade, have encouraged me to keep reflecting on this theme. In particular, I am grateful to Janette Murray and Eileen Slack for their careful scrutiny of the draft text.

MICHAEL CASEY, OCSO
MONK OF TARRAWARRA
JULY 11, 2003

An Introductory Note
on Cistercian Spirituality

The Cistercian tradition of spirituality, of which this book is an expression, began with a renewal of traditional Latin monasticism following the Rule of Saint Benedict at the abbey of Cîteaux (in Latin *Cistercium*) in Burgundy in 1098. Despite its rigor and austerity, the Cistercian reform spread rapidly through Europe in the twelfth and thirteenth centuries, and a particular spirituality developed that was well served by scores of highly literate authors, some of whom have been translated into English and are still reasonably well known today.

The Cistercians were part of a mystical tradition that drew much of its content from the Latin liturgy and from general theological sources. Although its boundaries cannot be defined rigidly, we can discover in the writers of the Cistercian tradition a common "feel," a shared spiritual vocabulary, and some degree of thematic focus. Most of the authors were abbots for whom practical and encouraging teaching was part of their pastoral responsibility. As a result, there is an emphasis both on inner experience and everyday behavior. In contrast to the prevailing pessimism, there is an overriding air of confidence in the mercy of God. The traditional themes of love and Christocentric devotion are omnipresent, but they are treated robustly, with a remarkable absence of sentimentality. The most typical literary genre used by the Cistercians was the *sermo,* or discourse, with an emotive, freewheeling oral idiom and the unabashed intention to draw a response from the readers. The style is consciously lyrical and personal, sometimes uplifting in its poetry, sometimes challenging in its trenchancy. According to a well-known phrase, these authors "renounced everything except the art of writing well." Over the last fifty years, as translations have become available, many people in many different situations have appreciated their contact with these sources.[1]

Following is a list of the mostly monastic authors who have guided the reflections that have issued in this book. They are either Cistercians or Church Fathers who influenced them. Their writings are cited according to the best original text available to me. Many are included in more than three hundred volumes edited in the nineteenth century by J. P. Migne, the *Patrologia Latina* (PL) and the *Patrologia Graeca* (PG). Better editions for some works are found in the series *Corpus Christianorum* (CChr), published by Brepols of Leiden, and in its *Continuatio Mediaevalis* (CCM). The French series *Sources Chrétiennes* (SChr) provides a critical text, translation, and notes. For the works of Saint Bernard of Clairvaux, I use the *Sancti Bernardi Opera* (SBOp). English translations of many medieval Cistercian writers are published by Cistercian Publications, Kalamazoo, Michigan.

Principal Authors Cited

Aelred of Rievaulx (1109–1166)
Aelred was an English recruit who became abbot of the now famously ruined abbey of Rievaulx in Yorkshire. He began to write at the suggestion of Bernard of Clairvaux. His best-known works are *The Mirror of Charity* and *Spiritual Friendship*. He has also composed several series of discourses.

Augustine of Hippo (354–430)

Saint Augustine is one of the most important figures in the development of Latin theology. He was a prolific theological writer and polemicist, but the early Cistercians were influenced by his more personal and spiritual works, particularly his *Confessions* and his commentaries on the Psalms and on the Gospel of John, which were much used in the liturgy.

Baldwin of Forde (d. 1190)

Baldwin was born at Exeter and became successively Abbot of Forde, Bishop of Worcester, and Archbishop of Canterbury. He was a well-read scholar and the *Tractates* he composed as discourses while abbot are profound personal reflections within the context of monastic tradition. His subsequent career as a churchman was ambiguous, to say the least. He took part in Richard I's crusade and died during the siege of Acre.

Beatrice of Nazareth (1200–1267)

Beatrice was a Flemish Cistercian nun whose writings were destroyed after her death to avoid trouble with the Inquisition. By accident, one work survived in the original vernacular: *The Seven Modes of Love*. This mystical treatise reexpresses the doctrine of the twelfth-century Cistercian authors from a feminine standpoint, in a language that is direct, simple, and poetic.

Benedict of Nursia (480–547)

Benedict founded the monasteries of Subiaco and Monte Cassino and wrote a Rule that has been the principal authority of Western monasticism. By encouraging his monks to read widely in Christian literature, he laid the foundation for the establishment of libraries and the flowering of scholarship which are the hallmarks of the Benedictine tradition. Although the Rule is a small text, the writings of those who have followed it and been inspired by it are vast.

Bernard of Clairvaux (1090–1153)

Bernard was the principal exponent of the spirituality of reformed monasticism in the twelfth century. The content of his theology was traditional, but it was reexpressed in a way that spoke strongly to the experience of his contemporaries. His literary style is warm, fluent, and very persuasive. His interventions in public life were not always well advised, but it was as a spiritual master that won him a reputation for holiness.

Evagrius of Pontus (346–399)

Originally from Cappadocia, he was forced by an indiscretion to take refuge in the Egyptian desert. There he became the theologian of early monasticism, combining the teachings of the Desert Fathers with the speculative framework of Origen. His *Praktikos* (a guide for monks) and his *Chapters on Prayer* are both available in English. Through his influence on John Cassian, his teaching and that of Origen became influential in both East and West.

Gregory the Great (540–604)

Gregory was a monk who became Bishop of Rome. He is the author of many works on the spiritual life, including the biography of Saint Benedict. His spirituality was influenced by both Augustine and Cassian, but his style was easier and more universal than theirs. The first books to be copied in the scriptorium of the newly founded Cîteaux after the volumes necessary for the liturgy were the twenty-four books of Gregory's *Moral Exposition on the Book of Job*.

Guerric of Igny (1075–1157)

Guerric of Igny was a Canon at Tournai Cathedral School until entering Clairvaux in 1125, aged about fifty. Thirteen years later he was elected abbot of Igny, a position he held until his death nineteen years later. Guerric is the most accessible of the Cistercian Fathers, his fifty-four *Liturgical*

Sermons traverse much of spiritual terrain experienced in a lifetime, paralleling our own experience with the different seasons of the Church's liturgy.

Helinand of Froidmont (d. after 1229)

Little is known of the life of Helinand. We possess a series of his discourses and some other writings. His doctrine was typically Cistercian and was influenced especially by Bernard and Augustine.

Isaac of Stella (1100–1178)

Born in England, Isaac studied in France. Isaac brought to his monastic career a fine mind and a sound education. His works include fifty-five discourses and other theological works. His doctrine is profound, strongly influenced by Augustine but with some highly personal positions and an engaging style.

Jerome (342–420)

In midlife Jerome became a monk in Bethlehem, devoting the rest of his life to sacred scholarship. His most famous work was the translation of the entire Bible from Hebrew and Greek into Latin. This translation was known as the Vulgate and remained preeminent in the Latin Church for fifteen hundred years after his death. His letters include many expositions of spiritual and monastic topics.

John Cassian (360–435)

Cassian was trained as a monk in the deserts of Egypt under the great Masters who lived there. He later founded twin monasteries near Marseilles and wrote for their benefit his *Institutes* and his *Conferences* (both available in translation). These works expressed in Latin and in a systematic form what he had learned in Egypt, and they were, in particular, a means by which the teachings of Origen and Evagrius reached the West. Cassian influenced Benedict and remained on monastic reading lists for nearly a century.

John of Forde (1145–1214)

John was an English monk, successively abbot of Bindon and Forde. Because of his polished style and sound doctrine, John was one of those chosen to bring to a conclusion Bernard's *Sermons on the Song of Songs*. He wrote a series of 120 discourses for this project, as well as some other works. He was one of the most important witnesses of Cistercian spirituality in the thirteenth century.

Origen of Alexandria (185–254)

Origen was the first major theologian of the spiritual life, interpreting the books of the Bible not only as sources of historical information and doctrine but also as guides to behavior and as incentives to prayer. Some of his philosophical and theological ideas were rejected as heretical, but much of his spiritual doctrine became embedded in subsequent mainline tradition.

William of Saint-Thierry (1085–1148)

William was a significant theologian and Benedictine abbot who was a close friend of Saint Bernard. In 1135, at the age of fifty-five, he resigned his abbacy and became a Cistercian monk at Signy. He has left more than a dozen profound literary works including a *Life of Saint Bernard* and *The Golden Epistle*.

CHAPTER ONE

Divine Humanity

Following the holy Fathers, we all with one voice teach
and profess that our Lord Jesus Christ, the one and same,
is perfect in divinity and perfect in humanity, the same
is genuinely God and genuinely a human being with a
rational soul and a body, the same is consubstantial to
the Father according to divinity and consubstantial to
us according to humanity, like us in all things apart from
sin. The same was begotten from the Father before the
ages according to divinity, for us and for our salvation
begotten in the last days from the Virgin Mary, the God-
bearer (Theotókos), according to humanity.

THE COUNCIL OF CHALCEDON (A.D. 451)

One of the clearest statements of faith concerning Jesus of Nazareth is that simultaneously he is fully divine and fully human: *perfectus Deus, perfectus homo.*[1] The words are easy to say, yet they contain a great mystery. The humanity and divinity of Jesus do not subsist side by side and independent, like chalk and cheese. Instead, humanity and divinity coincide in a single person so that the actions of Jesus are simultaneously the actions of a human being and the actions of God. For this inconceivable conjunction, the ancient theologians coined the unusual term "theandric"—belonging to both God and man. We may choose to be baffled or enchanted by their attempts to find a language to describe this unique situation, but we need to recognize that we are dealing here with a reality that is beyond our immediate experience—one that surpasses our ability to explain it with any certainty. Yet this central mystery of Christian faith is indispensable if we are to have a solid hope for salvation and eternal life. As a consequence, a clear understanding of the wonder of God's enfleshment is necessary if we are to come to grips with the equal wonder of our own divinization. In other words, we cannot hope to build a sound spirituality without a joyful appreciation of the incarnation.

At the time the Gospels were written, the humanity of Jesus seemed self-evident. Jesus of Nazareth was a man who lived and died; he belonged to a particular family, was formed in a particular culture, and was heard, seen, and touched by his contemporaries. Various assessments of the quality of his teaching and the nature of his mission could have been made without going beyond the assertion that Jesus was no more than an extraordinary man. This is the conclusion reached in the contemporary context of benevolent unbelief where Jesus is ranked with other spiritual giants, such as Abraham, the Buddha, Confucius, and Mohammed: All of them are accepted as great historical personages; all of them are religious giants, all of them are undoubtedly human.

In such circumstances, the assertion of Jesus' divinity is an unavoidable stumbling block to those outside the integrity of Christian faith. The New Testament consistently affirms that there was more to Jesus than mere humanity. For the next several centuries, the Church struggled to define this "something more" in terms that did not negate the unyielding monotheism of the Old Testament and yet offered a corrective to those reared in the facile polytheism of late antiquity. To us who do not much care about theory, this slow honing of theological concepts seems tortuous and unnecessary. The Councils of the early Church were passionate about getting it right—they did not want to lose anything of the deep mystery of Jesus' divinity. Unfortunately, the success of this theological evolution brought its own hazards. Once it became accepted among believers that Jesus was fully divine, the opposite error loomed.

The heresy named Docetism is almost as ancient as the Church. It represents a radical doubt about the reality of the humanity of Jesus, preferring to see it as no more than a kindly pretense adopted by God's Son to accommodate himself to our weakened perception. It is like an adult pretending to participate in a doll's tea party; or a visiting abbot, for the purposes of edification, sharing a morsel at the frugal table of the monks, before repairing to a more substantial repast away from the common gaze. Docetism insulates the person of the Word from the drama of human existence. Like most heresies, it means well. It has grasped the important truth that Christ's personhood is untouchable—not limited or defiled by moral weakness, ignorance, or malice. It has failed, however, to appreciate the astounding "condescension" of God, who has created human nature precisely as a receptor of divinity.[2]

Today, when speaking to believers, the Church faces the same challenge it met in refuting Docetism. It is necessary to affirm that there is nothing unseemly in the fullness of divinity dwelling bodily in Christ, because it was with this end in view that human nature was designed. We cannot emphasize enough that the humanity assumed by the Word was not the untainted boldness of Adam before the Fall, but the shriveled vulnerability we all share. As Bernard of Clairvaux reminds us: "Nothing so demonstrates God's positive attitude towards the human race as embracing my humanity. I repeat: *my* humanity, and not the flesh Adam had before the fall. What manifests God's mercy more clearly than that he would embrace such misery?"[3]

The credal statement that Christ is a "perfect" human being

is easily misunderstood. It can make us imagine Jesus as a youthful man with a great body, good teeth, an attractive face—endowed as well with charm, intelligence, and high culture. It is unthinkable for many that the historical Jesus may have been shorter than we, overweight by our standards, middle-aged and bald, with the mind and manners of a first-century Palestinian tradesman. We don't have any reliable data on what Jesus of Nazareth looked like; our personal picture of him probably reveals more about us than about him. Look at the devotional images that people have and ask yourself what these reveal about their owners' unconscious assumptions about the human condition and about themselves.

Much dubious Christology derives from the fact that many of us have trouble accepting the spottiness of our own concrete humanity, and loving what God has thus fashioned. In this scenario, perfect human beings demonstrate their perfection by being as unlike us as possible. And so we picture Jesus in such a way that he becomes a living reproach to humanity rather than its easily recognizable expression. By thus elevating him, we unprofitably abase ourselves and create a distance between us and him that defeats the purpose of the incarnation. God became completely human, omitting nothing that belongs to our nature. He was without sin, because sin does not belong to our nature.

The great mystery of God becoming human remains beyond our unaided comprehension. Our inability to make much progress in understanding Christ is not unrelated to the fact that we have a distorted view of what constitutes humanity. We have failed to liberate ourselves from a rejection of those very elements in our experience that demonstrate that we are human. On the one hand, we are attracted by the tempter's suggestion that we could become "as gods"; on the other, we easily dismiss from awareness anything that reminds us too emphatically that we belong to the earth. Pious people often feel that to assert that divinity and humanity can happily co-habit is to insult God. They are uncomfortable with any portrayal of Jesus that seems "too human." This conclusion results from our interpretation of divinity as that which is not human, that which transcends the human and, perhaps, even that which is antagonistic to humanity. It is hard for us to admit that our flawed humanity is the nearest thing to God on earth and that what gives humanity its special character is precisely its possibility and desire to become ever more like God.[4] If we misunderstand Jesus, it is not only because we have no comprehension of what divinity means; too often we have lost sight of what it means to be human and so we have not given to humanity its rightful place in our "spiritual" life.

If we look within and examine matters closely, we can notice in ourselves many failures in self-acceptance. In our fantasies, for example, we tend to re-create ourselves according to an alternative image and likeness: unconsciously we desire to be younger and more "perfect" than we are, without blemish or wrinkle, without any of the liabilities that stem from our genetic endowment and personal history. Without being fully mindful of it, we may be dissatisfied with what we are. We tend to assume that there is something inherently wrong with us. We think something needs fixing. Ponder, for a moment, some of the uncreative ways by which we manifest our fear of being ourselves and of being seen as we are.

(a) **Disguise:** We use clothing to present an image of ourselves as we want to be perceived. We are scared of being seen as nature made us. Clothes interpose an interpretative barrier between our reality and the eye of the beholder. Uniforms give the wearers an authority they do not have as private persons. Corsets and cosmetics change shapes and colors, and wild hair is tinted and tamed. We prefer bottled aromas to those produced by our own bodies. There are those who pay large sums

for "cosmetic surgery" on the grounds that they feel better if they look better. For some, the worst thing that can happen is that another will see them as they are; the primal curse of Adam and Eve was to be driven by shame to hide themselves with a few leaves and a torrent of words. We know from experience how they felt because we also are sometimes deeply ashamed of what we have become and we also try to hide.

(b) Conformity With the Crowd: To avoid possible ridicule and rejection, we often allow ourselves to merge with others so that we become invisible as individuals. Even our protests against conformity are often expressed as an alternative compliance. Instead of solitary dissent, we wear the uniform of other recognizable nonconformists. Few men and women dare to stand absolutely alone—most need to associate themselves with a group or a movement, whether this association involves adherence either to majority or minority opinions. So often we are afraid to be ourselves: with hypocritical sincerity, we parrot the opinions of others and mimic their positions because we are unsure of the validity of the conclusions that we ourselves generate. By quoting authorities and hiding behind them, we hope to shore up the fragility of a selfhood that is perceived as being under constant threat of extinction and unworthy of continued existence.

(c) Noncommitment: To be intense and passionate can make us targets for other people's sarcasm and scorn. If our beliefs, values, and practices stand out from the common ethos, we may feel vulnerable and exposed to mockery and misunderstanding. Our safe solution is not to allow ourselves to become committed to anything, to keep an "open mind" and a loose grip, tempering our preferences to the prevailing winds of opinion drummed up by the mass media. Even if we are private recusants, we take good care to hide our distinctiveness

under a mask of nonchalance. The result is that we become confused—we lose a strong sense of selfhood, and our personal identity is slowly dissolved into an amorphous blob. Because we do not know who we are, we cannot calculate how far we have strayed from true selfhood into the "region of unlikeness" where boundaries are blurred and no one ever feels fully at home.

(d) "Self-Improvement": There is a dissatisfaction that is creative, that energizes us in realizing our latent potential. This usually involves giving fuller scope to something already present within us, though inactive. Another species of discontent merely drives us to make endless adjustments to the superficial layers of our lives, in the hope of enriching our impoverished self-esteem. A new outfit, a new job, a new house, a new partner, need not necessarily quench the inner sense of inadequacy. Sometimes our efforts to improve our lives do no more than confirm us in our status as consumers, when what we really need is to commit ourselves to operating as generators or producers. The only process of self-improvement that works is one that does not reject what we are to begin with. Any other attitude will lead us to concoct ever-higher goals until eventually we are defeated by their impossibility. Unless we start with what we are, all our projects for growth will collapse, because their foundations were in the shifting sands of delusion and wishful thinking.

If we do not accept our own concrete humanity, we will be less capable of appreciating the humanity of Jesus. Otherwise our love and admiration for him may take the form of refusing to see in him the qualities we experience most in our own humanness. We project onto Jesus a "perfection" that is, in fact, incompatible with humanity. Jesus becomes more like an angel than a man. By thus making the incarnate Word superhuman—one who was only slightly like us—we deny the reality of the self-emptying of the Son of God. We also weaken the link that our common nature gives us. If my humanity was not good enough for Jesus, if his divinity required something better, then how can it be said of him that he was "like us in all things—excluding sin"?

The Fathers of the Church saw the humanity of Christ as a bridge between us and God—but it was a bridge on which traffic passed in both directions. Christ became human so that we might become divine, that we might see and learn from him the infinitude of love of which the human heart is capable.

Divine nature and human nature have begun to be closely united, so that by its intimate communion with what is more divine, human nature itself strives to become divine. This transformation that occurs is not only in Jesus but also in all of those who, in faith, embrace the life Jesus taught, which leads to friendship and communion with God.[5]

The Incarnation makes no sense without the corresponding doctrine of our divinization. God's Son descended so that we might ascend, that we might share the divinity of him who humbled himself to share our humanity.[6] In the Prologue of the Fourth Gospel (Jn 1:1–18), we see enunciated the three prime moments of Salvation History, as understood by the evangelist. "The Word was with God...the Word became flesh...and of his fullness we have all received." Our participation in the life of God is an essential part of the whole project. Our vocation is to be receivers of the fullness of the Word made flesh. The extent of the resultant assimilation is indicated when the evangelist adds "grace for grace." Here he employs the same preposition used in the Greek Bible to denote equivalence: "An eye for an eye and a tooth for a tooth."[7] Everything the Word was by nature, we become by grace.

Each of the believing and reasoning members of Christ

can truly say of themselves that they are what he is—even God's Son, even God. But he is so by nature, they by association (*consortio*). He is so fully; they by participation. Finally, what the Son is by virtue of being begotten, his members are not only by a legal decree or by the giving of a name but by adoption. So it is written: "You have received the Spirit of adoption by which we cry 'Abba, Father.'" It is by this Spirit that they were given power to become children of God so that they may be instructed by him who is the firstborn of many brothers and sisters to say "Our Father."[8]

There is a paradox involved in this doctrine: it is only by becoming divine that we begin to be fully human. Conversely, if we are not divinized we become subhuman—beings whose innate potential has been left unrealized. The dual nature of Christ finds its echo in our own progressive transformation. "Proclaiming Jesus of Nazareth, true God and perfect human being, the Church opens to all people the prospect of being divinized, and thus of becoming more human" (*Gaudium et Spes,* 41).[9]

That the divinization of human beings is a neglected doctrine powerfully reveals the impoverishment of Christian faith that we have allowed to occur. It is easy enough to reduce the mystery of God's plan to a few "metaphysical and ethical crumbs."[10] Such oversimplification does not succeed in making Christianity more accessible to the ordinary person, but simply renders it banal and boring.[11] No wonder exotic religions continue to attract new adherents at the expense of mainstream churches. Religion is not merely a self-serving institution, nor a shaper of events divorced from spiritual reality. Religion is about the transformation of sinful humanity. This miraculous process can be protected and even sustained by ethical constraints and rational discourse, but its essential origin is elsewhere. Faith is a gift from God that catapults itself into human experience with a high degree of unpredictability. Even where there is human intermediacy, faith seems to be caught rather than taught. It is a living flame that springs from an ardent heart and kindles a fire in another. Packaging, public relations, and salesmanship can never be adequate substitutes for the attractive power of a believer who is personally open to God. There is always the danger that theological and moral rectitude (orthodoxy and orthopraxy) loom so large on our religious horizon that relationship with God recedes into the background. In this age, more than any other, we need the divine boldness to affirm that Christianity is not a matter of being good but of becoming God. It is only by the whole-hearted acceptance of the truth that God's Son fully shared our humanity that we can be emboldened to find in him our way towards an intense and transforming relationship with the God who exists beyond human experience.

In approaching this topic, I want to celebrate the weaknesses and limitations that God's Son lovingly accepted for our sake.[12] It is far from asserting that these impairments somehow water down Christ's divinity. It is in the opposite direction that our reflections point. Throughout this book I shall insist that many negative qualities of which we are so desperately ashamed are not impedances to divinization because, mysteriously, they were found also in Christ. It makes no difference whether these perceived liabilities are essential and universal, or historical and private. There is no reason to exclude ourselves from salvation. Only an obstinately loveless heart separates us from God. The quality of our experienced communion with God will be largely shaped by our image of Christ. If we need to reframe our spiritual lives, there is no better means than returning to the Gospels to rediscover the features of Jesus of Nazareth and attempting to reproduce them in our own behavior.[13]

The method to be followed in this book is to ponder different aspects of Jesus' humanity as these are presented in the Gospel of Mark and, then, in alternate chapters, to turn our attention back to ourselves. Jesus' willing embrace of our common humanity invites us to a more profound self-acceptance—an attitude that already puts us on the road to divinization. In this procedure I am doing no more than continuing Mark's own method. Three times in the middle section of the Gospel he presents us with Jesus' predictions of his passion and resurrection. After each of these foreshadowings, he includes teaching about how we must follow the path that Jesus initiated. We will comprehend the mind of Jesus best if, in our own small way, we try to inculcate in our daily lives the values by which he lived and died. We shall better understand the experience of Jesus if we attempt to read our own inner landscape alongside his.

I have chosen to link these reflections to the earliest Gospel because Mark gives us the rawest picture of Jesus and so preserves the Church's most primitive memory of his humanity. In general, the Gospels are in no doubt that Jesus was human—they are more concerned to expound the evidence for his uniqueness: as a prophetic teacher, as a miracle worker, as the fulfillment of Old Testament hopes and promises, and as God's Son. This fundamental purpose is as true of Mark's Gospel as of the other three, but there is a grittiness in this primitive proclamation that was smoothed out by the later evangelists. By isolating Mark's work, we can perhaps glean some insights which are not available when all four Gospels are jumbled together.

Notwithstanding his repeated reference to Jesus as "God's Son,"[14] Mark presents him as a man engaged in many ordinary activities. Jesus seems to have left Nazareth and has a house in Capernaum (Mk 2:1, 3:19–20). His relationship with his family is, at least, ambiguous (Mk 3:21, 3:31–35, 6:1–6).

Although he has loyal followers, he frequently goes off on his own into the wilderness or the mountains (Mk 1:35, 3:13, 6:46). He gets hungry (Mk 11:12), he eats (Mk 2:15–16, 14:3, 14:18–25), sleeps (Mk 4:38), is so busy that he misses meal-times (Mk 3:20, 6:31), shows himself comfortable with plain speaking (Mk 7:18–22), he spits (Mk 7:33, 8:23), he sighs (Mk 7:34, 8:12). Jesus prefers to teach elliptically using parables and images drawn from his own shrewd observation. He experiences the fluctuations of human emotions. He loved (Mk 10:21), he knew anger (Mk 1:41,[15] 3:5), grief (Mk 3:5), compassion (Mk 1:41, 6:34, 8:2), amazement (Mk 6:6), indignation (Mk 10:14). He cursed the fruitless fig tree (Mk 11:14) and cleared out the Temple (Mk 11:15–19). In Gethsemane, he was distressed, upset, and weighed down with sadness (Mk 14:34). The Marcan Jesus is not a wimp; he could be stern (Mk 3:12, 8:30) or strict (Mk 5:43), make demands (Mk 8:34, 10:11–12, 10:21, 10:24–25, 10:42–44), refuse requests (Mk 5:19) and even be insulting (Mk 7:27), and Peter was very severely rebuked (Mk 8:33). Jesus' magisterial style is often indicated by a certain irony in his dealings with his feckless followers: affection and patience with just a tinge of exasperation at their slowness to pick up their message. We note also a complete fearlessness in confronting those who opposed him.

Mark presents Jesus as a tactile man, at home in his body. As a result Jesus is also a companionable person; he moves around in a group, the press of the crowd often creates difficulties and he seems always ready to share the jostling intimacy of a communal meal. And, at the end, he secures his continuing presence among his disciples not by words or thoughts but by the physicality of table fellowship and the charged elements of bread and wine.

Several times, especially in the chorus-endings of the miracle stories, the people are described as being amazed and astounded at what Jesus had done: but this wonderment drew them closer to him; it did not cause them to hang back abashed. Despite Jesus' fame and his attractiveness to common folk, his contemporaries were scarcely overawed by his presence.[16] Mark presents two series of controversies in which Jesus is challenged repeatedly by the religious establishment (Mk 2:1— 3:6 and 11:27—12:37). Nor were his adversaries afraid to insult him, often to his face. He was seen as a blasphemer (Mk 2:7), a table companion with tax collectors and sinners (Mk 2:16), someone who was out of his mind and in need of being restrained (Mk 3:21), possessed by Beelzebul (Mk 3:22), with an unclean spirit (Mk 3:30). He was laughed at (Mk 5:40), his neighbors took offense at him (Mk 6:3). Eventually he was betrayed, arrested, mocked, tortured, and put to death in the firm belief that this would be the end of him.

That Christ assumed human weakness was essential to the mechanics of our salvation: *Caro salutis est cardo*: "The flesh is the hinge of salvation"[17] since "what was not assumed was not healed."[18] Contrary to Gnostic thought, Jesus was not a mystical "universal man" but a specific individual, with a unique genetic signature, composed of particular molecules which were continually being recycled as ours are, subject to spatio-temporal limitation, nurtured in a particular culture. Being what he was meant that many qualities were absent: being male he was not female, being Jewish he was not Irish, being a builder he was not a rocket scientist. A rural villager living in the first century, Jesus probably assumed the earth was flat. If only we can learn to accept the "imperfections" of this "perfect" human being, we might become less discouraged about our own, and perhaps more open to receive the love that God unconditionally shines upon us.

This book is not only about Jesus; it is more directly concerned with us. If God's Son did not disdain to assume our human condition, then nothing that is part of our humanity need cause us to be dismayed. The enfleshment of God encourages us to accept, love, and understand our own carnality, with all its limitations. We are flesh and our journey to spirituality is dogged by difficulties. We do not have to regret this "rocky road" because God has designed us in this way. Jesus is one of us, and by word and example he guides our homeward journey. To us, as to the disciples, he says simply: "Follow me."

CHAPTER TWO

The Recalcitrant Body

The misery of human beings is nothing other than their own disobedience against themselves. Once they were unwilling to do what they could, now what they cannot do what they will. In paradise before sin, even though they were not able to do everything, yet they did not will to do what they could not. In this way they were able to do whatever they willed. Now we recognize in their descendants what the divine Scripture testifies: "Human beings have become like vanity" (Ps 144:4). Who can count how many things they will which they cannot do, because their mind and the flesh which is inferior to it will not obey them, that is, obey their will? Unwilling, their minds are often troubled and their flesh experiences pain, grows old, dies, and suffers other things. We would not have to endure these things unwillingly if our nature were in all things in and every way obedient to our will.

SAINT AUGUSTINE, THE CITY OF GOD, 14, 15 (CCHR 48, P. 437)

Despite the fact that we should know better, most of us are harried by the delusion of human perfectibility. We may not know what exactly it means to be perfect, but we feel secretly aggrieved because whatever perfection is, we are far from it. Each culture creates its own paragons: the warrior, the scholar, the artist, the winner, the doer, the fashion model, the communicator, the scientist, the healer. Some societies reverence the old, seeing in them the embodiments of ancient wisdom and experience. We, on the contrary, seem to hanker after illusory youthfulness, so quickly and so irretrievably left behind. In this instance, as in all others, we do not pause to consider the unreality of the fantasy. What we desire is a harmony of contradictory qualities. We seem to be seeking an innocence that is not inexperienced or naive, and a freedom that is not irresponsible. We do not want to give up the knowledge, power, and accumulated resources that the years have yielded. We forget the confusions, frustrations, and conflicts we encountered in arriving at an adult identity, and we would prefer our hormones to sit down and be quiet. The point is that all these archetypal models are similarly unattainable dreams, ectoplasmic ideals drained of every tiny skerrick of genuine humanity. We can learn from them if we engage them reflectively and critically, but we will make ourselves miserable if we allow them to tyrannize us.

We probably do not admit to being so crassly unrealistic as to take at face value the shallow characters of pulp fiction or the flickering celebrities engineered by the mass media. We have learned to live within our limitations and find comfort there. We do not much mind being nobodies. Yes, we have learned to accept what we think we are, but there is a certain uneasiness surrounding what we do. We may not admit to having many skeletons in the closet, but unless we are colossally repressed, we are compelled to confess that there are patches of our personal history of which we are deeply ashamed. I am not necessarily speaking here of great crimes or sins. What I have in mind are those many occasions in which we have failed to act out of the values and ideals that constitute an essential part of our identity. Or worse still, when we have acted in clear defiance of them. Not that we cherish our ideals less but, mysteriously, we do not carry out the good that we will, but the evil that we do not will is what we do (see Rom 7:19).

There is a dichotomy between what we are and what we do; and this creates an inclination toward a certain muddiness of spirit that Jean-Paul Sartre terms "bad faith."[1] We are often guilty of hiding the truth from ourselves—or hiding ourselves from the truth. We are identifying ourselves with an insubstantial entity that has no reality in the practical world. Our actions shout aloud what we are, but we do not accept the truth of what they proclaim. "It may *seem* that way," we say to our accusers, "but we are different, we are the exceptions."

The beginning of all reflection about who we are needs to take into consideration the dissatisfaction due to the fact that our deeds do not adequately express what we feel within. On the other hand, when others misinterpret our actions we feel a terrific chagrin, but we find it hard to say exactly why they are wrong. Neither our external behavior nor the judgments of others can express who we are. We are like children who lack the language to convey complex emotions; all we can do is stamp our feet in incoherent frustration. We honor eminent artists because they have the skill to externalize the inner movements of the spirit. Yet even the most gifted of them are conscious that no single work can express the lofty vision they have no more than glimpsed. Even great saints cannot fully embody the mystery by which they live. All of them are poor enough specimens of "Christian perfection" if viewed up close. Hagiography does us a disservice when it portrays them without fault or blemish. Correctly, they never see themselves that way.[2]

Readers of literature are conscious of how an otherwise heroic figure can be destroyed by a "tragic flaw." We feel the poignancy of this vulnerability and wish that it could have been otherwise. Yet is it possible? It is all very well for psychologists to track down dangerous and destructive inconsistencies within the very structure of personality, but how on earth do we get rid of them without results even more dire? Sometimes I think that the practice of virtue is a little like old-fashioned whale-bone corsets. The rolls of fat are constrained within rigid limits for the time being, but they are still there. Given half a chance they bounce back to their original fullness. Nothing substantial has changed. I remember hearing the *Imitation of Christ* quoted as saying that if we were to overcome a single vice every year, we would be doing well. Thus spoke an optimist! As an author of books on spirituality, I reproach myself for not practicing what I sincerely preach but, quite frankly, I know that such integrity is beyond me. The truth, however, deserves to be spoken even if those who speak it have not fully succeeded in shaping their own lives according to its considerable demands.

The ancient monks placed before their followers the gospel ideal of purity or undividedness of heart and advocated an extreme asceticism to promote its realization. It was a noble project, worthy of our admiration. The only problem is that it did not and cannot work. Even those hoary heroes of the spiritual life found that, at the end of long decades of spiritual warfare, the most that could be hoped for were occasional brief truces or breathing spaces. Even those who devote their entire lives to living in holiness soon discover that complete integration of energies is impossible while we are still "in the body." This inner conflict means that we remain permanently imperfect and we will pass into eternity imperfect. Our only hope is to rely on the mercy of God. In a sense, this necessary transition from self-reliance to ultimate dependence on God is the meaning and purpose of the struggle. Victory over our vices is an illusory ideal. If our sins are the only things that make us rely on God, then it seems unwise to get rid of them too quickly.

"There is no reason to suppose that an entity built, bottom

up, from the ambitions of individual genes will be harmonious."[3] We were created as a war zone. The battleground where this war is fought is the flesh where, in this present life, spirit and "body" overlap and grapple for supremacy.[4] If we are not to be overwhelmed by the attack of interior and often invisible assailants, we must understand the field of battle.

When I say "body" as distinct from "soul," I am not suggesting that our true selves are somehow distinct from the physical organism, a high-class parasite occupying its space.[5] When I say "body," I am referring to the self insofar as it is conditioned and sustained by that living, changing complex of molecules that fills our clothes and stamps its face on our passports. It is hard to say what part of us is not "body," since intelligence, memory, language, instincts, emotion, and even character have genetic and therefore organic foundations, and can be found to some degree in the "higher" animals. But there are subtle tonalities in our personality that are not "body" and are not found in animals: our occasional rising to free, disinterested choices, mature interpersonal love, our disinterested admiration of nonutilitarian beauty, the passion for abstract thought, poetry and art, laughter and humor, our capacity for mystical experience. These typical human activities are qualitatively different from similar operations in animals, and suggest an exponentially higher integration of the potentialities inherent in organisms not much different from those of animals. Such "higher" functions inhere in the body and make use of its instrumentality, but they belong to the sphere of the spirit. There is a significant point of discontinuity between the organic substratum and spirituality that cannot be bridged from the side of matter alone. A spark is needed before the kindling leaps into flame. Like life itself, humanity makes its appearance as an explosive miracle erupting from the otherwise predictable progress of evolution.

Despite our higher endowments, we remain animals, even

though we are animals with a difference. We cannot function for long without food and drink, rest and shelter. As concerns the rest of our life, what we once thought were willful choices we now recognize as often a matter of blind obedience to instinctual imperatives. Our sexual drive, in particular, seems to go its own way without much reference to our current priorities. To complicate matters further, social and cultural needs can get entangled with instinctual drives in a degree unknown to the animals: power and prestige develop aphrodisiac qualities, insecurity and anxieties may interfere with eating and sleeping patterns, fear and abuse inhibit intelligence. In the lives of high achievers, soaring feats of artistic or "spiritual" creativity are often interspersed with degrading bouts of compulsive sexuality, substance abuse, panic, or depression. Even our "higher" functions can get mixed up with emotions. We can activate bodily reactions of fear, anger, or lust simply by memories, thoughts, and imaginations, though it is often hard to determine whether the thought or the feeling came first. One may well conclude that humans are more the slaves of passion than animals since, even in the absence of body chemicals and external provocations, the mind can simulate and stimulate the organism.

Normal human beings, whose capacity for self-assessment has not been extinguished by repression, feel debased when their "higher" selves are overruled by bodily drives. Especially in the West, guilt intervenes, sometimes magnified out of proportion. We feel ashamed even to think about the possibility that others might find out about our subordination to lower lusts. For people with principles, every contrary indulgence carries a bitter aftertaste and often causes a sad hangover, as the axiom attributed to Galen suggests: *Post coitum omne animal triste.* Furthermore, such physical phenomena as adrenalin surges, sexual reflexes, a roving eye, and the embarrassing tendency to blush are not amenable to normal self-discipline and seem to us public indications of a divided king-dom.[6] It is as though the body is at war with the spirit and we, who take the side of the spirit, may sometimes feel betrayed by our "body." Not only that, we feel unsure that we can ever gain the victory and live in peace.

I often think that the "virtue" attained after decades of practice is no more than the effect of a decline in what the author of the fourteenth-century *Cloud of Unknowing* ter-med our "boisterous bodiliness." In other words, the absence of certain vices may be merely the effect of old age. A few good habits may have contributed slightly to the process, and maybe some change in outward circumstances, but mostly it is a matter of the inner fire slowly consolidating prior to ex-tinguishment.[7] It is almost amusing that the virtues we com-mend so eloquently to the young: self-control, abstemiousness, prudence, quietness, orderliness, are naturally easier in old age than in youth. When the body is young and vigorous, it has other strengths that ought to be utilized without excessive guilt due to the collateral damage that results. Enthusiasm remains a great gift even when it sometimes leads to excess, and spon-taneous generosity is beautiful even if it lacks a full measure of prudence. As for temperance and moderation, these quali-ties can scarcely be learned from others: it is only by person-ally experiencing the unfortunate effects of "too much" and "too little" that we learn to steer a middle course. It is not easy to allow others to learn from their mistakes as we our-selves had to.[8]

If we concentrate too much on our liabilities or the diffi-culty of the task, we may come to the conclusion that our efforts to live an "ordered" or "spiritual" life are futile and illusory. The theory of an orderly spiritual life is fine; it is just that we may feel that, personally, we lack the conviction, strength, or moral fiber to make it work.

On the other hand, the body is real; if we cannot control

its tendencies, why not let them govern us? An inner voice may suggest that instead of trying to impose a rational order on our wild nature, maybe we can find peace by relinquishing the ambition to live in accordance with reason or a sense of a loftier vocation, and letting life take its own course. This desire for a freewheeling existence is naive. We will soon discover that though we abandon spiritual and even moral priorities, there remain many other sources of constraint; our personal tally of inhibitions, public order, financial concerns, other people with different ideas, social and cultural expectations, and even a certain polyvalence among the bodily drives themselves.[9] This renunciation of mind-based living is not freedom; it is just a less conscious form of enslavement. It is like consenting to form an addiction in the hope that once we are hooked we will be relieved of the burden of choice—and thus no longer responsible for the ineffectuality of our attempts to be good. The decision to opt out includes the responsibility for all the consequences of that choice, just as we are deemed guilty of negligent driving if we close our eyes and take our hands off the steering wheel. Freedom is the result of proactive choice, it does not just happen.

To choose not to choose is a way of avoiding the admission that our wills are inherently weak. We can assign the blame to others, to events in our life, even to elements in our own character for which we are not responsible. We can become professional victims. All such behavior is an excuse made in bad faith to avoid effort. It is laziness. The opposite error is to think that we can rise above our lower nature and act like angels; this presumption is the deadly sin of arrogance, *hubris*. There is more going on in our life than the serene governance of sovereign willpower. The will is no more than a puppet king, appearing to give assent but more often than not caving in before the imperious demands of underground forces. We are caught in the middle. We are like a sailboat running before a storm. Our power of direction is reduced to 5 percent or less, but we can use that remnant of control not to confront the storm head-on, but to lessen its buffeting and survive. Maybe we can even steal some of its force to arrive at a more favorable situation from which recovery is possible and so reach our destination. If we deny the storm exists or refuse to take any countermeasures, our boat will certainly capsize.

To live a spiritual life means accepting and honoring the "body" and being prepared to negotiate. This realistic willingness to compromise involves recognizing that the "body" has its own distinctive ambitions, and not overestimating our own capacity to subsume or subordinate these. To believe that there is some system whereby we can be liberated from the otherness of the flesh is a surefire recipe for disillusionment. You may be determined to live an ordered life, but you will find it very hard to maintain that orderliness twenty-four hours a day for the rest of your life. Better, though it is a bitter pill for our pride to swallow, to walk the golden path of honorable compromise and attempt some damage control.

There is a persistent recalcitrance about our bodies that is significant enough to confront directly. The body and its drives subvert any attempt to derive norms of behavior from reasonable beliefs and values. "I take pleasure in the law of God in my inner self, but I see another law in my members that makes war against the law of the mind making me captive to the law of sin that inhabits my members" (Rom 7:22–23). This is not a case of my individual deviancy, but it is the universal human condition. This native inconsistency is like a preexisting state of sin, innate wickedness lurking at the door (as it is described in Genesis 4:7), ready to erupt in actions that are more or less deliberately malicious. "If we say that we have no sin we deceive ourselves and the truth is not in us" (1 Jn 1:8). We exist in a state of disorientation because the "body" aspect of our being seems to prevent our living constantly in the presence of

God. "So long as we are at home in the body we are away
from the Lord" (2 Cor 5:6).[10]

It is foolish to expect that the Ten Commandments are de-
scriptive of the way that anybody lives. I may have so far avoided
murder and the grosser forms of idolatry, but this scarcely en-
titles me to claim immunity from all prosecution—especially
since there is little evidence that the positive values underlying
the prohibitions have been implemented in my life. Jesus
pointed out that to be honest we have to extend the definition
of malice beyond deeds to thoughts and words (Mt 5:21–48),
and that leaves us all tarnished. To underline my culpability,
Saint James insists that to fail to keep the law in a single point
is to be guilty of violating the law as a whole (see James 2:10).

There is, as it were, an inherent defect in human nature
that is the foundation of all personal sinfulness. Instead of
having recourse to the hallowed expression "original sin," I
can explore the concept of "eschatological sin."[11] We necessarily fall short of the glory of God (Rom 3:23). We have not
yet become what we are to be in the future. In strict terms this
defect has nothing to do with the past, although that is how
the Bible and much of tradition portrays it. It has much to do
with our present and our future. We are inherently imperfect
because our journey is not over. We are still on the road. Humanity is, perhaps, like a blossom on a fruit tree, pretty enough
to look at but useless to eat. It has not yet appeared what we
shall be (1 Jn 3:2), but our transformation presupposes that a
natural or physical body dies and that a spiritual body rises
(1 Cor 15:44).

That happy outcome is, if you are reading this, still in the
future. In the meantime, a lot of patience is needed to cope
with the ambiguities that every life enfolds. We may not enjoy
being likened to whitened sepulchers (Mt 23:27), but the fact
is that most of us are careful to present as better than we know
ourselves to be.[12] Rare indeed are those whose goodness is

totally transparent; most of the saints seem readier to recognize themselves among the ranks of the sinners. Paradoxically, it is probably true that those who do not have a concern to hide their sinfulness from others embody more visibly the inner beauty of true holiness.

The consciousness of sin and its verbal expression are an essential part of any realistic spirituality. "Behold I was conceived in wickedness and when my mother conceived me I was a sinner" (Ps 51:5). Cultivating this global sense of sin because of our distance from God, our inner fragmentation and our unwillingness to accept what we are is more worthwhile than compiling an exhaustive shopping list of all the things we have done wrong. Who can count them, and who can discern where malice begins and where weakness and ignorance end? Perhaps certain actions can serve as symbols of our total need for God's mercy, but the mystery of our resistance to God can never be reduced to particular actions or habits that are within our power to reform. Counting sins, grading them, and assigning appropriate penalties or remedies is probably the fastest way to lose any sense of the inherent horror of sin as the rejection of the God of love.[13]

Meanwhile, on a more positive note, we can consider investing some effort in reducing the level of inconsistency, in training the body to keep to reasonable limits, so that it does not disturb our commitment to "spiritual" goals and our devotion to God. Accepting our ordinariness and trying to live peaceably with others will demand of us a great deal of bodily and emotional self-governance. I am convinced that, for many people, rigorous fasting and penitential practices do not have much to contribute to this process, especially when they are self-designed and self-implemented. Much more effective in bringing us to the frontiers of the spirit is the patient and proactive acceptance of illness, pain, old age, loneliness, rejection, and deprivation. It is true, however, that all physical suffering

tends to heighten our body-sense so that we become more
acutely aware of its ultimate impotence. "The flesh yields no
profit," says Jesus (Jn 6:63), and Saint Paul confirms this when
he states unequivocally, "I know that what is good does not
dwell in me, that is, in my flesh" (Rom 7:18). The discovery
of the boundaries of carnal possibilities can motivate us to
look beyond visible reality and to God, but they can also lead
to disillusionment and despair. Random attempts to punish,
tame, or train the body are unlikely to have enduring efficacy
in bringing us closer to God because they attempt to deal with
the symptoms of our rebellion from God without recognizing
its causes. In moderation and under direction, however, bodily
disciplines may be useful both in forming good habits and in
reminding us of how far from the ideal we have strayed. But
wise spiritual directors will always be on the lookout for secret and more suspect motivations.

Perhaps we need to think more creatively about involving
the body in personal prayer—through physical stillness, a concern for posture, and a sense of place, putting on or taking off
clothes, the engagement of the senses.[14] The spiritual life is
not so interior that it can survive without the body. We will
find from our own experience that appropriate places, sounds,
and words can induce in us a deep peace that quickly leads to
a tranquil receptiveness to spiritual mysteries. We also discover that there is no universal, surefire prescription for what
will work. Our bodies are different and so the manner in which
they provide access to the spirit differs from one individual to
another.

Above all, zeal for harnessing the body's potential for spirituality will prompt us not to underestimate the potency of the
body corporate. The body is not merely our area of subjectivity; it is also the basis of intersubjectivity. It is by the agency of
the body that we enter into and sustain relations with others.
This also is a war zone, as we shall see in a later chapter.

CHAPTER THREE

Jesus Baptized in the Jordan

It happened in those days that Jesus came from Nazareth in Galilee and was baptized in the Jordan by John. Immediately as he was coming up out of the water, he saw the skies split and the Spirit coming down like a dove on him. And there was a voice from the sky saying, "You are my son, you are loved by me, in you I find my delight."

MARK 1:9–11

Karl Rahner wrote somewhere that the modern (that is, mid-twentieth century) version of the ancient ecclesiastical discipline of public penance was lining up in the pews outside a confessional—to be seen by all as needing absolution. Imagine what a stir it would make if Jesus were to be found among these self-avowed sinners! The theologians would try to haul him out of the line. The confessor would, no doubt, implore him as Matthew's Baptist did, "I have need to be absolved by you and do you come to me?" But, if the Gospels are to be believed, Jesus would be undeterred by the outraged sensitivities of his admirers.

Mark tells us clearly that John's baptism was a public and external rite that expressed an inner change of disposition, and had as its effect the remission of sins (Mk 1:4). It was a penitential act. Those who were baptized confessed their sins without dissimulation or denial in the presence of a vast multitude. The extraordinary thing, on which all the Gospels are agreed, is that Jesus took part in this ritual cleansing.

The liturgy of the eastern Churches explodes in wonder at this impossible paradox. Even in the more prosaic West, the Latin antiphons for the feast of the Lord's baptism register amazement by lyrical texts and untypical melodies that leap through large intervals. If the incident strikes us as unremarkable, maybe it is because our senses have been dulled by habituation, so that nothing in the Gospels has the power to surprise us or stimulate us to deeper reflection. Mark begins his version of the Good News with the proclamation that Jesus is the Messiah and (at least in some ancient manuscripts) God's Son (1:1). Yet the Messiah's first public appearance is as a participant in a communal ritual intended to remit sins. What does it mean that Jesus numbered himself among sinners?

There can be no doubt that the purpose of Jesus' life was to deal with sin. Indeed, where a sense of sin is lacking, Christology inevitably is impoverished. "God was in Christ reconciling the world to God, not taking account of their transgressions" (2 Cor 5:19). The meaning of Christ's life is to be found in his breaking down the barriers of resistance and hostility that separate us from God, and which find concrete expression in our inhumanity to one another.

The question to be asked is *how* Jesus neutralized the intimate malice inherent in wills divorced from love. We are free agents who have voluntarily withheld love. In our own particular microcosm, we have said "No," and it is not at all obvious how the actions of another can reverse that firm negation. It is not sufficient to say that Jesus by his teaching showed us the right way to live. The "mystery of lawlessness" (2 Thess 2:7) is far deeper than mere morality. It cannot be cured by guidance and exhortation. What Jesus has done is to destroy the universal inevitability of sin and to offer us a freedom that is both prevention and cure. The New Testament gives us many avenues to explore the "work" that Jesus did for us. Christ was a priest, offering sacrifice to atone for our sins. He redeemed us, that is, he bought us back from slavery and set us free. He "justified" us, declaring us innocent although we were guilty. He gave his life for us. In all of these approaches, we can see that Jesus has accomplished some unique and irreversible good on our behalf. But perhaps we do not quite understand *how* it all happened.

A key word in understanding the mechanics of salvation is *koinonia*, commonness, communion. Both the act and the effect of sin consist in alienation from God—and from others and from ourselves. We are like the willfully stupid sheep that separates itself from the flock and is on the point of perishing in the wilderness. We cannot return because we are both stubborn and ignorant, and each moment our weakness grows. If we cannot go to the mountain, then the mountain must come to us. Jesus comes seeking the lost and infirm, carrying us back to the flock on his sacred shoulders, reestablishing us in the communion that willfully we had ruptured.

Sin is self-perpetuating isolation; salvation consists in the restoration of relationship. The initiative comes from God—our own efforts are futile. We cannot go to God, so God's Son has to "visit" us where we are, and to "remain" with us while the homeward journey is completed. This embrace involves accepting us in our weakness, blindness, and malice, bearing with our fallen state and neutralizing its effects by supporting us, guiding us, and sweetening our bitterness with unconditional love. It is by the direct action of Christ that we are restored to communion.

We can see this reconciliation taking place in so many Gospel incidents—what happened to those people in Palestine is a pattern that is repeated invisibly throughout the centuries. Jesus comes to search out and save what is lost, to heal what is diseased, to restore us to the table of friendship and to transform our lives in the pattern of his own. In Mark's narrative of Jesus' baptism, the same dynamic is operative.

Baptism is a physical rite; it takes place in the territory of the body. Jesus, having assumed our flesh with its universal liabilities, accepts its weakness as his own and seeks a remedy. He empties himself of dignity and joins the sinful throng. He becomes humbler yet, and lays aside his garments to stand exposed to all in his bare humanity. He submits to John and is entombed beneath the waters of the Jordan. Let us pause at this point.

I would like to suggest that, at this moment, Jesus was acutely burdened by sin—not as the result of any personal transgression or deflection of will, but simply as the effect of his total solidarity with sinful humanity. He instinctively understood the reality of what recently has been termed "social sin."[1] Each of us carries the burden of every sin that is committed: by every sin we are diminished and infected. This being so, it is possible as a member of a sinful race lovingly and gratuitously to accept responsibility for sins to which one has never given personal assent.[2] We become guilty, as it were, by association. We who have unknowingly profited from the injustices of our ancestors are not totally powerless to undo the harm. We can own the evil. We can apologize. We can make amends. We can try to minimize the ongoing pain caused by reprehensible actions. More than this, we can choose out of love to absorb within ourselves the venom of others' sin and experience its effects and, thereby, to shield them from the consequences of their own actions. Throughout his career, this is what Jesus did. Because he reached out to the marginalized, he was charged with consorting with sinners. It is true; he manifests a preferential option for the wayward. He saves them by sharing their lot. Not primarily by preaching or teaching but by being for them Immanuel, the God of compassion in their midst. He is the one whose heart was large enough to make him want to carry the sin of the entire world.[3] "Surely he has borne our infirmities and carried our diseases…the Lord has laid on him the iniquity of us all" (Isa 53:4–6). Saint Paul goes even further in a statement that sets theologians aflutter: "For our sake, God made [Christ] who knew no sin to be sin so that in him we might become the righteousness of God" (2 Cor 5:21).

The loving completeness of Jesus' self-emptying and its significance for us are celebrated in one of the letters of Saint Antony of Egypt (d. 356).

> Therefore, also, Jesus emptied himself of His glory, and took upon himself the form of a slave, that His bondage might make us free. And we were foolish, and in our foolishness committed every kind of evil; and again He took the form of foolishness, that by His foolishness we might be made wise. And we were become poor, and in our poverty lacked all virtue; therefore again He took the form of our poverty, that by His poverty He might make us rich in all wisdom and understanding. Not only this, but He even took upon himself the form of our weakness, that by His weakness He might make us strong. And He became obedient to the Father in everything unto death, even the death of the cross, that by His death He might work the resurrection of us all, that he might destroy the power of death, that is, the devil.[4]

Jesus' consciousness of sin coincides with his sense of total solidarity with all humanity. "I am a human being and I consider myself no alien to anything human"—even sin.[5] For us, humanity begins at—and in some cases never goes far beyond—the level of self-absorbed individualism. The frontiers between self and nonself are rigidly defined and systematically policed. It takes a lifetime of growth for us to begin to breach these borders and to feel a limited communion with others. With the Son of God it seems to have been otherwise. Without speculating about how Jesus of Nazareth conceptualized it, his self-awareness was always and necessarily an awareness of self-in-relation—fundamentally with the Father in the Spirit but, as a consequence of the Incarnation, also inclusive of all humanity, sinful though it is.

The many references in the Gospels to the prayer of Jesus need not be interpreted in terms of a detached communion of Jesus with his Father. The long nights spent in prayer may well have been fraught with an urgent awareness of human weakness. "Because I am human, I am weak. Because I am weak, I pray."[6] The prayer of Jesus constantly reflects his dual nature: it is the expression of divine intimacy and, at the same time, it is shaped by human fragility, fragmentation, and inconstancy. When Jesus prays, it is in a voice that is familiar to us all. He prays as one of us. His prayer is also ours.

In assuming our humanity, Jesus embraces it in its totality. In coming to baptism, it is as our representative and the mysterious bearer of our collective guilt that Jesus seeks forgiveness.[7] The weight far exceeds the capacity of any one man to sustain it and so he sinks beneath the surface of the waters into the darkness. First-century Jews were not an aquatic people. Wild water was something to be feared, representing, as it did, the power of unreasoning chaos. To be baptized involved yielding control. As Jonah's canticle indicates, to be swallowed up by the waters was a departure from the ordered universe for the deeper unknown, where no solid footing could be found and life itself was not guaranteed. The symbol of baptism was more than a ritual cleansing of the stain of sin. Past identity must be dissolved.[8] When Jesus comes to be baptized, bearing our sins, it was in full awareness of the radical separation sin has created between us and God. Here, as at

Calvary, he enters into the depths of that estrangement. His immersion in the Jordan is an anticipation of his death.[9]

It is as Adam that Christ enters the Jordan. In him the whole human race stands before God "confessing their sins." Jesus does not attempt to save himself but freely submits to the human instrument whom God has provided. There is no denial of guilt, no avoidance of shame, no dissimulation. It is a moment of honest avowal of the true state of fallen humanity. Civilization and all its trappings are mere sham. Bare, fragile flesh teetering on the brink of extinction is the only reality. In Luke's account Jesus is praying (Lk 3:21). What words would this Adam use to express the universal longing for the restoration of the broken relationship with God? Perhaps with our voice he utters the words he later praised, "O God, be merciful to me a sinner" (Lk 18:13).

The moment of descent has ended and Jesus begins to rise. Implicit in this rising is the death-resurrection motif of the paschal mystery. Immediately the miraculous occurs. At the very moment when the death-dealing power of sin seems triumphant, God intervenes. Several things happen. The bowl of the sky is split so that there is no longer any obstacle to traffic between heaven and earth.[10] The Spirit descends upon the new Adam, and Jesus is addressed by a voice from heaven, affirming that he is God's much-loved Son in whom his Father finds delight.

These words, unlike those used at the Transfiguration (Mk 9:7), are addressed to Jesus; there is no indication in Mark that the Baptist heard them. They are a statement that in Jesus the whole sinful mass of humanity is accepted and loved by God. At this moment, Jesus knows something that nobody else knows. Despite sin, there is no separation between heaven and earth, between God and the human family. Nothing, not even sin, can separate us from the love of God. Even while we are sinners, God's love is undeviating and God's Spirit acts tirelessly. This message will be the kernel of Jesus' preaching, and is still today the Good News which seems both scandalous and foolish to those outside the community of faith (1 Cor 1:23).

The timing of this revelation is important. Jesus, the bearer of our sins, does not encounter divine coldness. As the representative of our sinful race he is received with prodigal tenderness. This is the surprise that God has in store for us. As long as the consciousness of sin is kept at bay, the gratuity of God's love is undiscovered. To believe that we are without sin (or at least without really shameful sins) is to falsify our relationship with God.[11] Somehow, in a manner that baffles human intelligence, it is the awareness of our concrete need for forgiveness that provides us with access to the mercy of God. It is only through the door of mercy that we can find access to the heart of God.

The early Church understood that Jesus' public mission began with his baptism (Acts 1:22). Something happened at that point to transform a village builder into a herald of God's kingdom. At this sacred moment, it became clear to Jesus that the relationship he experienced with the Father in the Spirit was accessible to all. But the doorway to this relationship was the recognition and acceptance of the truth that he is one with us. All that he did was for our sake and for our salvation.

When Jesus came to John the Baptist, he was a long way from home. We may understand him as being on a journey of self-discovery—seeking means of putting into words his subliminal sense of God's presence and of solidarity with all. In a typical gesture of humility, he embraces communion with sinners and thereby experiences the truth of what Saint John would later write, "Even though our hearts condemn us, God is greater than our hearts" (1 Jn 3:20). God knows all and yet love is undiminished.

CHAPTER FOUR

Ourselves and Others

You are mistaken, O holy Thomas, you are mistaken if you hope to see the Lord apart from the college of the Apostles. Truth does not like corners; private places do not please him. Truth stands in the midst: discipline, the common life, common pursuits—these are the things which bring him pleasure.

BERNARD OF CLAIRVAUX, *SERMON FOR THE ASCENSION* 6.13

T he humanity of Jesus is a mirror in which we can see our own humanness more clearly. Because he was willing to be associated with us sinners, we find in him no trace of that attitude typified by the Pharisee who congratulated himself on not being "like the rest of men." We are saved by the initiative of Jesus who incorporates within himself the totality of our race. We are lost to the extent that we exclude ourselves from this all-inclusive embrace. We cannot hope to receive salvation if our relationship with God is confined to a private chapel from which others are excluded.

Community corrects individual defects; what one lacks another supplies, what one breaks another repairs, when we fall there is someone to lift us up (Eccl 4:10). One body has many irreconcilable inconsistencies; many bodies together neutralize their potential to do harm. In a choir of thousands, who notices if I sing a wrong note? Perseverance in the spiritual life demands a community of common faith—with one heart and

one mind, as Saint Luke says in Acts 4:32. This sharing involves not only the universal Church but also a more local-
ized communion. The closer and more complete the bonding,
the more effective such community will be in bringing us to
that simplicity of heart in which God becomes progressively
more apparent. But beware! The "body" will rebel against
any curtailment of its autonomy or any limitation placed on
the fulfillment of its desires. Quickly the mind will join the
chorus of dissent to rationalize the resistance to any authority
outside the self.

An overdeveloped sense of our own distinctness easily leads
us to undervalue the rights of others. We do this, for example,
when we attempt to make exclusively our own what, of its
nature, is common to all. At its most obvious level, this happens when we amass material goods at the expense of others,
or exploit for our own advantage an earth intended for the
equal benefit of all. Associated with this acquisitiveness are
the various forms of violence with which we seek to enforce
the fulfillment of our desires. Their side effects are the anger
and sadness which are aroused when our wishes are opposed
or frustrated. Most of the common catalog of sins involves a
rupture of human community due to exaltation of self. As
Saint Paul says, "The whole Law is summed up in a single
commandment: 'You shall love your neighbor as yourself'"
(Gal 5:14). Before the violation of the neighbor's rights there
is a deeper manifestation of sin—a pernicious self-centeredness
and, beyond that, isolation from the brothers and sisters God
has given us. To overvalue our own rights necessarily distorts
our judgment of the relative importance of the rights of others.

This is the vice that ancient monastic authors term
singularitas. Singularity is a cutting oneself off from the community by denying to others the right to have any input about
the way I live, to make any demands on me, or to restrict my

freedom in any way. Since the late nineteenth century, the word "solipsism" has been used in philosophical circles to denote a radical subjectivism which emphasizes personal experience to the extent that other people have only secondary significance. In Vatican documents and in many European languages, this tendency is termed "individualism." The word has some currency though, perhaps, it would be better avoided in English if a better substitute were available. In our language, the term is more often assumed to refer to no more than appropriate self-assertion, or a fondness for doing things one's own way or harmless eccentricity. However, when Pope John Paul II denounces individualism as something that "leads to the denial of the very idea of human nature" he was speaking about something far more destructive than mere personal style. Real individualism tramples on the rights of others, destroys the foundation of human community, and inevitably corrupts and saddens those who embrace it.

By "individualism" is meant the systematic denial of the social component of human nature; it is a practical rejection of the truth that we belong together. It is a self-perpetuating isolation that refuses to take others as being of equal dignity and so reduces them to objects to be exploited—albeit unconsciously. Individualism is manifested in my overvaluing my own roles, rights, and opinions, refusing to others any input about the conduct of my life. Philosophers distinguish between two words often used interchangeably: "person" and "individual." Being a person means being in relationship with others; being an individual indicates that we are distinct, separate, and unique. Personhood involves the possibility of self-transcendence through interaction and cooperation with others; individuality merely asserts that we are different. In Western cultures, it is easier to give effective priority to individuality over relationship, and it has been so since the sixteenth century.

Individualism isolates us from the herd and makes us competitive. Instead of reaching a goal in association with others, I seek to go it alone, to get ahead of others. "Sibling rivalry" has been around since Cain and Abel and, if it seems a mild enough deficiency, perhaps we should remind ourselves of the outcome of the biblical story: envy quickly becomes all-consuming and leads to violence. In ventures of limited scope and duration, individualists can accept the importance of attempting to create a "team spirit," but in the business of life itself they are mostly on their own. They can combine with others on a short-term basis to fill in a particular area of their dream's mosaic, but they do not have a collective dream that is all-embracing. Too often in Western culture, the realization of our own hopes seems possible only by frustrating those of others. For me to win the gold medal of my dreams, others need to compete with me and lose.

Individualism allowed to run rampant within me progressively produces a hard edge of perfectionism: an inconsiderateness that demands much of others because I am dissatisfied with my own level of achievement. Any evidence of weakness or failure in myself must be denied, repressed, and projected onto others. Individualism begins to reshape the person into an anti-image of God. "If someone lives only for himself and for his own advantage, and considers only himself in deciding how he should live, we can understand [this entire life] to be wholly dark."[1]

Five particular characteristics of this monster begin to assert themselves in different degrees as time goes by. I shall exaggerate their features a little to help us to see them more clearly. Consequently, our own experience may be less intense than what follows.

(a) *Isolation:* Sometimes a feeling of loneliness can be a positive reality. It alerts us to our need for companionship and motivates us to make the effort to build bridges to other people. This subjective loneliness is, therefore, an advance on what we might term "objective" loneliness. In this sorry situation, persons live isolated and self-contained lives, without any real attachment to others. They see to the fulfillment of their own needs and pleasures, exploiting others where necessary. Popularity, parties, and promiscuity cannot protect such people from deep affective frustration, yet often they are unaware of their situation and unable or unwilling to take steps to remedy it. Affectivity atrophies to the point where its absence is no longer noticed, and the saying "No man is an island" appears ludicrous.

A particular form that loneliness takes is the refusal to be bound by any of the ties that are constitutive of human community. At one level, this reluctance means a failure to accept that every group will have its own rules and roles, structures, and expectations. To be constantly recalcitrant regarding the harmless particularities by which members of a group identify themselves to one another inevitably leads to disaffiliation. Because one refuses to be an insider, one becomes an outsider. The triviality of such coded signals as the pronunciation of particular words or the adoption of particular rituals should not be mistaken as indicating diminished importance. Often they transmit a serious symbolic meaning. Those who do not enter into bonding behaviors progressively exclude themselves from belonging.

I can become lonely through too much independence or by wanting to avoid any sense of indebtedness to others. Asking for help and receiving it is an important way of building a relationship and breaking down interpersonal barriers. If I design my life in such a way that I do not need anyone else, I am almost certainly condemning myself to an affective wilderness. If I am reluctant to rely on anybody else, it means that I have to see to everything myself. The price I pay for wanting to remain permanently in control is that I am never "off duty." Since I have no confidence that others will take care of my interests, my life will tend to be rigidly overcontrolled, lacking lightness, spontaneity, and a spirit of play. Trusting others is liberating; failing to trust binds me up and leads to misery.

Not being a willing member of a group means that I become a stranger to the kind of inspiration, encouragement, support, and guidance that come from participation in group activities. I may undertake schemes and projects of my own, but without the interest of others these often stagnate or are blocked so that our perseverance in them is problematic. If I am somewhat involved in spirituality or religion, as an individualist I will not be comfortable with the corporate ideals of the Church and tend to drift towards the fringes. My participation in liturgy will be passive—if not passive-aggressive. For pious individualists, spirituality is a matter of a personal relationship with God, without too much input or feedback from others. Verticality without horizontality.

(b) Sadness: Happiness is often the gift of other people: too much of my own company can lead to sadness. I hesitate to use the term "depression," because what I am referring to is more the result of personal choices than an illness due to biochemistry or trauma. Because I have barred access to the heart in order to secure my personal freedom, I may find myself deprived of that unconditional support, affirmation, and good cheer that is never self-generating. The sense of being understood and accepted by another human being has been excluded. In attempting to make myself invulnerable, I have put myself beyond the healing touch of love. Effectively, I have chosen lifelessness or misery, though I may not be fully aware either of the choice nor of its effect.

(c) Meaninglessness: The will for meaning collapses when I make myself the measure of all things. A certain hardness creeps into my assessment of people and events that leaves little room for sentiment. To give meaning to something outside myself is to give it power over me, and I am determined never to yield control of my life. This apparent strength robs me of the feedback that I can receive from others that makes life and all its efforts worthwhile. I can admire myself all day in a mirror, but a sincere compliment means much more. I can achieve my goals brilliantly and yet all seems hollow. We can find meaning in life only to the extent that we give something outside ourselves the power to command us. In individualism there is no commitment to anything outside ourselves; the enthusiasm and commitment we find in others is beyond comprehension.

(d) Arrogance: Arrogance stems from a deep dissatisfaction with being ordinary. It leads us to treat others in a way that prevents their asserting any equality with us.[2] Some people act this way out of deep feelings of insecurity, but individualists sincerely believe that they are not like the rest of humanity. An essential part of their defensive system is to make it uncomfortable for others to approach them. Predictably enough, most of us do not like being gratuitously treated as inferiors and so we tend to stay away from such people or to handle them with care.

(e) Delusion: Individualism is such a powerful denial of human nature that it is constantly being eroded by experience, life, and other people. To protect itself, it has to put a spin on the data of experience and weave delusional fantasies that cocoon it further in a self-sustaining world of unreality. There is a fundamental untruth about such a life, and whatever superficial charm masks its evil intent, it has as its ultimate effect the diminishment and even the destruction of the person. There

are many paths by which we can flee from the truth of our being and, to remain intact, the individualist has to make use of most of them. We may be amused or affronted by their actions, but we should be in no doubt that this is more than immature narcissism. Individualism negates the essential purpose of human existence.

The physical body is our sole means of forming the corporate body. Our existence is collective insofar as we are physically close, exchanging information, doing things together, and bonding. The recalcitrant resistance our bodies offer to being ruled by our "higher" functions is replicated in our reluctance to yield our autonomy to the nonself whether this nonself is conceived as other persons, a collectivity, tradition, conventional wisdom, or accepted standards and structures.

God's Son precipitated himself into the midst of a humanity divided by thousands of years of warfare and apartheid. Jesus took upon himself our human fragmentation with all its consequences. In his baptism, he experienced that he was part of a conflicted humanity and by his "body" he was away from God, yet his relationship with the Father remained effective.

CHAPTER FIVE

Jesus Tempted

Immediately the Spirit drove [Jesus] out into the wilderness. And he was in the wilderness for forty days being tempted by Satan, and he was with the wild beasts and the angels were serving him.

MARK 1:12–13

Mark's accounts of Jesus' baptism and temptation are located in Judea and are outside the geographical scheme he has used to order his Gospel. This choice of location may be because they represent two permanent polarities in Jesus' consciousness; on the one hand, a sense of affinity with God and sonship, on the other, a prevoluntary resistance to God that will come to the fore especially in Gethsemane. What we see in the temptation of Jesus are the same two elements that figured in his baptism: divine sonship and solidarity with a sinful people.

The temptation narrative in the earliest Gospel needs to be read in its own right and not confused with the details Matthew and Luke added to suit their particular approaches. The two later Gospels present the incident as an unequal debate between Jesus and the devil. Jesus easily demonstrates that, unlike Israel, he is God's faithful Son, not diverted from his mission by appetite, acquisitiveness, vainglory, or presumption. In Matthew, the tempter is vanquished and leaves Jesus, at which point the angels come to minister to the victor (Mt

4:11). In Luke, the devil departs but only temporarily; he or she will return when the Hour comes (Lk 4:13).

Mark's account is extremely brief and follows quickly on the narrative of Jesus' baptism. In an astonishing reversal of mood, Mark tells us the Spirit immediately and violently drives God's Son out into the desert—the same verb is used for the expulsion of demons. The effect of being admitted to divine intimacy is instant dispatch to the front line of battle. I wonder whether the evangelist is trying to communicate to us that sonship and temptation are two faces of the same reality. For Jesus to live consciously as God's Son here on earth necessarily involves a struggle. To be with God means contending with "Satan" who, in the Old Testament, is not so much an anti-God but the adversary of humanity, the recorder and accuser of every misdeed. Our relationship with God is constantly undermined by the querulous murmur, "How can you be a child of God when you do such things?" The loving trust to which we give the name "faith" allows us to affirm God's unconditional love without denying or dissimulating our own guilt. We are, at the same time, sinners and yet saved: *simul peccator et iustus*. Jesus is the one who, par excellence, holds together these contrary realities.

Far from being shielded from this perennial contest, Jesus is flung into it. The desert is a harsh and hostile environment, considered in the ancient world to be the lair of demons. This is no romantic escape into golden sunsets and solitary meditation, but a life-and-death struggle, the outcome of which is not immediately clear to the principal protagonist. Nor are the ground rules of such warfare predictably defined. Temptation rarely involves a full frontal assault on God by open rebellion. More often it is a matter of putting God's claims on hold "temporarily," while other more immediate matters are attended to. God is absent from our awareness: we are directly concerned with other more tangible realities, like food, possessions, and reputation. We can agree, therefore, that the expanded version of Matthew and Luke was a fair interpretation of Mark's laconic statement. However, we know from our own experience that the overt content of temptation is often irrelevant, just as eating the fruit in Eden was a harmless enough activity. The malign meaning of the forbidden act is to be found in its capacity to rupture the relationship of dependence on God. An action becomes a sin when it is a means of claiming an inappropriate autonomy. Jesus' lifelong temptation was to allow his mission from the Father to become dormant, to do nothing, to spare himself the trouble, to take life easy. What a sin of omission would that have been!

The Fourth Gospel makes it abundantly clear that Jesus' chosen priority in life was the accomplishment of the Father's plan of salvation: "My food is that I do the will of the One who sent me and bring his work to completion" (Jn 4:34). But it was not a choice lightly made. "Now my very soul trembles. Should I say, 'Father, save me from this Hour'? No, it is for this that I have come to this Hour" (Jn 12:27). Let us not water down the heroism of Jesus in pursuing his mission. Perhaps he experienced something of the seething inner duality of which Jeremiah wrote:

> O Lord, you have seduced me,
> and I was seduced;
> You have overpowered me,
> for you are stronger than I...
> If I say, "I will not mention him,
> or speak any more in his name,"
> then within me there is
> something like a burning fire
> shut up within my bones.
> I am weary with holding it in,
> and I cannot.
>
> JEREMIAH 20:7, 9

From the outside, Jesus' life may have appeared to be like a boat tranquilly holding its course in midstream. The inner reality, as suggested by this narrative, was more energetic—a constant battle to hold the rudder steady against contrary currents, with much vigilance and heavy toil necessary to avoid coming aground.

Mark does not say that Jesus undertook a fast, but simply that he was being tempted by Satan for forty days, a standard period of time in many Old Testament narratives. To engage in fasting or any other practice of self-inflicted suffering does not involve yielding up control. The measure of pain can be moderated at will. This is not how the temptation is portrayed in Mark. Jesus has no choice in the matter. To be picked up by the hair, like Habakkuk (Dan 14:36), and dumped in a hostile environment means separation from the sphere of reasonable expectations, and being totally at the behest of whatever chaotic forces inhabit that place. Mark is appealing to our mythic imagination in an effort to avert the conclusion that Jesus' life was all plain sailing. Jesus' solidarity with fallen humanity was not merely a polite gesture that left him untouched by the storms that so often make our life a misery. More practically, Mark is preparing us for the fact that Christian life, likewise, is "not without persecutions" (Mk 10:30). We have been called to follow the one who was tempted in the desert, and we must expect that fidelity to our life of discipleship will involve us in substantial and sometimes earth-shuddering struggles.

The modality of temptation is further specified by the addition of two other elements: "He was with the wild beasts and the angels were serving him." Notice that in Mark the two relationships coexist, whereas in Matthew the angels make their appearance only when the temptation terminates. This sentence could easily be understood as a statement of Jesus' dual nature, with one foot in the world of the beasts and the other in that of the angels. In a different sense, it is an enigmatic summary of the human condition. It is this duality that precipitates human beings into the dilemma of temptation. We are simultaneously beastly and angelic but we are not mere beasts, and we are certainly not angels.[1] What we become depends on a self-determining act of will. But to which polarity will our voluntary assent incline? We can recognize something of our authentic selves in both extremes. Tragedy results when we single-heartedly pursue one and, in the process, are obliged to deny the other. The result is falsity. To be true to ourselves we have to maintain our links with both the physical world and the spiritual world, and there is no simple formula that can give us lifelong balance. We have to adapt as we go. And mostly we do it badly.

Mark is telling us, perhaps, that Jesus was not immune from the wavering inconstancy of the human nature. "He was tempted in all things like us, but did not sin" (Heb 4:15). The condition was the same as ours, the struggle was similar; only the outcome was different. "He is able to help those who are tempted because he himself suffered temptation" (Heb 2:18). Viewed from a certain aspect, our earthly sojourn is a prolonged experience of being alienated from our spiritual home.[2] If we allow ourselves to be conformed to our ambience, we progressively lose our identity as God's children and become alienated from our deep selves. We are in the wilderness in the sense that the only way we can be true to what we are is to resist the deformative influences that surround us.

Perhaps the wild beasts of the desert had intrapsychic echoes. In dreams and in phobias, animals often serve as covert representations of unrecognized wild streaks in our own makeup. Because we are too fearful to acknowledge the presence of violent urges that run counter to the willed direction of our lives, we refuse them admittance into consciousness.[3] The result is that we tend to project onto exterior agents the desire to rebel against conformity that is being generated secretly in our own hearts. In such an interpretation, Jesus being with the beasts is another way of saying that he experienced interiorly some instinctual revulsion at the mission he had received.

Another way of interpreting the reference to beasts and angels is to read the text in terms of security and trust. Jesus was under constant threat in a physically harsh environment where roaring lions were abroad, looking for someone to eat. As a man outside his familiar territory, Jesus must have experienced prudent fear for his safety. No doubt questions concerning food and shelter came to consciousness, and a prayer for daily bread must have been often on his lips. Ancient Israel was sustained by manna and miraculous quails, but no such portents attended the testing of God's Son. Yet he was mysteriously protected and sustained, as Mark expresses it, by the ministry of angels. The overcoming of such existential fear by an ample trust in Providence will later figure largely in his preaching to the people.

Did the sojourn in the desert begin as a sort of retreat, like Saint Paul's withdrawal into Arabia (Gal 1:17)? Impelled by an urgent need to unravel the significance of the gift he had been given, Jesus sequestered himself and wandered off alone to ponder. What transpired came as a surprise. Instead of a receptive soul, full of gratitude, the Good News encountered resistance. In ordinary existence, many distractions divide our attention so that we can live happily enough with ambiguity for long periods; conflicts often sort themselves out in time. There are no distractions in the desert; the stark opposition between human sin and the divine presence cannot be eased away from sight; it must be endured. Because the magnitude of divine mercy utterly transcends human experience, it casts doubt upon the rational constructs by which we live. Reason retaliates. The tempter's whisper bade Jesus' query whether there ever could be peace between the holiness of God and the insistent unrighteousness of humankind. Was not this sense of harmony he experienced a delusion? Why should he take upon himself the unlikely mission of proclaiming God's bounty— an activity that will certainly result in suffering and probable failure?

Perhaps, as Matthew and Luke suggest, Jesus drew solace and insight from the Hebrew Scriptures as he wrestled with such counter-suggestions to his call and commission. Certainly, as the later narrative of Gethsemane will insist, his time of temptation was also a time of prayer. And as the will begins to give a more comprehensive assent to the Father's plan, peace returns. And, it seems, Jesus reappears on the public stage.

Once temptation had been overcome, Jesus continued to defer to John. When Herod removed the Baptist from the scene, Jesus succeeded him. His initial preaching had two principal points (Mk 1:14–15). The first was proclamation: the time is now. The second was exhortation: be changed at the level of heart and mind, as John had preached before him. Jesus offers a new meaning for *metánoia*: it is a matter of trusting in the Good News that God and sinful humanity are reconciled.

The preaching of Jesus flows from his vanquishing of temptation. Within the microcosm of his own psyche, Jesus experienced the encounter of the prodigal Father and his errant child. As the representative of our sinful race, he had heeded the call to return despite the massed voices of discouragement and despair. Jesus understood that his moment of enlightenment was of significance for the entire human family; the history of our race would never be the same. It is in this sense that he proclaimed the Hour of fulfillment in which God's rule over humanity has become accessible.

CHAPTER SIX

Contrary Imaginations

Watch out for the double soul for it is an evil and sense-less thing, and it uproots many from the faith, even those who are very firm and faithful. For this double soul is a daughter of the devil and does great harm to the ser-vants of God. Despise the double soul and overcome it with everything that you do. Be clothed in a faith that is strong and powerful, since faith promises all things and achieves all things. The double soul, however, cannot believe even in itself and frustrates all the work that it attempts. See then that faith comes from above, from the Lord, and has great power. The double soul, on the other hand, is an earthly spirit which comes from the devil and is powerless. You, therefore, must serve faith which has power and keep away from the double soul which is impotent. Thus you will live to God, and so to will all who think thus.

THE SHEPHERD OF HERMAS, 39

W hen the remnant of Judah returned from exile in Babylon, the people brought with them a certain openness to the phi-losophy of their Persian liberators. For the followers of Zarathustra, the experience we know as temptation was due to the fact that, within human consciousness, two contrary thoughts or spirits permanently cohabit; one good and one bad. This approach to the dynamics of wrongful choice was adopted and adapted by postexilic rabbis who spoke of two tendencies or inclinations (*yetserim*) resident in the human heart (see Gen 6:5, 8:21). This notion evolved on the fringes of Judaism during the intertestamental period. We find clear statements of it in *The Testaments of the Twelve Patriarchs*[1] and in the Dead Sea scrolls.[2] The double soul, manifested in doubt, hesitation, wavering faith, and inconstancy, is the result of choosing to follow now one, now the other, side of this inherent polarity.

Only one strand of New Testament doctrine maintained contact with contemporary Jewish thought and produced a Christian version of this theme.[3] Apart from the well-known passage in Romans 7, we find an example of such teaching in the Epistle of Saint James.

> If any of you lacks wisdom, let them ask for it from the God who gives to all simply and without reproach and it will be given to them. Let them ask in faith, without hesitating, for those who hesitate are like waves on the sea blown by the wind and tossed about. Someone like that cannot expect to receive anything from the Lord, for anyone who has a double soul will be unstable in all their ways.
>
> JAMES 1:5–8

The state of a person with a double soul (διψυχία) is characterized by inner division, the experience of conflict in decision making and in frequent inconsistency of external actions with inner aspirations. It is expressed by tepidity and mediocrity, a desire to find easy compromises and an avoidance of commitment. A double soul leads to a double life, which the person attempts to cover up by repression, rationalization, and lies. In philosophical terms, it is the preference for multiplicity over unity; morally, it is the failure to subordinate the passions to personal choice; at the level of feeling, it leads to a long-term sense of malaise and a crippling sense that something is seriously wrong.

We find many examples of this idea in early Jewish-Christian writers.[4] Often it is associated with the theme of the "two ways" between which a choice must be made, one road leads to life, the other to death.[5] There is, within this tradition, a persistent tendency to personalize these options or tendencies. Eventually, the evil principle was subdivided into a host of resident spirits, each identified with a particular vice. Although this tendency was more common in the immediate post-apostolic period, we still find traces of it in the late twelfth century,[6] and perhaps even in our own times.[7] The tradition seems to have lasted longest around Alexandria. This is how Hermas describes the situation.

> Hear then concerning faith. There are two angels within the human being: one belonging to righteousness and one belonging to iniquity....The angel of righteousness is delicate and modest, meek and even-tempered. When she rises up in your heart, immediately she speaks with you about righteousness, self-control, and every just work and glorious virtue. Look now at the angel of iniquity. First of all, she is sharp-tempered, sour, and unreasonable. When she rises up in your heart, you will know of her presence from her works....When sharp temper falls on you or bitterness, know that she is in you. The same holds for the desire for many things to do, for foolish expenditure on feasting and drinking, for all sorts of superfluous luxuries, sexual desire, wealth, pride, boastfulness, and all this sort of thing. When these things rise in your heart, know that the angel of iniquity is in you.[8]

Origen of Alexandria also makes use of the same imagery.

It is certain that at the moment of sinning it is the
Spirit of Evil that is acting in the heart of the sinner.
Immediately he gains access and, when we welcome
him by evil thoughts and evil desires, the Holy Spirit is
quite saddened and thus under constraint, if I may thus
express myself.[9]

To me it seems that the number of counter-virtues is
infinite since there are spirits [assigned] to each human being, promoting in them the different kinds of
sins. For example, there is a spirit of fornication and
one of anger. There is another spirit of avarice and
another of pride. So if it happens that people are upset
by all or even many evils, they may be reckoned to
have within themselves many hostile spirits. These spirits are present to each person in plurality because individuals do not have single vices or commit single sins,
but everyone seems to give entrance to many....I do
not consider the Prince of Fornication to be a single
spirit, for there are innumerable spirits who present
themselves for this duty—different ones for each person—fighting under that leader and urging them towards these sorts of sins.[10]

What we see emerging is a certain sophistication regarding the dynamics of temptation. Evagrius of Pontus, a disciple
of Origen, will take the process a step forward by speaking
not about indwelling spirits but about "thoughts" arising
within in apparent independence from the will. "It is not within
our power to determine whether these thoughts disturb the
soul or not. But it is within our power to choose whether or not
we prolong them and whether they arouse passion or not."[11]

Having established the universal presence of such disturbing thoughts, Evagrius attempts to explore their specific content. All are alike in seeking to undermine our faith in the gift of God and to divide, distort, and diminish the love that the Spirit has poured into our hearts. This generalized resistance to God uses different strategies according to our changing circumstances. The names Evagrius gives to these unholy thoughts may be unfamiliar, but we all have experience of the realities to which the names refer.[12] Evagrius is particularly interested in the mental processes and rationalizations which precede the external acts. We can say, perhaps, that the following are the principal kinds of temptations that human beings commonly experience.

*(a) **Gluttony:*** At first sight this seems to be such a gross tendency that most of us would prefer to ignore it. A glutton is not merely a person with a gargantuan appetite for food, as we are reminded by the presence around us of eating disorders, widespread obesity, and various forms of substance abuse (alcohol, nicotine, narcotics, and pharmaceuticals). Gluttony is a matter of ingesting for its own sake without reference to the health of the body which the satisfaction of appetite is intended to assure. According to the classical definition, gluttony is evident when a person eats an excessive amount of food or eats with excessive eagerness or too fastidiously. When our appetite for food comes adrift from our conscious priorities and seems to have a life of its own, then, whether we like the term or not, we are being tempted to gluttony.

*(b) **Fornication:*** Yes, we all accept that it is easy for the sexual instinct to rule and ruin our lives. This is probably why "immorality" is often taken to mean "sexual immorality." It is a difficult area to survey because of the shame that characterizes it. The frontiers between what is voluntary and what is

not are often fuzzy. Evagrius notes a difference of opinion about whether lust begins at a mental or physiological level. What is certain, however, is that our innate sexual tendency can be aroused not only by internally generated thoughts, but by external stimuli acting directly upon us or through the agency of the imagination.

(c) Avarice: Nobody likes to be considered a miser and so, often enough, we are slow to recognize this tendency in ourselves, and meanwhile we can be unconsciously controlled by it. In a consumerist society where worth is measured by possessions, avarice becomes a virtue. Many of us are ashamed of our lack of wealth, manifested by our inability to join the race to compete in "conspicuous consumption." We can never have enough money. How many crimes are committed to get more money, even when the perpetrators are already rich! Often avarice is disguised as legitimate concern for our security in later life, as Evagrius records.[13] Such preoccupation with our own welfare goes against one of the most frequently attested themes of New Testament moral teaching: the avoidance of anxious care.[14] Furthermore, there is a competitiveness involved in the acquisition of wealth; the goods that we accumulate are unavailable to others—as a result, many relationships are threatened and countries plunged into war as a result of disputes over material assets.

(d) Sadness: We do not always see sadness as a source of temptation, preferring to see it as sorrow or grief caused by external events and/or depression due to psychochemical imbalance. While it is true that in particular situations sadness is an appropriate or unavoidable response, there are other situations in which our movement into misery is deliberate and malign. More than a century before Evagrius, Hermas had written that sadness "is the most evil of spirits and the one most to be

avoided by the servants of God."[15] What is at issue here is more than a melancholy disposition. Sadness is the opposite of vitality; it is best understood in terms of a lack of energy for appropriate good works. One who is sad is self-preoccupied, unable to be adventurous, or to reach out to others because of a lack of nerve or verve, or from an excess of caution or timidity. Indeed sadness and fear are often intermingled, producing a chronic condition of self-doubt and a reluctance to move beyond familiar parameters. Like acedia, the end result of falling under the influence of this temptation is a failure to interact creatively with the real world.

(e) Anger: Many of us confuse anger and aggression. Anger is a feeling or a passion which registers our negative response in a particular situation; aggression is a learned strategy for dealing with that feeling by attacking somebody else. Most of us disapprove of aggression and do not permit ourselves to participate in it overtly. Meanwhile, we do not always recognize the anger that is within us, and so we express it in different and often invisible ways. Passive aggression, detraction, involvement in campaigns are just a few of the ways that anger can control our life without our being fully aware of it. We attempt to excuse our negativity by seeing it as a response to others' anger, but often it is our own anger that we are projecting onto them. According to Evagrius, "Anger is the sharpest passion,"[16] and "Anger has a greater need of a remedy than lust."[17]

(f) Acedia: The vice of noninvolvement is said to be endemic in the Western world.[18] The acediac is a person without commitment, who lives in a world characterized by mobility, passive entertainment, self-indulgence, and the effective denial of the validity of any external claim. It is a butterfly existence, lived only for the moment, supported by a comprehensive fantasy

life that cocoons the individual from any undesired intrusion. Acedia is the temptation to live as though life had no ultimate meaning or purpose, to eat, drink, and be merry, and to give no thought to tomorrow. Sometimes it is identified with sloth or idleness, but that is only the external face of an attitude marked by chronic withdrawal from reality into the more comfortable zone of uncommitted and free-floating fantasy. The temptation to acedia is an invitation to abandon involvement and leave the pangs of creativity to others.

(g) Vainglory: We are all inclined to do things that win us the approbation of others—in fact most teaching depends on approval as a means to stimulate progress. It is only when our need of affirmation and praise becomes so paramount that it swamps other considerations that it is dangerous. In such a situation we are tempted to do or omit to do something not because of its intrinsic rightness or wrongness, but according to whether it is likely to win us the applause or blame of bystanders. Sometimes we will be led into crime for fear of being rejected by our companions. On other occasions, it will be a matter of doing "the right deed for the wrong reason" so that our improper motivation changes an otherwise worthy act into something self-serving. We become like politicians jumping through hoops in order to gain a few extra votes on polling day. In the process, morality is sidelined. Evagrius notes that vainglory often besieges the virtuous; many secretly hope that their good works will become widely known.[19] This desire to be called holy before being so runs counter to Jesus' teaching in the Sermon on the Mount where the right hand is encouraged to hide its virtuous deed from the left (Mt 6:3). When we are overcome by the temptation to vainglory, all our virtuous efforts are degraded and our actions become tainted. The disinterested altruism of which only the human species is capable has disappeared from our conduct and has been replaced by a

spirit of cunning and exploitation. We are using good deeds to extract approval from others. Just as reproof disproportionately upsets us, so praise puffs us up and makes us arrogant; when such self-exaltation become habitual, we are led into the most fundamental of all the temptations: pride.

(h) **Pride:** If humility is a matter of accepting our own earthiness[20] then, as its opposite, pride must be constituted by denying our dependence on God and severing the bonds that express our solidarity with other human beings. The prideful mind is dominated by thoughts that undermine every relationship. The signs of pride correspond closely with the attitude of individualism which was the subject of an earlier chapter. It is not mere arrogance or haughtiness—both of which demand an audience. This vice is a tendency to such radical self-containment that others are shut out. Mercifully, pride is a tendency rather than an accomplished fact; it secretly nibbles away at the integrity of our good actions; usually it does not devour them entirely. Evagrius is in no doubt about the malign outcome of a life lived under the banner of pride. "Anger and sadness follow in its footsteps and the final evil is derangement of mind, mad raving, and visions of a crowd of demons in the air."[21]

Whatever we may think about the anthropology inherent in an approach such as that of Evagrius, we have to admit that its strength is that it offers an explanation for the everyday experience of temptation. The persistence of imaginations that run contrary to the conscious direction of our lives troubles us, and the evenness of our life is upset by the chemical, physiological, and emotional reactions they trigger. Cumulatively, such temptations engender a degree of mental confusion. Why is it not possible for us to live the kind of life to which we aspire? Why are our ideals so consistently betrayed by our own minds and bodies? Is all desire for a spiritual life merely delusion?

Here it has to be stated clearly that from the teaching of Evagrius and John Cassian it is clear that although such thoughts come from deep inside us, and the fantasies in which they are inserted draw their energy from events in our real life, they are to be viewed as fundamentally unwilled. They are prevoluntary. For good people, it can be a consolation to know that the cause of such contrary imaginations is not personal choice, but an outcome of human nature. There is a certain amount of evidence to suggest that the more strongly we seek to channel our energies in a particular direction, the fiercer the temptation. One who is merely drifting knows no such torment. George Bernard Shaw is reputed to have quipped, "The only way to get rid of temptation is to give into it." Temptation is often the sign of a good life. It is almost as though our nature is protesting against the stern discipline we attempt to impose on it. "The demon of fornication...attacks more violently those who practice continence."[22] It seems that only when a person attempts to live chastely and piously that sexual fantasies and blasphemous thoughts attack.[23] The bottom line is that, mindful that Jesus was also tempted, we should not blame ourselves for being tempted, nor should we ignore or deny our vulnerability. Instead, we should accept temptation as a normal part of a good life and try to develop tactics that minimize the influence that our particular demons have over us. Beyond that, we have to recognize that with us temptation is not always unsuccessful. As Saint Augustine notes, sometimes even the strong yield to temptation.[24]

The typology of temptation which Evagrius adapted from traditional teaching reminds us that temptation assumes different forms. It varies from person to person and from one stage of life to another. We need to remember, however, that there is but a single purpose in all temptation: to separate us from God. Here are some features which are common to all temptations.

(a) Temptations occur only in areas of weakness and vulnerability. An option becomes a temptation only when there is a good chance that we be strongly attracted to it. Knowing our current weaknesses gives us some opportunity to take preventative measures.

(b) Temptations habitually catch us unprepared and wrong-footed. Weeks may pass without a ripple, then suddenly a thought will come to mind that quickly propels us towards acts that hitherto seemed unlikely. We will often notice, for example, that temptation seems to have easier access when we are tired, disgruntled, or otherwise in bad form.

(c) Temptation is often very clever in that we are sometimes allowed to make some progress against one vice and, while we are celebrating, the doorway to another is left unguarded. While claiming victory over lust, we are defeated by anger. While reducing anger we succumb to sadness.

(d) Temptation can become so undramatic that it passes by unnoticed. By repeated action, vice becomes a habit or even a sort of addiction. At this stage, we easily slip into sin without much of a struggle. This is the most dangerous form of temptation precisely because it troubles us the least.

(e) Luther referred to reason as "the devil's whore." In this scenario, we are led away from the simplicity of the Gospel by twisted thinking that blurs the distinction between good and evil. Once we find ourselves in a situation where sin has taken root in our lives, we often resort to rationalization to convince ourselves that everything is OK. We deny the overt content of our acts, we repress our feelings of guilt, and we often embark on a campaign to prove to ourselves that what we are doing is perfectly natural, morally neutral, harmless, and, in any case, unavoidable.

(*f*) One of the gravest effects of temptation is that it often causes us to lose heart. Our failures in the struggle against lust or gluttony lead us into sadness. We doubt our own worth, we lose our nerve, and we may be so overcome by defeatism and despair that we give up the struggle altogether.

(*g*) Oddly, temptation and failure can coexist with genuine spiritual progress and attainment. Often, as we grow in spiritual self-awareness, we become more conscious of the compromises that hitherto have been comfortably accommodated in our habitual behavior. We are disturbed by these and try to do something about them; but casting off a long-familiar pattern of behavior is not so easy.[25] In this way, progress ushers in a phase of struggle and defeat. We may be surprised that our desire for God increases apace with our perceived failures.

(*h*) It is important for us not to identify with our temptations. They may say a lot about us, but they do not tell the whole story. "Even though our hearts condemn us, God who knows all is greater than our hearts" (1 Jn 3:20). "God knows of what we are made, he remembers that we are dust" (Ps 103:14). Temptation tends to make us forget that, fallen though we are, we are greatly loved by God. There is more to us than our sin. Especially in time of temptation and afterwards, we need to avoid attributing to God the reproach we direct at ourselves.

(*i*) To speak to another about the specifics of our temptations greatly reduces their power over us.[26] Such conversation not only subverts any incipient process of repression, but it also offers us the benefit of a wiser counsel which reinforces a more positive identity. Our confidant may not always be able to offer us spectacular advice, but we will find the experience of being listened to and heard is itself a source of comfort and new resolution.

(j) At some stages, we may find it useful to explore with another person the fantasies which fuel our temptations. Usually these are not entirely bad. Often enough, the images that shout for our attention point to neglected elements in our own depths. To make contact with these images through active imagination or in some other way can help us to get out of the trough of temptation and set us more firmly on paths that lead to progress.

(k) When there is a case of obsessive thoughts that are probably due to some deep repression, it is probably best to bite the bullet and seek the help of a therapist. It may take time and effort but the freedom and lightness of being that can result will make everything worthwhile. Without some professional attention, we will be burdened unnecessarily, maybe for the rest of our life.

Jesus was tempted and so the fact of our own temptation should occasion no surprise. What disguises the ordinariness of the experience is that the content of temptations is woven out of the fabric of our life so that we think that what we are experiencing is unique to ourselves. The first stage in resisting temptation is being aware of it. We will become aware of it only when we are not afraid to own that, being human, temptation is our lot. And we will probably pray with greater fervor the petition of the Lord's Prayer, "Lead us not into temptation."

CHAPTER SEVEN

Jesus Exorcises

And they entered Capernaum. And immediately he was teaching in the synagogue on the Sabbaths. And they were struck at his teaching, since he was teaching like one with power and not like the scribes. And immediately there was in the synagogue a person with an unclean spirit. And he cried out, "What is there between us and you Jesus Nazarene? Have you come to destroy us? I know who you are, the holy one of God." And Jesus rebuked him saying, "Be silent!" and "Come out of him!" And the unclean spirit shook [the man] and shouting with a loud voice came out of him. And all were amazed, so that they asked one another saying, "What is this thing? This is a new teaching with power so that he subdues unclean spirits and they obey him." And the story of this immediately [circulated] everywhere in the whole region of Galilee.

MARK 1:21–28

Mark's first account of a miracle shows the effect of Jesus' struggle with Satan in the wilderness. From this solitary contest, Jesus emerges as one with power to expel demons and restore those troubled by them to the "cleanness" of full humanity. The demons, for their part, recognize in Jesus "the holy one of God" whose power they could not withstand. This title should astonish us. In the Old Testament, holiness is the prerogative of God. By extension, it is a quality associated with objects or persons consecrated to the worship of God and is set forth as an ideal for the people called by God's name; "Be holy as I, the LORD your God, am holy" (Lev 19:3). It is almost never used of human beings.[1] It is used of Jesus relatively rarely in the New Testament.[2] By the mouth of the demon, Mark presents Jesus as one so powerfully under the influence of the Spirit that he constitutes a threat to the continuance of demonic dominance. Because Jesus belongs to the sphere of God, his mission is not dependent on human reception; it operates of its own irresistible power. Nor is his sphere of activity confined within the boundaries of God's people. As we shall see in the course of Mark's unfolding narrative, the hegemony of God which Jesus proclaims is universal, even reaching beyond and below the limits of human awareness and control. If we can hear in our imagination the thundering stampede of the two thousand Gerasene swine as they plunge into the abyss (Mk 5:13), then we will have some idea of the power of holiness which Jesus represents. Thus the words of the demon turn this encounter into more than a routine exorcism. It becomes the raw confrontation of holiness and uncleanness, in which the will of "the holy one of God" prevails.

Yet Mark's account is worth pondering for more reasons than that. The evangelist has interwoven two themes which, at first sight may seem to us unconnected. The power which Jesus manifests in expelling the demon is deployed through the instrumentality of his teaching.[3] The reaction of the bystanders to the miracle is significant: "What is this thing? This is a new teaching with power so that he subdues unclean spirits and they obey him." Not a word is said about the beneficiary of the miracle, nor about the exorcism itself: the wonderment is directed towards the "new teaching" which is a channel of contact with the wonder-worker and mysteriously purifies those whom it touches from demonic influence.

Power on this earth and in this age is habitually oppressive (Mk 10:42). Jesus' contemporaries suffered under the power of the Romans, their puppet kings and tax collectors, the power of the priestly oligarchy and that of the village "experts" in religious matters. They were familiar with the hostile force of nature expressed in floods and storms and earthquakes. They witnessed for themselves the violence of demons, and they dreaded the appearance of ghosts (Mk 6:49–50). Ordinary people fervently hoped that the powers would keep their distance. Here, however, was something new. The power which Jesus communicates to his hearers is benign; it is a force for liberation, not a new level of enslavement. The "teaching" whereby the change is effected is more than a plethora of pious platitudes or a body of moral exhortation; mysteriously and wonderfully, it has the inherent capacity to bring forth good fruit automatically—αὐτομάτη—as we read in Mark 4:28.

Much more than the other evangelists, Mark is at pains to present Jesus as a teacher. Jesus' perception of the most urgent need of the people is that they lack care and guidance. "And going out [Jesus] saw a large crowd, and he felt compassion for them, because they were like sheep that have no shepherd; and he began to teach them many things" (Mk 6:34). In the parallel account of Matthew 14:14, the outcome of Jesus' compassion was that he healed their infirm. But, according to Mark, Jesus' visceral response to the people's situation led him to teach them. The crowd's hunger for a wisdom to live by occasioned in Jesus a greater compassion than the mere lack of visible food or the burden of physical ailments.

Jesus is most often addressed as "Teacher" in Mark; and in some cases, the vernacular titles *Rabbi* or *Rabbouni* are embedded in the oral tradition Mark is following. Jesus' interaction with the disciples or with the crowds is habitually described by using the verb "to teach," often in the imperfect tense, signifying an activity that continued for a period, or with a participle describing a state of teaching, or in the phrase "he began to teach," again signifying an activity lasting some time. When the crowds came, "it was his custom" (Mk 10:1) to teach them. Mark never uses any expression that might signify that Jesus taught them a particular thing and then moved on. Jesus' "teaching" was a matter of an ongoing and lasting relationship, closer to personal formation than to the mere communication of information or knowledge. In Mark, Jesus teaches in synagogues, by the seaside—and in one memorable vignette, sitting in a boat on the water (Mk 4:1)—in the villages, on the road, and at the end of his journey in the Jerusalem Temple. Unlike Luke 4:20, Jesus is never presented as being seated in a formal posture of teaching; this remains the prerogative of the scribes (Mk 2:6, 12:39). Teaching is for Jesus a formative relationship and not a tenured position.

When the crowd remarks on the newness of Jesus' teaching, they are not referring to any novelty in its content. Jesus continues the work of John the Baptist, announcing the imminence of the reign of God and the need for repentance and faith (Mk 1:15). During the period of Judean ministry, Jesus finds common ground with at least one scribe on what is most important among all the commandments of God (Mk 12:28–34). His principle had ever been to include rather than exclude (Mk 9:39, 10:14). Not all his contemporaries would have agreed with particular aspects of his teaching but rabbinic texts dating from the second century A.D. seem to indicate that the bulk of Jesus' teaching was located within the accepted range of Jewish opinion. The Sadducees may have scoffed at his teaching on resurrection (Mk 12:18), but it is likely that the Pharisees would have accepted it (see Acts 23:6). There were different schools of thought among the rabbis, and the content of Jesus' teaching would have seemed unexceptional to many who heard it.

There are four areas in which the distinctiveness of Jesus

was sufficiently apparent to have generated a mortal hostility among those teachers who occupied the chair of Moses.

(a) Compassion: In Mark 6:34, it is clearly stated that Jesus was moved by the unhappy confusion of the crowd: they were like shepherdless sheep. The Greek word that is usually translated as "having compassion" is very physical. It is not an abstract benevolence reaching out from a great distance, like a philanthropist in his penthouse feeling pity for the homeless. The verb ἐσπλαγχνίσθη means that at this moment Jesus felt the tightening of the muscles of the solar plexus and the constriction of his innards—just as we feel when we experience strong emotion. It was, literally, a gut reaction. It was as though Jesus absorbed into himself the chaos of the crowd and allowed it to generate within his own awareness the sharp anxiety and pain which they dimly experienced. Taking their condition on himself, he acted to reduce their confusion by clear and authoritative teaching which was simultaneously comforting and challenging. The important thing to note, however, is that Jesus did not see himself merely as a supplier of unmet needs whose task was to remedy the deficiency. His response was, rather, to open a relationship in which all that was his would be accessible to those who approached him. His solidarity with their pain led him to invite them to a solidarity with his connectedness to his heavenly Father.

(b) Personal authority: The preferred mode of teaching in a traditional society such as first-century Judaism was by quoting precedents and authorities. As the number of quotable personages increased, so opinions multiplied. This profusion of possibilities meant that with sufficient scholarly diligence almost any position could be supported by an appropriate reference. Furthermore, reliance on ancient tradition demanded a large amount of book knowledge and was thus restricted to

educated professionals. So abstruse and abstract could such
reasoning become that ordinary common sense and humanity
were factored out of the equation. Who in their right mind
would equate nibbling a few grains of corn with the menial
and sabbath-breaking work of bringing in the harvest (Mk
2:24)? Who would think that God is better served and the
sabbath preserved by omitting a life-giving deed (Mk 3:4)? Of
course, Jesus' contests may have been more with literal-minded
local enforcers rather than with the genial scholars like those
whose views are transmitted in *The Mishnah*. Jesus regularly
cut through these multiple layers of tradition and precedent.
To the pharisees who found fault with his disciples' easygoing
ways he thundered, "You leave aside God's commandment
and cling to human tradition" (Mk 7:8). "The sabbath came
to be for the sake of people, people did not come into being
for the sake of the sabbath" (Mk 2:27). Not only in his teaching or in his debates did Jesus distance himself from the dehumanizing fundamentalism that some expected but also in his
practice. He was so happy to find faith in the ritually unclean
woman who touched him that he was unconcerned about any
defilement he may have incurred from the contact (Mk 5:25–
34). On the other hand, when issues impinged on the honor of
God, Jesus could be strict, not allowing anyone to take a short-
cut through the Temple carrying a vessel (Mk 11:16). In general, Jesus went to the heart of the matter without the appara-
tus of scholarly discussion; he spoke directly to the people's
own experience and he was not afraid to challenge them. In
many such encounters, Jesus particularly showed himself as a
master of the pithy axiom that embeds itself in the memory
where it continues to goad.

(c) Parables: Jesus' preferred mode of discourse, as attested
by the various strands of Gospel tradition, was to make use of
images, metaphors, similitudes, and stories that beckoned their

hearers to participate in ongoing reflection on their meaning. The parable of the unworthy tenants (Mk 12:1–11), for example, is intended to be interactive. As the story unfolds, it invites readers to fill out the narrative by interpreting it against the background of their own particular situation. In computer parlance, readers are expected to provide a hypertext from their own experience. Jesus' adversaries certainly did this. They saw in his words their own condemnation and so they wanted to arrest him (Mk 12:12). Jesus here shows himself to be politically astute. A story can be subversive, but it is hard to prove it. His figurative words were complemented by symbolic acts typical of a prophet, such as the cursing of the fig tree (Mk 11:12–14, 20–21) and the expulsion of merchants from the Temple (Mk 11:15–19). Although not lacking in rational content, we could say that much of the strength of Jesus' message operates at the level of intuition. Much of his teaching was directed to the right hemisphere of the brain and thence to the heart.

(d) "Good news": The term "gospel" seems to have been especially important for Mark. Everything that Jesus said or did was good news. Even though the moral teaching of Jesus is exigent and the demands of God's reign are absolute, they are communicated to us in a way that inspires optimism and confidence, not fear and dread. We might say that the Gospel is user-friendly even when its demands are uncompromising. If we accept that "the medium is the message," then we must come to the conclusion that if Jesus was able to sell his hard words to the crowds that followed him, he must have been a very attractive man with a lot of charm and a persuasive manner. Mark is at pains to show throughout the Gospel that the principal disciples had extreme difficulty in comprehending Jesus' message and even more difficulty in putting it into practice. Despite all their reverses, however, they remained glued

to him by personal loyalty and friendship. Paradoxically, I suppose this is "good news," especially for us who find ourselves in a similar situation—desiring to be with Jesus yet not always able to internalize his message or to live in accordance with his values.

Jesus was for his disciples, and can be for us, a teacher who imparts himself rather than some external knowledge or expertise. Nobody else can reproduce the power inherent in Jesus' teaching. Jesus the teacher is an aspect of his personality, and his manner of teaching expresses his relationship with us. Mark's approach is echoed in loftier language in the Fourth Gospel. Jesus is presented as the preexisting divine word that relocates in the human sphere. Discipleship is described in terms of the believer remaining in the word, and the word remaining in the believer. There is a high significance given to the process of remembering, whereby words once spoken and heard can be retrieved, reexperienced in a new context, and reactivated. The words that Jesus speaks give concrete expression to his solidarity with us. They reach out to heal what is wounded and defective in us. They are our salvation—our means of access to the divine sphere: "The words that I have spoken to you are spirit and life" (Jn 6:63).

Jesus becomes a teacher only because there are those who are willing to learn from him, and once this relationship is established anything can happen. To attend the school of Jesus is not merely a matter of filling our minds and hearts with beliefs and values. Mysteriously, our discipleship involves, at a deeper level, the confrontation with and the eventual expulsion of our own particular demons. It concerns salvation and not merely instruction.

CHAPTER EIGHT

Detoxification

All the recesses of our heart must be kept under constant surveillance and the traces of whatever arises there must be prudently considered. This is in case some mental beast—lion or dragon—might, in passing through, leave there its harmful traces. If we are neglectful with regard to thoughts, access to the sanctuary of our heart will be permitted to others also. We will be able to get rid of the dens of wild beasts and the hiding place of poisonous snakes if at every hour and moment we open up the soil of our heart with the plough of the Gospel, that is, with the unceasing memory of the Lord's cross.

JOHN CASSIAN, CONFERENCE 1.22

J esus' victory over indwelling forces of evil is both dramatic and consoling. It is not, however, the end of the story. Both Matthew and Luke record a saying of Jesus that reminds us that even after we have been delivered of our demons, danger remains.

> When the unclean spirit has gone out from a person it roams around the waterless regions looking for a place to rest, but it does not find one. Then it says, "I will go back to my own house from where I came." When it comes, it finds the place unoccupied and swept, with everything in order. Then it goes and brings with it

seven other spirits worse than itself and they come in and take up residence there. So the last state of that person is worse than the first.

MATTHEW 12:43–45 = LUKE 11:24–26

The inner forces that assail the integrity of our discipleship are not easily recognized and are eliminated only with great difficulty over a long period of time. We experience a slippery plurality about our "demon" that makes it hard to establish whether we are assailed by one or many, and where the "demon" ends and our own shadow side begins. So the unclean spirit in Mark 1:24 speaks of itself as "we," and that in 5:9 gives its name as "Legion," claiming to number as many as six thousand. So it is that as soon as we neutralize one source of inner division and temptation, we suddenly become aware that another "demon" is ready to step forward and take its place. We substantially reduce the level of chaos in the area of sexuality only to find ourselves preyed upon by anger or laziness or self-righteousness. There is a danger that by investing all our resources to fight on a single front, we become blind to the danger of attack from elsewhere. "Many times we have seen that those who observe fasts and vigils most severely...are suddenly deceived so that they cannot bring what they have begun to an appropriate conclusion, and they finish their high fervor and laudable lifestyle with a hateful outcome."[1] We may feel that it is not fair to be flung back into battle after all our efforts. Alas! Such is the reality of the human condition.

The ancient masters of spiritual living were mainly concerned with matters of motivation. They used to look beyond sinful actions and the momentary weakness of will which assents to them to the less obvious infrastructure that makes sin possible.[2] If we honestly survey the landscape of our personal sin, we will begin to appreciate why these old monks were concerned with both the remote and immediate antecedents of sin. At the crucial moment we are often too distracted to make a fully free choice. This is why we regularly attempt to excuse our wrong actions by pleading that what we consented to was far less malevolent than what actually happened. It all *seemed* so harmless; I did not *know* the gun was loaded; I *thought* I was sober enough to drive home; I *meant* only to hurt a little bit; I didn't *realize* that my passion would get out of control so quickly. The machinery of denial cranks into action and before long we have absolved ourselves with a plea of diminished responsibility and, perhaps, projected the blame onto another.[3]

I am not questioning our sincerity in reaching this conclusion, and I am certainly not trying to water down the traditional teaching that full knowledge and deliberation are required for grave sin. I am suggesting that our self-scrutiny needs to be much more demanding if we wish to find an answer to the question of where our sin comes from. Temptation is not totally unpredictable; it usually occurs when several of our defense systems fail simultaneously. We may experience this collapse as a "moment of weakness" but, in reality, it becomes more and more inevitable as the incentives to sin increase and the restraints are restricted. In the case of sexual temptation, for example, it is not merely a matter of hormone levels, although these may play a part. Consider a man in the following situation.

- He is outside his normal environment with its supports and limits.
- He goes to a place which he dimly knows to be *risqué*.
- His values have been eroded gradually by living in an environment that does not honor chastity.
- His spiritual life has been allowed to lapse.
- He has permitted bad habits to flourish unregarded.

- He has actively allowed his imagination to be saturated with sexual images.
- He is somewhat repressed, alienated from his body or otherwise unable to be aware of when his actions are being dictated by sexual instinct.
- He has developed the capacity to rationalize almost anything he does and is generous in acquitting himself of blame.
- He is cultivating the company of someone who is sexually attractive to him—whether he is fully conscious of this or not.
- His inhibitions have been lifted by alcohol or drugs.
- He allows himself to transgress, one after the other, all the appropriate boundaries.

Knowing all these things, we who observe his conduct are not surprised that he gets himself into trouble. The point is that what seems to us inevitable often catches the person concerned unaware. It is either experienced as a sudden, overwhelming temptation or it is scarcely noticed at all, disregarded as one of those things that "just happen." Certainly no responsibility is accepted for the final act. In themselves, none of the contributory factors may be seriously sinful; but, collectively, they exert a force that is practically irresistible. The major failure has been a defect in prudence: there has been no oversight of life and, as a result, choices have been made in isolation without regard for their impact on the concrete situation taken as a whole.

Our response to such a scenario must be this: to understand sin you have to go back beyond the moment of sin to look at its antecedents. Grand strategy in war is more than battleground tactics; it includes attention to the unheroic area of logistics. If you can maintain your own supply lines while cutting those of your enemy, you will win the war. When it

comes to fighting sin, we need to identify and neutralize whatever nourishes its growth and increases its strength. We find
this process difficult because often enough it involves renounc-
ing things that are harmless in themselves but which, for one
reason or another, happen to trigger a disproportionate reaction in us.[4] Just as those with celiac disease have to avoid glu-
ten because of a kink in their physiology, each of us needs to
be aware of potential stimulants of unhealthy passions, be it a
matter of lust, envy, jealousy, anger, or self-depreciation. What
is perfectly harmless for somebody else may be deadly for us.
And so we need to be aware that for us, if not for others,
certain events are plague carriers. We need to protect our frontiers against them; if this is not possible, we need to consider
quarantine measures and inoculation. Cut off the supply lines
and the vices will wither. Leave them intact and we will certainly have a battle on our hands, the outcome of which is in
no way certain.

Whether we care to admit it or not, we all find ourselves
in a situation where weeds grow alongside the wheat. There is
a fifth column within us, sabotaging our efforts to live in accordance with our sincerely held beliefs and values. Within
the core of our being, we discover prevoluntary incentives to
sin that often carry us in a direction we do not consciously
want to go and that continually undermine the authority of
our reason and will. This is the reality that the Council of
Trent described with Saint Augustine's term "concupiscence."[5]
In part, concupiscence is an innate and universal condition,
the result of a tension between what we are now and what we
have the potential to become. In this technical sense,
concupiscence is the resistance of nature to the personal will.[6]

It is possible to take the notion of concupiscence to a further stage. Human nature resists any course of action that
summons it to transcendence whether this course of action be
a matter of accepting the governance of reason and will, or

the more intense self-transcendence involved in the following of Christ. The energy deriving from our interior duality has, therefore, a particular antipathy to the action of grace. It is only with extreme reluctance that our nature consents to be trained to live a moral life; the demands of the Gospel and the life of grace are just too much.[7] "We proclaim Christ crucified, a scandal to the Jews and to the Gentiles foolishness" (1 Cor 1:23). Concupiscence is most fiercely experienced when we are most energetic in our dedication to the Christian life. It operates concurrently in three channels whenever we incline to some virtuous act: it tries to distract us by waving before our noses a more attractive and less noble alternative, it lowers our energy levels and inclines us to let the opportunity pass and, third, it contaminates the moral quality of the action by connecting it with unworthy motivations.

Concupiscence is unruly; it is not essentially bad. We are diminished by it only to the extent that we permit it to govern us without reference to our higher faculties and vocation. It is by struggling against its dominance that our Christian character is formed; this is the process termed by the medieval Cistercians as "the ordering of charity" (*ordinatio caritatis*), whereby all "lower" affectivity is subordinated to and formed by the "higher" loves, especially charity. To say this in another way, "We must strive to overcome concupiscence by progressively integrating it into the ethical order sustained by grace."[8]

The most powerful ally of concupiscence is our desire to embrace pleasure and avoid pain. We associate the idea of the pleasure principle with Freud, yet we find it also expressed in the Middle Ages, for example in Baldwin of Forde, a Cistercian monk who ended his life as Archbishop of Canterbury.

Since I am speaking of sins, the thing which we seek, the thing which lies deepest, seems to be none other than the pleasure which sin provides. At the beginning of sin, during it, and at its end, the sinner craves and desires only this one thing: the pleasure which he feels—or hopes to feel—by sinning. It is true that one often seems to enjoy sinning for reasons other than pleasure, but the motive of pleasure must always be there, either directly or indirectly.[9]

Most of the time the choice between pleasure and pain makes compromisers of us all. The danger is greatest when we try to avoid the drama of decision making and attempt to sail through the situation on automatic pilot. Then ingrained habit takes over to do nature's work in supplanting the rule of reason. "Reason is overwhelmed first by the corrupting action of nature and afterwards by habit, which according to the philosophers, is a second nature."[10] Experientially, it is often in the dominance of bad habits that we feel the brunt of concupiscence. This is probably why the Council of Trent insisted that concupiscence was derived from sin and leads to sin.[11] Concupiscence links up with sinful behavior to create, as it were, a residue of past sin which remains after the sin itself has been forgiven and forgotten and which retains the capacity to regenerate itself, given the right conditions; a bad habit may be compared to "cookies" planted in computers from the Internet to expedite future dealings. The stronger the habit, the shorter the distance between the first suggestion and the completion of the act, and the feebler the resistance.

None of us wants to sin, yet we are continually being hustled willy-nilly towards the precipice of consent by habits, rituals, and addictions. We make matters worse when we repress our feelings of guilt and rationalize our crimes to such an extent that repetition is almost inevitable. Even an isolated transgression can easily create memories that offer shortcuts for the future. Fantasies can dress up a situation with a glamour or significance that makes it more attractive. Each time we sin we make the path by walking. The next time it will be easier—soon it becomes an expressway. The result is that the passions become identified with the actions they lead to. Anger is a passion with physiological attributes, but aggression is a learned strategy that is only one way among many of dealing with the impulse. When the habit takes root, the first stirrings of anger are immediately translated into aggression. Lust is a passion that is felt: acting it out through sexual behavior is an acquired technique of returning to normal. In both anger and lust, there is the possibility of cultivating other less automatic and, perhaps, more moral ways of responding to the urging. Habit makes it less likely that we will look for them.

There is scope for what may seem like old-fashioned resistance: once we have arrived at an honest understanding of our situation, perhaps we need to make an act of the will and dig in our heels. I am not going to pursue that course of action as I have in the past, even though I am strongly drawn to do so. Sometimes we arrive at this point only because a dramatic event has shocked us into reality and exposed the delusion inherent in the life we were living. It takes a lot of courage to reverse course. It takes even more to keep resisting our impulses when our resistance itself is far from complete and when old habits reassert their dominance. Ask those who have tried to control their weight or to give up smoking. Some measure of direct action is always necessary, but it is much better if we can go behind the overt behavior and deal with its causes.

The point about seeking to understand the origins of sin is that it provides us with the possibility of working out realistic strategies for bringing more consistency into our life. In this, we need an uncommon degree of common sense and patience.

We cannot turn back the tidal movement of concupiscence with a snap of our fingers, nor is there any point in doing so. We can, however, take token steps that signify our will to move in another direction—to do good, to minimize suffering, or to resist evil. It does not matter how small the steps we take since "quantitative judgments do not apply."[12] First of all, it is a question of overcoming our negative inertia, of being proactive and patient while a positive momentum builds. Further, part of any strategy for spiritual warfare is eliminating, as far as possible, any thoughts that contribute to temptation's vigor and replacing them with more wholesome thoughts. Most often, the first betrayal is mental. If we can offer effective resistance at this level, we will save ourselves from the complications that ensue when sin is externalized.

We are aware of how much we are stirred by words and images that we encounter in daily life and in our contact with mass media. We know that the impressions we receive often trigger strong emotions in us which, in turn, modify our behavior. It follows that we can modify our behavior by exercising some control over what enters through the windows of the senses. In theory, this means making some effort to filter out whatever is going to lead us astray. We are often frustrated by the pace of events: an image is captured long before we can take practical steps to block it out, and there is no way of unseeing what we have already observed. There is, however, a complementary process: we can fill the chasms of our mind and imagination with good thoughts and good images.

We do not want to spend all our energies dealing with our vices: identifying, quarantining, and eventually neutralizing them. By being too vigorous in scraping off the rust, we may end up putting a hole in the bucket. The key word in Matthew's warning about the return of the demons to their former home now refurbished is "unoccupied" (12:43–44). The devil finds work for idle hands. It is not enough to work hard to eliminate the unsavory thoughts and imaginations that set up our descent into sin. We have to expend some energy in the task of injecting positive thoughts that might offset the malign influence of concupiscence. Listen to what Bernard of Clairvaux says about this.

> Therefore I encourage you, friends, to turn aside for the time being from troubling and anxious reflection on your own progress, and to escape to the smoother paths of remembering the good things which God has done; so that instead of becoming upset by thinking about yourself, you can draw breath by turning your attention to God. I want you to experience for yourself what the holy prophet advocates: "Delight in the Lord, who will grant your heart's desire." Sorrow for sin is certainly necessary, on condition that it is not constant. More joyful recollections of God's generosity should interrupt it, lest the heart become hardened by too much sadness and so perish through despair.[13]

This advice is in the same line as Saint Paul's directive in Philippians 4:8: "Think about whatever is true, whatever is honorable, whatever is just, innocent and lovable, whatever is of good repute, whatever is virtuous or praiseworthy." Some translations paraphrase the verb as "fill your minds" and that makes a lot of sense. By evangelizing our own inner spaces, we water down the impact of concupiscence and provide a springboard from which good thoughts and virtuous actions may take their origin.

Filling our minds with God's good news means building into our lives a regular intake of words and images that counterbalance the contrary messages that have their origin in the interaction of concupiscence and the world around us. We need constantly to be reminded of the invisible aspects of our existence: our spiritual origin and destiny, our value in the eyes of God, the loving and forgiving presence of God in our life, the mysterious overlap of time and eternity. These things will slip from awareness unless we deliberately remember them, and then our spiritual life will slowly fade away. "Forgetfulness is the death of the soul," as Bernard of Clairvaux reminds us.[14]

To remain spiritually alive the best means is to become fervent disciples of God's revealed word. This means spending time reading the Scriptures and listening to them, meditating on them in such a way that they speak to our hearts and throw light on our lives, setting the Gospel as standard against which we measure the options we face in daily life. It is amazing how difficult it is to find a few minutes each day for holy reading, meditation, and prayer—notwithstanding the hours we squander watching television, reading newspapers, and surfing the Internet. I need to keep reminding myself that if I drift away from interactive contact with the Bible, my prayer will soon become very self-centered and then will either degenerate into meaningless formalism or disappear altogether. When prayer goes, I soon lose the spiritual orientation of my life, and it is only a matter of time before major infidelity will occur.

This is not the place to repeat all that I have written elsewhere about holy reading.[15] In the present context I am suggesting merely that its regular practice is one of the best ways of reducing the imperiousness of certain thoughts that lead us into temptation. There is no magic about it. To maintain this practice, an effort of the will is required and a certain spirit of practicality.

What we take in must be processed. We need to ponder the words of Jesus quietly, until their import for our lives becomes evident. This means holding the message while we absorb its meaning. The ancient monks were encouraged never to finish their reading until they had selected a short text to carry with them during the day so that, almost imperceptibly, they would be led deeper into the meaning of the text and at the same time bring into the light some of the shadowy corners of their own hearts.

> Some part of the daily reading should, each day, be stored in the stomach of the memory and thus it will be digested. At times it should be recalled for frequent rumination. You should select a text that is in keeping with your calling and in line with your personal orientation—something that will seize hold of the mind and not allow it to think over alien matters.[16]

Beyond what we absorb from our meditative reading of the Scriptures, from our participation in the liturgy, from reading books and listening to discourses, there are many topics with which our minds may be profitably occupied:

- The recalling of scenes from the life of Jesus, perhaps establishing links between what we are experiencing and particular incidents
- Pondering the meaning of the good and bad examples with which experience and reading provide us
- Retracing some stages of our own life's journey
- Counting our blessings
- Seeing the hand of God at work in the beauty of creation
- Trying to understand the deeper significance of daily events
- Being open to receiving a word of life from anyone we meet
- Being mindful of death, and
- Reactivating our hope in eternal life

All of these add an extra dimension to our perception of issues. In particular, we can grow in appreciation of the possibilities of every day if we serenely admit into consciousness the awareness that our time on earth is limited. Most of our contemporaries do not want to think about death, yet nothing is more certain for each of us. Death is the ultimate instance of our loss of control, and we fear it so greatly that we avoid even thinking about it. Yet the thought of death is one of the most effective means of impelling us to take every day and every moment seriously: to live each day as if it were to be our last. "Assiduous reflection on death is the highest philosophy," writes Arnulph of Boheries.

> If spiritual laziness does get a hold, one should cure oneself of it by making a meditation about the stone slab on which the dead are washed. One should remind oneself how corpses on the way to burial are handled there, how they are turned face upwards and face downwards, how the head hangs, the arms are limp, the thighs cold, the legs lie stiff; how the corpse is clothed and sewn up, how it is carried to the grave, left in the tomb, covered with earth, how it is devoured by worms and rots away like a stinking sack.[17]

Maybe the imagery is a little graphic for our modern sensibilities, but the point is that a time will come when life as we know it will come to an end, and we will have no more opportunities to do good. The message is about making optimal use of the present. "Today, if you hear God's voice, harden not your hearts" (Ps 95:7–8). Tomorrow is always too late. How would I live today if my life were not to extend beyond a year, a month, or even less? Today is the day when infinite possibilities remain open before us if only we can shake off our torpor and reimagine a different future.

We cannot procrastinate forever; a day will dawn which will
be our last.

Christ overcomes the inherent power of the evil one
through his teaching, by filling our minds with truths that
drive out the poison of evil suggestion that rises within us. Of
us this process requires that we listen with the ears of our
heart and allow ourselves gradually to view life against a different perceptual horizon. As our consciences are reeducated
we learn to serve a different master, and progressively to cede
control of our lives to him. In this way Jesus says to us, as he
once said to the Twelve, "You have been purified already by
the word that I have spoken to you" (Jn 15:3).

CHAPTER NINE

Jesus the Sower

[Jesus] said: The Kingdom of God is comparable to a person who sows seed on the ground. While that person sleeps and rises during nights and days, the seed germinates and grows. How the sower does not know. Of its own accord the earth bears fruit: first the blade, then the ear, then the full grain within the ear. When the fruit is ready, immediately the sower sends in the reaper because the harvest is ready.

MARK 4:26–29

In the parables of Jesus we come closest to understanding something of his personal philosophy of life. Disputation and controversy use the currency of external authorities—pitting one witness against another to convince, confuse, subvert, or demolish a contrary opinion. Although Mark presents Jesus engaging in this sort of debate in two important series of episodes (2:1—3:6 and 11:17—12:40), he notes that what attracted the people was his personal "authority" rather than his skill in argument. Instead of the barrage of texts and cold deductions used by his opponents to buttress their opinions, Jesus spoke directly from experience. His hearers understood that he knew what he was talking about. Because he spoke from the heart, Jesus revealed something of himself as he spoke; it was this openness that won over those who listened. Jesus taught by relationship.

A preferential option for teaching in parables indicates that Jesus did not see the action of God in this world as capable of being defined strictly, or confined within the ordinary categories of human experience. It is not so easy for us to accept that the ways of God transcend our powers of reasoning. We anticipate that, with enough diligence in collecting data, we can define all events in terms of cause and effect. Whether we like it or not, divine intervention in human affairs can be described only obliquely: by allusive language, poetry, and similitude. Such activity belongs to another order of being.[1] Any attempt on our part to measure, explain, and predict what God does is necessarily deficient. That is why revelation is necessary and why the interpretation of Scripture is so difficult. In the presence of the Holy, we quickly become aware that our rational mind is a much blunted instrument, of its nature unable to analyze or describe the divine and, in any case, too often subverted by instinctual desires to perform at its peak. "Woe is me! I am lost, for I am a man with unclean lips, and I live among a people of unclean lips" (Isa 6:5). All that we can do in our moments of enlightenment is to look and to see, to wonder and admire. We can never comprehend or encompass God. And there is, more often than not, a divine darkness cocooning God's deeds on earth that makes them unsearchable by mortal intelligence.

The three parables that Mark presents to us as a bloc in Chapter 4 compare the operation of the "kingdom" of God—that is our entry into a state of being connected to God in response to revelation—to the growth of seeds. There are three distinct messages given in Mark 4 that are applicable both to the whole Church and to ourselves personally. They seem simple and straightforward, but if taken to heart can lead to a change in our perceptual horizons.

- **Mark 4:1–9: The Parable of the Successful Harvest:**
  The sowing always results in a harvest, despite many
  vicissitudes and setbacks.[2] Furthermore, numerically
  the seeds that are lost are few in number compared
  with those that bear fruit.[3]
- **Mark 4:26–29: The Parable of the Fruitful Soil:** We
  who are the beneficiaries of God's action in our lives
  never really understand the process and so can contribute little to it.
- **Mark 4: 30–32: The Parable of Surprising Growth:**
  Present appearances give no indication of what the
  final result will be: the outcome of God's work is
  superabundant.

This is optimistic teaching addressed to those liable to become discouraged at what they see around them. But it is more
than that. The implicit message of these parables is a call to
confidence that God who has begun a good work is in the
process of bringing it to completion. It is an invitation to go
beyond visible evidence and reasonable prospects and to trust
in forces that cannot be seen or measured.

Although the sower may appear to be in charge of the
operation, he does not even touch the heart of the seed's mystery. Despite the busy necessity and visibility of his task, the
sower has contact only with the outer shell of the seed. He
makes his small contribution in bringing the seed into contact
with the earth and, after that, his work is ended—he sleeps
and he rises and the dynamism of growth operates independ-
ently of any human effort or skill. This is in clear contrast to
the work of tradesmen. A carpenter leaves his work and goes
to bed; the next morning he takes up from where he left off.
There has been no progress in the interim. Everything depends
on the application of his skill to the wood. It is different for
the sower. Once the seed has been cast on the earth, he can do

no more. Well might he sleep and devote himself to other activities. He has become redundant. Growth and harvest will
be determined by factors beyond his control. The mystery inherent in nature takes over. A house does not build itself; the
builder needs constantly to assess and to measure, to work in
sequence and within strict limits, according to plan. In nature,
all this is automated. For the farmer, intervention is often interference and it may jeopardize the outcome of his crop. He
has to learn to stand back and let nature take its course.

The parable implies an even greater degree of estrangement between the sower and his seed. Not only can the farmer
do nothing to help his crop along, he does not even know
where to begin. What is happening is not only beyond his
control; it is beyond his comprehension. No doubt modern
agronomists could provide the poor man with an abundance
of scientific information on the process. Their purview, however, is limited. Who really knows the answers to the deeper
question of *why* a dry seed becomes a luscious fruit. Perhaps
the experts have only scraped the surface of the mystery of
life. How did biological imperatives infuse dead matter with
such purpose and precision? Perhaps this is a case where science needs to be supplemented by wisdom.

Sidelined by his own crop, the sower can do no more than
watch as it goes through its predefined stages of growth. To
describe the earth's fruit-bearing, Saint Mark uses two rare
words which describe an inner dynamism in the seed. The
first is μηκύνηται which points to the purposeful vigor of growth;
and the second is αὐτομάτη, which means "of its own accord"
or "automatically." Both emphasize that the work of growing
belongs to the seed, not to the sower; the power of growth
comes ultimately from God.

Saint Mark distinguishes three stages in the plant's journey towards its destiny. First, the green blade breaks through
the crust of the soil; then it continues growing until an ear is

formed, and finally the grain develops within the ear. This pattern of growth is not mere quantitative expansion; each stage of the continuum is qualitatively distinct. The blade develops into a stalk which grows until it has reached its correct height. Corn as high as an elephant's eye is useless if it has no ear or grain. So, there is a spurt of growth in a particular direction and then it stops and a new phase is entered. When the stalk is complete, the plant's energy is directed to forming the ear, and later the life-containing seed that is the goal of the process. Natural growth is nuanced and differentiated; it is not simply endless and mechanical repetition of a simple operation.

There is a certain inevitability about this growth. The impedances described in Mark 4:1–9 are all external. Once the conditions are right, nothing can stop the seed from producing superabundantly. We can see visible signs of growth, but the dynamism that produces it is internal and unseen. A latent energy that is inseparable from what the seed is pushes it towards fulfillment.

There is, however, another consideration. Passing through fixed stages means that growth occurs at its own pace; it cannot be hurried, nor can any of its moments be bypassed or abbreviated. The needs and desires of the sower are irrelevant, clocks and calendars have no input: the seed follows its own measured trajectory. Only in its due season will the harvest be achieved.

Once growth is complete and the harvest is ready, it is time for the farmer to act again. He sends in the reapers to collect the fruits of the earth's toiling. We are reminded of the proverb quoted by Jesus in John 4:37. "One sows, another reaps." Those who gather in the harvest are benefiting not only from the sower's work but also from the invisible and secret operation of God's Providence, as it travails to bring to birth from the earth "the bread that strengthens our hearts" (Ps 104:15).

As we attempt to enter more fully into the imagery of this parable, we begin to see more clearly why Jesus used it to instruct us about the nature and dynamics of the "Kingdom of God."

Malcolm Muggeridge, the former editor of *Punch* and a Catholic apologist well known in England in the 1960s, used to speak with some asperity about the "Kingdom of Heaven on Earth, Incorporated." We are, he thought, too ready to reduce the Church to this-worldly forms and manners and, consequently, there is a tendency to exclude anything otherworldly if it cannot be understood rationally or easily marketed to the doubting majority. For him, the demystification of the Church in the West was a fact to be lamented since it was a tendency that would lead inevitably to the Church's decline. The lesson we can learn from his rather extreme point of view is valuable: fully to understand the Church as the sacrament of our salvation requires us to transcend rational inquiry, to unbind our poetic intuition, and to allow ourselves to be drawn ever deeper into mystery.

God's work of bringing the human race to full fruition can never be reduced to human strategies and interventions. It remains an enigma, as Saint Paul says (1 Cor 13:12). This reality was brought home to him when he spoke before a sophisticated audience in Athens (Acts 17:22–32). They, like many of our contemporaries, found Christianity acceptable so long as its preaching remained at the level of ethics, aesthetics, and social welfare. Begin to talk about a future life and the resurrection of the body and you have lost them. The fact is that at the very heart of Christianity there is a mystery which needs to be accepted in the luminous twilight of faith. It cannot be fully understood, explained, or proved by the exercise of reason. Yet, though salvation can never be understood fully in this life, it may be pondered with awe by the humble, but first we need to stand back and contemplate. God's

"Kingdom" can never be tamed, manipulated, or confined to convenient categories. It has a will of its own; it produces results by its own means and in its own season; it acts αὐτομάτη. This means that often it is better for us to back off lest we court frustration by trying to reorient God's action to suit our limited perceptions.

One of the traditional qualities of the Church is that it is "catholic" or all-inclusive. If it is faithful to its nature, the Church may never allow itself to degenerate into a sect with clear boundaries between insiders and outsiders, between "us" and "them." Catholicity is not a claim to some universal hegemony that permits the Church to impose its will on all and sundry. Authority in the Church is service: this service is unrestricted in scope and permits no exclusion of persons. If it is true to itself, there are no collateral advantages in its exercise. Service is a privilege only in the sense that following the way of Jesus is always a privilege, even though such discipleship leads unavoidably to the sacrifice of self for the sake of others.

Throughout history, there has been a tug of war between the essentially otherworldly mission of the Church and the practical necessity for a great deal of this-worldly organization. By choosing to portray the community of salvation as powered by invisible energies, Jesus provides us with the broader context of our contribution to the coming of the Kingdom. God is the primary agent. Grace (or the Holy Spirit) is what drives us forward. Our hardworking efforts are, in God's plan, necessary, but they do not define the end result. We do what we can, but our labors are subsidiary. This is a reason not for gloom, but for celebration. "This depends not on [human] willing or running but on God showing mercy" (Rom 9:16). God is at work in our world: the outcome is secure. Our relatively minor efforts will share disproportionately in the glory of the inevitable victory.

What does this tell us about Jesus himself? The Gospel

tells us that Jesus was a builder (Mk 6:3): a worker in stone and wood. As such, he was accustomed to the calculating manipulation of material in order to achieve the anticipated result. Yet he knew that such purposeful diligence mirrored God's way of working less accurately than the wild ways of the natural process of growth. For him, the Kingdom of God is not a matter of human skills or resources; it is, as the Fourth Gospel reminds us repeatedly, the Father's work.

The first quality of Jesus' personal philosophy that this parable indicates is his renunciation of control, even concerning the most important element of his own life, the advancing of God's Kingdom. Such an attitude is possible only on the basis of a supreme confidence that someone else is taking good care of matters. Jesus does what he can and leaves the rest to the Father, whose work he does and whose will is irresistible. We find the same conviction expressed by Saint Matthew in the Sermon on the Mount. After telling us to learn a lesson from the carefree existence of birds and flowers under the Father's overarching care, Jesus continues: "Do not be concerned saying, 'What shall we eat?' 'What shall we drink?' or 'What shall we have for covering?' These are the things with which the nations are concerned. Your heavenly Father knows that you need all these things" (Mt 6:31–32). Jesus lived a carefree life because he made the Kingdom his priority—and all other elements of his life slotted into that basic option.

This inner freedom, so typical of Jesus, is not unlike the attitude described by the Letter to the Hebrews as "faith." The eleventh chapter begins with a definition of this basic stance before God. "Faith is the assurance of what is hoped for"; and more importantly for our purposes, "it is what convinces us of the reality of things unseen" (Heb 11:1). Subsequent verses spell out the two opposite qualities of hope: it connects us to the invisible world which God inhabits, and it fits us to live a godly life amid the contradictions and frustrations of this world. From the standpoint of this present age, there is darkness; faith however is luminous, because it opens a window to a hidden world of light. Of Moses it is said that "he continued steadfast as if seeing the unseen" (Heb 11:27).

Once the hidden treasure is discovered (Mt 13:44), then there is a joyful movement of renunciation, since lesser things have lost their hold over us. Once having felt ourselves come alive through our participation in the life of God, we are gradually disenfranchised from this world. We have another source of identity: "Our citizenship is in heaven" (Phil 3:20). God is our homeland and even though we are at a great distance, we cannot avoid becoming "strangers and foreigners" in matters considered by many to be crucial to a successful and fulfilling life. Our treasure is not here, it is in heaven; and that is where our hearts find their home (see Mk 10:21; also Mt 6:21 = Lk 12:34).

We notice this detachment in Jesus, as presented in the Gospels, and consider it a great freedom. It was, however, a freedom purchased at the price of substantial renunciation. Jesus seems not to have been bound by family ties (Mk 3:31–35) or by a concern for material possessions (Mt 8:20). He was free to move beyond his native village and not afraid to transgress even religious conventions (Mk 7:1–8), or to upset those in authority (Mk 11:17–18, 12:38–40). He dissociated himself from others' ambitions (Mk 10:45), fled crowds (Mk 1:35), resisted pressure for miracles on demand (Mk 8:11–12), and imposed silence on those who would spread his fame abroad (Mk 1:44, 3:12, 5:43, 7:36, 8:30, 9:9).[4] For those wishing to join Jesus' company, his demands were extreme and must have seemed life denying (Mk 8:34–35, 10:21–25). Mark even attaches a fearsome rider to the promise of the hundredfold in this age; the blessings will come packaged "with persecutions" (Mk 10:30). And although this Gospel has nothing paralleling the stern judgment of Luke 16:15 ("That which is highly esteemed by human beings is an abomination in the sight of God"), Jesus' words to Peter are uncompromising. "Satan, go away, out of my sight; your human way of thinking is not from God" (Mk 8:33). The converse of the same theme is more consoling, even the weakness of God surpasses human strength (1 Cor 1:25): "What is impossible to human beings is possible to God" (Mk 10:27). The point is: there is a vast discontinuity between the ways of this world and the sphere of God. Jesus' inner freedom is not the easy result of dispensation from all external imperatives. It is the fruit of a steadfast and all-embracing renunciation powered by the immediacy of the spiritual world.

For many of us being free means being in control. For Jesus, inner freedom was the opposite: a matter of yielding control of his life to his Father and accepting that those who impacted on him were, knowingly or not, his Father's agents. This is a theme developed most fully in the Fourth Gospel. Jesus replies to Pilate, "You would have no authority over me if it were not given you from above" (Jn 19:11). This Gospel asserts repeatedly that Jesus' whole philosophy of life was dominated by a proactive search for and conformity with the Father's will. "My food is to do the will of the one who sent me and to bring his work to completion" (Jn 4:34). This Johannine theme of obedience parallels Saint Paul's "obedience of faith" (Rom 1:5 and 16:26). It is not enough to glimpse the spiritual world and identify with it. We are also obliged to conform ourselves to its imperatives and that submission involves a certain rejection of this-worldly standards (Rom 12:2). Contrary to what we who cherish our autonomy might expect, Jesus was free because he chose to obey.

Such a capacity for obedience is not the result of a tendency to compliance that is related to timidity or fear. It stems from complete confidence in the one who is obeyed. Jesus' intimacy with the Father was such that his trust was absolute. He was able to yield control because he understood that all progress is from God and that it happens in a way that necessarily transcends human understanding. Jesus was aware that in his human nature he could not survey events from the standpoint of eternity but that, like us, he was dependent on impressions received through his senses and the conclusions he drew from them. He was undoubtedly more conscious than we are of the limitations inherent in such knowledge. He was prepared to suspend his own judgment and to defer to the clear mandate and mission he had received and to follow the serene and subtle guidance afforded by his intimacy with the Father.

Jesus accepted unknowing. This is a hard word for us whose peace of mind we make dependent on complete knowledge. We do not like being in the dark. We are apprehensive in dealing with matters of which we do not have previous experience. The unknown occasions fear in us. There is a feeling component in knowledge. We feel comfortable when we have all the data and ill at ease if our information is incomplete. We are slow to welcome an invitation to move beyond what is familiar. Jesus, the teller of the parable, reveals that he is different. He can leave things in God's hands; he does not have to know all the details. He is the sower of the seed who works while he can but knows that a time is coming when further work is impossible (Jn 9:4) and unnecessary. This is not a source of frustration for him, but simply the way things are. In emptying himself, he set aside the privileges of divinity; now he is constrained by the limitations of spatio-temporal existence. He has become weak, like us, but understands that God is potent. His knowledge, like ours, is partial, but Jesus does not care that he is ignorant of when the final Hour will come; it is sufficient for him that the Father knows (Mk 13:32).

This childlike trust made Jesus comfortable in accepting the limitations of his humanity, fearless in a degree that most of us will never attain. Boldness in word and deed is the natural

concomitant of faith and confidence; this is clear from the
Acts of the Apostles. Jesus is certainly not a timid man in any
circumstances. A sudden storm that fills professional fishermen with terror finds him calmly asleep on a cushion (Mk
4:38). He easily navigates the transition from nowhere
(Nazareth) to the town (Capernaum) to the city (Jerusalem)
with forays into foreign territory in between. He deals with
all classes of people with equal deftness and is uncompromising in the face of opposition and hostility. He continues his
journey to Jerusalem even when he knows that it will result in
a death whose very mention terrifies his disciples (Mk 8:31,
9:31, 10:32–34). During the events leading up to his crucifixion, his spirit is uncowed; he confronts his captors with dignity and forthrightness (Mk 14:48–49, 61–62, 15:2). This
courage is more than obstinacy; it is an indication that Jesus is
conscious that what we experience in this world of space and
time is only a tiny part of infinite reality. Saint Paul knew this
also. "This small momentary trouble is preparing for us an
eternal weight of glory that is beyond measuring. We do not
fix our gaze on things seen, but on what is unseen; because
what is seen is for a moment, what is unseen is for eternity"
(2 Cor 4:17–18). Of Jesus also it can be said as was said of
Moses in the text quoted earlier: "He continued steadfast as if
seeing the unseen" (Heb 11:27). Living in immediate contact
with otherworldly realities relativizes the impact of what happens here. Those who go willingly to martyrdom understand
this. "I consider the sufferings of this present season insignificant compared with the future glory to be unveiled before us"
(Rom 8:18).

It is his connection with eternity that stamps Jesus' every
action. Free of many of the enslaving attachments that limit
human beings to present realities he is able to stand back
and see the world around him in the light of eternity. This
vision so fills him with hope and confidence that he is able to

approach life without fear. In fact this total absence of anxiety must have made a deep impression on his disciples since freedom from care (μέριμνα) is a consistent theme of New Testament teaching.[5]

The three parables about seeds embody this liberating perspective. There is no need for anxiety because the harvest will be good despite current setbacks, despite the fact that we do not understand what is happening, and despite appearances to the contrary. Jesus would have us to be like him. This means vacating the driver's seat and allowing the Father's plan to unfold, playing our small part proactively and energetically, but never for a moment assigning to ourselves the supervisory role that belongs to God alone. It is God's Kingdom, not ours; we merely plant and water, it is God who makes things grow (1 Cor 3:6).

Reflecting on this simple parable, unique to Mark, we glimpse something of the heart of the teller of the parable. Jesus appears to us as a man who

- draws wisdom from the world around him
- sees beyond appearances
- renounces control
- respects the Father's will
- trusts the Father's word
- cooperates in the Father's plan
- is patient for the coming of the Hour

This is what Jesus was; this is what we also are called to become.

CHAPTER TEN

Trust in Providence

My dear friends, this is a good peace and tranquillity of heart: to maintain oneself in evenness of disposition, and to listen with reverence to everything that takes place under heaven. To bless God in everything, for it is God who arranges everything. Not to will to change anything for it has been well done and contributes to the beauty of the whole. To maintain in all situations that charity which, as it is said, does not rejoice in evil but rejoices with the truth.

ISAAC OF STELLA, *SERMON* 47.20

It has been said that suffering is the only truly universal human experience. From the time we are cast forth from the womb until we teeter on the edge of the grave, we continually feel pain at different levels of our being. We all have experience of the pangs that signify that it is time to attend to our biological necessities for food and drink, for rest, warmth, and shelter. We know what it is like to be sick, to be hurt, or to carry an injury. We suffer when we are deprived of good company, solidarity, and intimacy. Because our bodies are such that they permit "higher" functions, we also suffer when things go wrong and these operations are curtailed. Even when our basic organic needs are met adequately, our bodies can be thrown into emotional disarray by unknowing, unreasonable fears, shame, frustration, disillusionment, disappointment, meaninglessness, and a host of other factors that are not directly life threatening. We have a much greater capacity for anxiety than any of the animals. Even purely mental events have the capacity to interfere with the physical organism and make us ill.

This somber aspect of human experience is generally not well integrated into our philosophy of life and that makes the suffering more acute. Usually when a culture identifies a situation that is a source of pain, it develops structures to minimize the suffering of those who find themselves in that situation. In traditional societies, there are rituals for birth and death and for the confusing passages of transition. These soothe anxieties and surround these passages with meaning. The same happens in all cultures. Today, for instance, it is generally recognized that persons who have undergone a traumatic experience can be helped by providing them with that specialized form of human solidarity that counseling offers. We understand well the need for support and empathy in certain grave situations. The pain has been noticed and a partial remedy has been prescribed. When we are reluctant to identify a general source of hardship, the situation goes unattended.

Mostly, we rise to the occasion at a time of major disaster. It is easy, however, to underestimate the weight of suffering that many people carry with them throughout their daily lives. It is not unusual to find a great ocean of misery lurking behind a brisk and efficient facade; it takes only a sympathetic listener, and sometimes a little alcohol, for a vast torrent of sadness to overflow. An unfaithful spouse, a wayward child, missed opportunities, dashed hopes, conflicts, anxieties, guilt, shame, envy, suspicion, desperation. At the time of such disclosure we are surprised, for somehow we have accepted the proposition implicit in much of our popular philosophy that it is possible to expel from human existence everything that is negative. We half-believe that most people pass their days pleasantly. Pain is not considered to be a normal concomitant of life. To us, suffering is something out of the ordinary: it means that something needs to be fixed; something has gone wrong and, therefore, somebody is to blame.

Technology and the division of labor have relieved us of many burdens, and "leisure industries" are booming. We have many more amenities than our parents and grandparents. Yet, it seems, we are no closer to utopia. Depression and suicide are on the rise in most developed countries, alcohol and substance abuse is at a peak, and no country is immune from random acts of violence. It may be said that such examples are at the extreme end of the spectrum, and that is true. It needs to be remembered, however, that all of us are subject to the same grinding pressures, even though we do not react to them in such visibly antisocial ways. For many of us, the negativity seethes inside instead of being expressed by observable changes in behavior. Often enough, the buildup of this hidden plaque of malaise is gradually changed into a sense of nameless dread. I do not know if anyone has attempted to measure the level of fear in contemporary society, but I suspect it is high.

When we are troubled we perceive the cause as being outside ourselves—the result of the interaction of external forces beyond our control. So, we project onto others the fear we dare not face, and they become our enemies. The list of potential candidates includes all those who are in some way different from ourselves: in race, religion, gender, sexual orientation, political opinion. We give them new names: they become perverts and deviants, terrorists, extremists, foreigners; and we cross the street to avoid meeting them. How seemingly blessed are those who blindly blame somebody else for their misery—they never have to repent of anything!

Perhaps it were more honest if we owned our fears and confronted them directly. The fact is that we are living in a world which we cannot control. Our intelligence enables us to see beyond the present sunshine to winter storms and chaos. Wars and rumors of wars, earthquakes, floods, famine, environmental degradation, asteroid strikes. What happened to the dinosaurs could easily happen to us! On a more domestic scale, we cannot exclude the possibility of bereavement, illness, unemployment, failure, disgrace, and a thousand other intimate tragedies. My parents lived and reared a family under the shadow of two world wars and the Depression of the 1930s. My generation has been luckier, many of us have little immediate experience of objective upheaval, and so have faint confidence in our capacity to survive troubled times. Sometimes it is easier to cope with actual hardship than with the vague dread of what the future might hold.

It is this metastasis of fear that Jesus addresses in the Sermon on the Mount. Our cosmic impotence is as real as it was for first-century Palestinians living under a cruel Roman occupation. It is not unreasonable that we feel insecure in the face of social change due to the expanding horizons of knowledge and the rapid subversion of traditional morality. There is a challenge inherent in such unease. We are called to reexamine the foundations of our inner security. To revel in pessimism and become apostles of gloom is to escape that challenge. This age as much as any other has potentiality for great good. Simply lamenting the state of affairs does nobody any good. Often enough, instead of preparing us mentally to deal with whatever the future brings, such predictions of doom may lead us in despair to adopt an attitude of "eat, drink and be merry for tomorrow we die!" (1 Cor 15:32). The world is a mess; there is no future life; God is dead! Let us squeeze from the present moment every precious drop of happiness.

Faith has to grapple constantly with the latent doubt that we may experience concerning the saying of Robert Browning that "God's in his heaven—all's right with the world." Faith means letting go of our ambition to control, understand, or even cope with what happens. It means releasing our anxieties into God's hands and seeing all that happens as coming from the hand of God. The fact that I cannot comprehend the logic of events means merely that my intellect is limited. It does not necessarily follow that the earth is spinning off into chaos and that we will all be ruined.

Our relationship with God is often undermined by our fears about impending disaster whether this be on a cosmic, social, or personal level. John Cassian recognizes that doubts about the effectiveness of God's Providence have a crippling impact on our attempts to pray. Our friendship with God is muddied when we find ourselves in rebellion against events whose significance is beyond our comprehension. Speaking of the phrase "thy will be done on earth as it is in heaven," he continues:

> Nobody can say this prayer sincerely unless they believe that God arranges all visible events, whether negative or positive, for our benefit and that God is more solicitous and provident for the salvation and welfare of his own than we are for ourselves.[1]

Most of us will find this to be a demanding prescription, especially in hard times and whenever we are confronted with what seems like unmitigated disaster or gratuitous ill will. Trust in God's Providence is a summons to go beyond appearances to the bedrock of reality that grounds our faith. God is the creator, conserver, and controller of everything that is. In some way that escapes our powers of understanding, "all things work together for good" (Rom 8:28). To some, this conclusion may seem like a cop out: the ultimate act of intellectual dishonesty, the smothering of human suffering with platitudinous piety. It need not be so. It can just as easily derive from a glimpse of

God that has left us convinced that God is a God of love, and that all that God permits is, in ways unknown to us, an expression of that love.

Of course it does not rain every day. There are also periods of sunshine and peace. Human nature is such that we need both good times and bad to bring out the best in us, and this is reflected in our experience. Even in the worst extremes there are breathing spaces and moments of respite and relief. Fortunately for us, neither happiness nor hardship are permanent realities in our life. Bernard of Clairvaux speaks of this.

> If sadness were our continual state, who could bear it? If, on the other hand, things always went well, then who would not think little of them? Wisdom, the careful controller of all things, alternates the course of the temporal life of his chosen ones with a necessary changing between good things and bad. By such a regimen they will neither be crushed by adversity nor lose discipline through too much joy. Also it means that joys are more appreciated and difficulties more readily endured. Blessed be God for ever![2]

There is a special mode of suffering that is particularly painful to those of us who are concerned for living a spiritual life. (This includes you; why would you bother reading a book like this otherwise?) Let me describe the scenario briefly. There have been moments in our lives in which God has seemed close to us and we have been attracted by the prospect of pursuing a spiritual life. We have begun to think different thoughts and to evaluate issues against a different horizon. We read a little. We pray more both in the church and privately. We begin to be concerned about the moral quality of our behavior. On the surface, everything seems to be going well, but underneath there is a certain uneasiness. This may be caused by some habitual infidelity that is so ingrained that we dare not look at it too closely and so we sideline it. Alternatively, it may be the result of a sudden fall from grace, either into some sin of which we had thought ourselves long quit, or into some new aberration to which we had considered ourselves somewhat immune. The worm of doubt gnaws at our innards: is there any reality to this so-called spiritual life that I am leading? Look at me, I am worse now than ever I was.

To translate this inner questioning into theological terms, we are asking ourselves how sinful acts fit into God's beneficent Providence. It was easy enough for Saint Peter to declare that the death of Jesus was in accordance with "God's determined plan and foreknowledge" (Acts 2:23). It is not so difficult to see others as blind instruments of Providence. It is a different story when it comes to our own willful rejection of God's call and grace. We know that this can be deliberate, cool-headed, and hard-hearted. How can God work through actions which are overtly rebellious? There is a danger that when we stop making excuses for ourselves and honestly face up to the moral import of what we have done, we might begin to despair.

There is a famous gloss to the text of Romans 8:28 attributed by Paul Claudel to Saint Augustine. "For those who love God, all things work together for good—*even sins.*" That even our personal infidelities bring about a happy outcome is bold teaching, but this is what we celebrate every year at the Easter Vigil: *O felix culpa!* It is indeed a happy fault that occasioned the sending of one who would die for us while we were still sinners (Rom 5:8). The practical implications of this we find in the following words of Pope John Paul I:

> I run the risk of making a blunder, but I will say it: the Lord loves humility so much that, sometimes, he permits serious sins. Why? In order that those committing these sins may, after repenting, remain humble.[3]

On this point the smiling pontiff, for all his diffidence, is in perfect accord with the ancient masters of Western spiritual tradition. Listen to this text from Gregory the Great where failures in small matters are alleged as the means by which success in large matters is kept untarnished.

> The dispensation of almighty God is large. It often happens that those to whom he grants the greater goods are denied the lesser, so that their minds might always have something with which to reproach themselves. Hence, although they long to be perfect, it is not possible for them. They work hard in the areas where they have not been given the gift, and their labor achieves no result. In consequence they are less likely to have a high opinion of themselves in the areas in which they have been gifted. Because they are not able to be victorious over small vices and excesses, they learn that the greater goods do not derive from themselves.[4]

For Gregory, it is precisely the pain occasioned by the co-existence of spiritual experience and repeated falls that motivates a person to pray earnestly for divine deliverance.

> Sometimes they are admitted to a particular, unaccustomed experience of inner sweetness and for a moment they are, in some way, new people, set afire by the breath of the Spirit. And the more they taste the object of their love, the stronger grows their desire for it. Within themselves they crave what they had experienced through the inner sense of taste. From love of that sweetness they become of less value in their own eyes. For after they discover that sweetness, they are able to perceive what sort of people they are without it.

They try to prolong the experience but they are driven back from its strength because they are still weak. And because they are incapable of contemplating such purity, they weep sweet tears and then fall back and lie down on the tears of their weakness. For the eye of the mind is unable to fix itself firmly on what it had so fleetingly glimpsed. It is subject to the restraint of inveterate habit which holds it down. In this state they are filled with yearning and they ardently try to transcend themselves, but each time they are beaten back by fatigue and they fall down into their familiar darkness. A soul so moved must endure a serious inner struggle against itself.[5]

Bernard of Clairvaux bases his approach on the largeness of God's mercy; he does not underestimate the squalor and shame of human sin. "Do you think that God has become a miser or has run out of resources? Do you think that God has become impotent or hard-hearted? Absolutely not! for God knows of what we are made."[6] It is in the light of this maternal care that Bernard is able to see how God deals with sin.

Bernard begins by contrasting the attitudes of good people who admit their sins and those who are not bothered by their evil deeds.

While we are in this body we must flee from the face of the temptation that pursues us. And if sometimes we flee less swiftly, then temptation catches us and we are knocked over—but the Lord catches us....It is necessary while we are detained in this world that we will fall sometimes; but some stay down, others do not.... "The just fall seven times a day." There are different kinds of falls. When the just fall, they are caught by the Lord and so they rise again, stronger than before.

But when the unjust fall, there is no one to help them rise again. For they fall either into a harmful shame or into hardness of heart. They may offer excuses for what they did and thus shame leads them deeper into sin. Or they show a bold face, like a prostitute, to indicate that they fear neither God nor human beings but, instead, like Sodom they publicize their sin. The just, however, fall into the hand of God and in a marvelous manner, even sin itself works for them towards righteousness. "We know that for those who love God all things work together for good." Does not a fall work for us for good if we become more humble and more careful because of it?[7]

In Bernard's view the inevitable falling of the just is into God's hand: we do not fall out of God's hands. His use of the phrase "it is necessary" means that sin is universal. The question is not whether we fall, but how we respond to the fact of falling. If we avow our fault and look to God for mercy, only good can come out of the incident. If our response is to cocoon ourselves more fully in the delusion of blamelessness, then sin is compounded and we end up further from God.

For it is a fact that the Spirit does come and go, and those who stand with the Spirit's support necessarily fall when this support is withdrawn. But they do not collapse completely since the Lord, once again, stretches out a helping hand to them. For people who are spiritual or, rather, for people whom the Lord intends to make spiritual, this process of alternation goes on all the time. God visits by morning and subjects to trial. The just fall seven times, and seven times get up again. What is important is that they fall during the day so that they see themselves falling and know when they have fallen and want to get up again and call out for a helping hand saying, "O Lord at your will you made me splendid in virtue but then you turned away and I was overcome."[8]

Bernard is saying quite clearly that our sins cannot hurt us, so long as we acknowledge them. Indeed they can become a springboard by which we leap into a fuller self-knowledge which, in turn, brings about a closer relationship with God.

This same teaching we find eloquently proclaimed in the fourteenth-century mystic Julian of Norwich. She speaks of Saint John of Beverley as one who, after a fervent youth, sinned seriously, but was yet granted the grace of recovery.

> In his youth and in his tender age he was a much loved servant to God, full greatly loving and fearing. And nevertheless God allowed him to fall, though mercifully keeping him so that he perished not, nor lost time. Afterwards God raised him to many more graces, and by the contrition and the meekness that he had in his life, God has given him in heaven many joys, surpassing what he would have had if he had not sinned or fallen.[9]

Elsewhere Julian takes this doctrine further. It is through our sin that we come to know the largeness of God's mercy.

> After this [God] allows us to fall harder and more grievously than ever we did before—as it seems to us. And then we think (because we are not all wise) that what we have begun has come to nothing. But it is not so. It is necessary for us to fall and it is necessary for us to see it. For if we did not fall we should not know how feeble and wretched we are on our own, nor should we know so fully the marvelous love of our Maker.

For, in truth, we shall see in heaven for all eternity that though we have sinned grievously in this life, we were never hurt in God's love, nor were we ever of less value in God's sight. This falling is a test by which we shall have a high and marvelous knowing of love in God forever. That love [of God] is hard and marvelous that cannot and will not be broken for [our] trespasses.[10]

For Julian, as for Bernard, the cause of our confidence is not that our actions are blameless or trivial. We are secure not in our own virtue but in our faith that God "writes straight on crooked lines." Our sins are good only because they remove our complacency and self-reliance, and thus they force us into the sphere of divine mercy.

I see that mercy is a sweet, gracious working in love, mingled with plenteous pity. Mercy works by preserving us and mercy works by turning all things to our good. In love, mercy allows us to fail somewhat, and in failing we fall, and in falling we die. For death is inevitable since we lack the sight and experience of God who is our life. Our failing is full of fear; our falling is marked by sin; our dying is sorrowful. Yet in all this the sweet eye of pity never departs from us, and the working of mercy never ceases.[11]

The ability to see the hand of God not only in global disasters and in what happens to us and to others is a first step. To go beyond this and believe (and it is a work of faith) that somehow God is not absent or dismayed by our grievous failures is a giant stride in the right direction. It means that we have transcended all those inner voices of self-reproach that we have accumulated in a lifetime and have begun to accept as true the Good News that Jesus brought us.

There is, however, something more to be said. If we consider the matter for a moment, we will see that there are two aspects of trusting in God's Providence. The first, as we have noted, is not to allow ourselves to attribute disproportionate importance to events that seem to go against us. The second is to recognize in every opportunity a divine imperative to surge forward and make the most of it. Every moment of our time here on earth may be considered as an open door, beckoning us to a more abundant life. Our faith prompts us to pass through that door, even though we cannot know for certain where such an adventure will lead. The image of sowing seed that Jesus used in his parables is a good reminder that although we can neither know nor control the future, we are expected to use our best efforts to make the most of present opportunities, recognizing always that it is God who gives the increase (1 Cor 3:6).

It is sometimes possible to see two opposing attitudes to the future among members of religious congregations. For some, the vow of obedience is a guarantee that they will be able to continue indefinitely in a situation which they are able to control. The rule and constitutions set boundaries around what may be legitimately asked of them in terms of ministry, lifestyle, and expectations. Since everything is prepackaged, surprises can be effectively excluded. No wonder stagnation easily results! For others, the vow of obedience is more dynamic. It is an invitation constantly to extend their horizons, to attend to the unanticipated, to grow beyond personally set limits, to be always discerning where the call of Christ leads. It is trust in Providence that makes it possible for such religious to take the plunge and accept a new and uncertain avenue of endeavor which, whether it "succeeds" or "fails" will almost certainly be an occasion of growth.

All of us are faced with similar choices. We are very inclined to stay in a known situation where the challenges are predictable and within what we consider to be reasonable bounds. We forget that such self-imposed limits are invisible to God. It may be that the real beginning of the story of our spiritual adventure begins with words similar to those spoken to Abram/Abraham: "Go forth from your country, from your family and from your father's house to the country I will show you" (Gen 12:1). Staying at home will get us nowhere. At certain stages of our life we need to move. Not being afraid of the uncertainty or the possibility of making a mistake but boldly to cast out into the deep (Lk 5:4). *Carpe diem.* Seize the day! The opportunity will not last indefinitely.

There is something more. Part of the good faith that trust in Providence engenders is the practical recognition that the present moment has an impact on the future. What we do today will affect what happens to us tomorrow. For this reason we are not totally passive in respect of the future, whether our present labor concerns building up an infrastructure for future development or being prudent in ensuring against potential mishaps. If we save for our retirement, our last decades may well be more comfortable than if we did not. If we work hard at school, then there will be better prospects of a university education. Saint Augustine was fond of the image of the hardworking ant. The balmy days of summer do not find it idle, but working hard to prepare for the rigors of winter. He recommends that we feast abundantly on God's word when the times are easy, so that when bad days come, we will have something to draw forth from our cellars to sustain life and hope. Speaking about his efforts to help a heretic, Augustine writes:

> We tried to console him with God's word, but he was not one of the wise ants who, during summer, have gathered what they need to live on during the winter. When things are tranquil people ought to gather God's

word for themselves and store it in the inmost part of their heart, just like the ant hides in the inner chambers of its nest the fruit of the summer's labors. If it has a holiday in the summer and does not do this then, when winter comes, there is trouble. If it does not have inside what it needs to feed itself then, necessarily, it will die of hunger. The man of whom I am speaking had not gathered God's word for himself so that, when winter came, he did not find what he was seeking. He did not have the means to be consoled by God's word. He had nothing within him.[12]

This is a salutary reminder that trust in Providence is not the result of a buoyant personality and an optimistic attitude to life. Such confidence derives from the theological virtues of faith, hope, and charity and quickly wilts unless it is constantly doused with prayer. It is in his moments of deep, solitary communion with his Father that Jesus deepened his bonds with the spiritual world (see Mk 1:35, 6:46, 14:32, perhaps also 3:13 and 9:2). By retreating from the tumult of involvement and going up to the top of a "mountain," Jesus was able to maintain a vision of human life that was not confined to this-worldly perspectives. We will find that the same experience will be ours. The more we pray, the easier it will be for us to view events and issues in perspective and in proportion. If we abandon prayer we will tend to leave God out of the equation and, when troubles come, we will find it impossible to view them otherwise than negatively. We could rephrase Augustine's exhortation thus. When the going is good, build a relationship with God; it will stand you in good stead when things inevitably go wrong.

CHAPTER ELEVEN

Jesus Stills a Storm

*On that day, because evening had come, [Jesus] said to
them, "Let us go over to the other side." Leaving the
crowd behind, they took him as he was in the boat, and
there were other boats with him. And there was a great
windstorm and the waves hurled themselves into the
boat so that it was already filling up. And [Jesus] was in
the stern sleeping on a cushion. They raised him and
said to him, "Teacher, is it no concern to you that we
are perishing?" And [Jesus] rose and rebuked the wind
and said to the sea, "Be silent! Be quiet!" And the wind
stopped and there was a great calm. [Jesus] said to them,
"Why are you timid? Do you still have no faith?" And
they feared with a great fear and they said to one another,
"Who is this, then, that the wind and the sea obey him?"*

MARK 4:35–41

This narrative of Jesus exercising his authority over the forces
of nature clearly connects with the account of Jesus walking
on the water (Mk 6:45–52), which itself is linked in the final
verse with the miracle of the feeding of the five thousand (Mk
6:35–44). All these events are termed "nature miracles," since
they involve some assault on the physical laws by which the
universe seems to be governed, and thus cannot be reduced so
easily to the beneficent psychological impact that Jesus had
on those around him.

We find the idea of Jesus suspending the laws of nature profoundly unsettling, since so many of our everyday choices presuppose a stable and predictable universe. We do not want to hear about a man who has the power to do extraordinary things, whose effects are empirically verifiable, but whose cause is unknown. We do not mind a man forgiving sins (Mk 2:10) because the supposed effect is invisible and beyond proof or disproof—even if it is associated with a miraculous cure (Mk 2:12). Cures can be dismissed as merely "psychological." Our weak faith can dodge the question if there is some possibility of a "rational" explanation. The nature miracles are different. They confront our faith directly.

Perhaps our difficulty with passages such as the account of the calming of the storm derives from our habit of looking at the event in isolation. The evangelist tells us that Jesus gave orders to the wind and the sea and they obeyed him. We want to know why and how this came about. We will arrive at more satisfying conclusions if we view the miracle in a broader context.

If we go back to the beginning of the Gospel, we see that Mark begins his Gospel (according to a probable reading) with the proclamation that Jesus is God's Son. If we accept this proposition at its face value, in terms of a first-century view of reality, nothing is impossible. It may be that Jesus' contemporaries reached this conclusion only gradually and painfully. We who are believers, and for whom the Gospel was written, have already accepted this credal statement. What we expect to find in the Gospel are stories which illustrate what we already know. We are already convinced of the reality of Jesus' otherworldly origins; the Gospel does not have to prove anything.

As God's Son Jesus has ἐξουσία: power, authority, the right, freedom, and inclination to act in order to bring creation back into the obedience which is the condition of its fulfillment.

This power was employed particularly against all forces that were hostile to God and to humanity: death, and its forerunner disease, demonic infestation, the binding power of sin. We may add to this Jesus' lifelong war against the crippling effects of the Pharisees' strict interpretation of the Law—an emphasis in the Gospel which reflects the situation of the early Church and is surely the result of Saint Paul's preaching.

Jesus also exercised dominion over the physical elements, which were considered to be ruled over by invisible spiritual powers. We read in Ephesians 6:12: "Our struggle is not against flesh and blood, but against the principalities and powers, against the cosmic rulers of this darkness, against spiritual forces of evil in the heavenly places." This is the battleground on which Jesus fought. He is the standard-bearer of God's campaign against the demonic forces which were believed to exercise their malign influence through their control of the physical world. First-century Palestinians did not have the same sentimental outlook on nature that has flourished since the Industrial Revolution. For them, the natural world existed to be feared, tamed where possible, and improved upon. Unlike us, they had no desire to preserve lions that went about looking for someone to eat (see 1 Pet 5:8). The world in rebellion against God was a hostile environment for human beings. Those who lived close to nature were aware of this. Biodiversity was not high on their list of priorities; they were too busy making provision for their own survival.

If the universe is considered to be under the sway of malign spiritual forces, it will be no surprise to us that God's Son is understood to be independent of the tyranny of the physical world and its unseen controllers. Once this presupposition is granted then his power over storms and his ability to walk on the sea seem obvious. In Mark's view, all the various instances of Jesus' exercise of authority are related. Curing the sick, forgiving sin, stilling the storm, giving orders to demons, teaching with authority, cleansing the Temple, are all expressions of Jesus' power or authority. All these extraordinary events raised the question of who Jesus really is (Mk 2:12, 4:41, 6:2, 7:37, 8:27–29, 11:28).

Jesus' identity is less clearly affirmed in the Gospels than in later theological developments. An aura of mystery remains. All the Gospels attribute to Jesus the enigmatic self-designation "son of man." Exegetes reach different conclusions about what exactly this solemn title was supposed to mean in the mouth of Jesus. Perhaps its use was deliberately ambiguous, straddling the two aspects of Jesus' life among us: the earthly (in which case "son of man" would simply mean a human being) and the heavenly (with an implied reference to the figure in Daniel 7:13 and other late Jewish literature). Perhaps it is an effort on the part of Jesus to retreat behind a wall of anonymity, as so often happens in the Gospel of Mark, and to leave us all guessing.

In the first place "son of man" is an assertion of solidarity with that first man of whom Genesis speaks, as Luke recounts, Jesus "was considered a son...of Adam, of God" (Lk 3:23, 38). In a certain sense, the attribution of the title "son of man" to Jesus is an owning of that lordship over the natural world which was given us at creation. The authority by which Jesus is free from cosmic powers is not his alone but is common to every man and woman descended from Adam. Even though it was damaged by sin, human dignity, deriving from our imagehood of God, remains intact. We were made to go beyond our material origins and to live in communion with God transcendent. Enslavement is contrary to our nature. This is why Jesus claims a freedom to act for the benefit of humanity even to the point of forgiving sin (Mk 2:10), and suspending the obligation of the Mosaic Law (Mk 2:28). This authority reaches beyond the present age into eternity. The "son of man," although subjected to a redemptive death, will rise (Mk 8:31,

9:9, 9:12, 9:31, 10:33–34, 10:45, 14:21, 14:41) and will come again in glory to judge the living and the dead (Mk 8:38, 13:26, 14:62).

This lordship over creation is not something reserved for the future.[1] In so many areas Jesus is presented as one who is not bound by boundaries, who repeatedly exceeds the limits that others have accepted. No wonder he is condemned as a transgressor. Furthermore, the freedom which Jesus claims for himself is a freedom to which he invites all his followers. During the ministry in Galilee, the objections of Jesus' adversaries are often aimed at the disciples rather than directly at Jesus himself (Mk 2:18, 2:24, 7:1–5). Jesus defends them: they have the right to the same freedom as himself.

Anyone who does the will of God becomes Jesus' brother and sister and mother (Mk 3:35), enjoying the same privileges. Such persons belong to an inner circle and the mystery of God's kingdom is communicated to them (Mk 4:11–12, 34). They share in the authority of Jesus to teach, to heal, and to exorcize (Mk 6:7–13). As it happened, the disciples' faith was wobbly and they did not always succeed, for example, when confronted with particularly difficult cases of healing (Mk 9:28–29). They did not respond to Jesus' invitation to feed the crowds themselves (Mk 6:37), and Peter's efforts to walk on water lasted only a few faltering steps (Mt 14:28–30). There must have been a certain amount of irony in Jesus' telling them if they had even the tiniest bit of faith they would be able to move mountains (Mk 11:23). In fact, there is no geological evidence of mountains in Palestine being moved. Yet, after the resurrection stranger things happened. Jesus' promise that the disciples' feats would be greater than his was realized (Jn 14:12): even Peter's shadow was sufficient to bring about miracles (Acts 5:15).

In the light of such data, perhaps it is better to see the actions of Jesus less as an epiphany than as a lesson for his disciples. The calming of the storm did fill the disciples with awe and wonderment, and this attitude persists right through the Gospel of Mark, until its very last words (Mk 16:8). But, at this point, Jesus is less interested in manifesting his hidden self to the disciples than in giving them a demonstration of the power of faith. The implication in his rebuke was that with faith they could have handled the situation as well as he. Without faith, he noted, they were cowards.

The episode begins at the end of a day's preaching. It is evening (Mk 4:35). The disciples take Jesus "as he was" (v. 36); presumably this means either in the boat from which he had been preaching (Mk 4:1)[2] or tired from the day's labors. In any case, Jesus went to the stern and fell asleep on the steersman's cushion.

The presence of resurrection words in the account gives notice of a larger canvas. The contrast between the sleep of Jesus and his "rising" to still the storm already points to a poetic transition to a more general message. When Jesus sleeps in death, the Church falls into disarray. At the resurrection, calm returns and with it, as the Acts of the Apostles repeatedly demonstrates, great boldness in proclaiming the good news.

> To sleep on the boat means to die on the cross....When [Jesus] sleeps, the sea rises under the impulsion of the wind, and the panicking disciples fear shipwreck.... When Christ awoke, as in the resurrection from the dead, he brought peace to the hearts, first of the apostles and then of the universal Church. He triumphed over the world and bound its ruler.[3]

From the description of the boat filling with water in verse 37 there seems to have been objective danger of sinking, unlike Mark 6:48 where the terror of the disciples was more subjective. These were professional fishermen; if they thought they were in danger, the situation was surely grim. Fear was an appropriate response. This terror was probably heightened since the Hebrews were not a seafaring people. The watery sea was understood as an embodiment of the power of chaos assailing human beings and drawing them into its mortal embrace. A storm at sea was more than a challenge to seamanship; it was a confrontation with death. Allied with darkness, it was enough to strike terror in the hardiest mariner.

Meanwhile Jesus slept on a cushion in the stern. There is a note of accusation in the reproach of the disciples. "Teacher, is it no concern to you that we are perishing?" Jesus' response is no more panicky than that of a man roused from sleep by a howling dog. He stands up in the heaving boat and rebukes the wind, telling the waves to settle down. There is a sense of majesty and serenity in Jesus' action. The effect is immediate. It is as though the power of stillness goes out from Jesus and quiets whatever it touches. "Let all mortal flesh keep silent." The disciples are astounded at the sudden abatement of the storm, unable to comprehend what has happened before their eyes.

The sleep of Jesus, like all his actions, was meant to be instructive. Its significance is revealed in the reprimand directed at the disciples. It was not that Jesus did not care about impending disaster—he denied that a disaster was about to take place. As he made his missionary journey to pagan territory, he was content to leave his personal safety in the hands of God, the Lord of history in whose Providence all temporal events are governed. We find a similar disposition in Saint Paul as he endured the storm which led to his being shipwrecked in Malta (Acts 27:8–44). It was indomitable confidence in God that was the source of Jesus' contagious calm.

There is an extraordinary Providence that goes beyond God's ordinary governance of events. We see this Providence in the parting of the Red Sea, the provision of manna and miraculous quails, and the other events associated with the exodus of God's people from Egypt. The ravens who fed Elijah in his wilderness retreat (1 Kings 17:3–6) and that which carried away the poisoned loaf from Saint Benedict[4] are certainly examples of God's extraordinary Providence. The fact is that in the Scriptures and in Christian literature we find countless instances of God apparently intervening to produce an intended result. Mere coincidences? It is not so easy to convince those who have been the beneficiaries of extraordinary "luck" that God has not been acting on their behalf. I know a man who, as a result of an act of kindness, failed to board a flight that was subsequently hijacked and from which no one survived. He, like the disciples, was filled with a great sense of awe— fully convinced that God had intervened to shield him from death. Theologically speaking, there is no reason why this intervention should not be so. The traditional idea of guardian angels is built on such a supposition.

Jesus' sleep is like the sleep of the sower (Mk 4:27). He has done the work that is expected of him. The rest is left in God's hands. This attitude of peaceful trust is the result of an unambiguous commitment to the Father's will. On the one hand, there is a fervent and proactive sense of mission, to complete the work given me to do. This is complemented, on the other hand, by the placid expectation that the rest of the pieces will fit in place without my being unduly concerned about them. Jesus could well have replied to the disciples what Luke has him saying to Martha. "You are concerned and disturbed about many things, and only one thing is necessary" (Lk 10:41–42).

The problem was not with the storm, but with the attitude of the disciples who felt obliged to remain in control of all that happened around them. So long as they were in control, their "faith" was strong—just as the "faith" of Thomas revived once the evidence for it stared him in the face (Jn 20:29).

For the disciples in the boat, when the elements start to go their own way and a life-threatening situation ensues, "faith" begins to falter. Loss of control leads to a loss in confidence. The obvious conclusion is that they had not yet learned to trust in a power that transcends human possibilities.

Jesus is stern in his assessment of the disciples' failure. He calls them cowards. They act as though there was no God and, as a result, their assessment of the danger is exaggerated. Not for them the sentiment expressed in the Latin translation of Job 13:15: "Even though God kill me, still will I hope in God."[5] Their fear was natural under the circumstances. The problem was that, to a large extent, their faith did not kick in to counteract it. So their fear made cowards of them all. Even though, as Saint Paul says, "God has not given us a spirit of cowardice" (2 Tim 1:7), even the best of us are often rendered powerless by timidity. It is as though, in the moment of danger, our horizons contract and we can see nothing except impending horror. "At the onset of such a violent and unforeseen attack, they all staggered and reeled like drunkards, and all their skill was gone.[6]

The faith that the disciples lacked did not consist in being blind to the dangers of their situation. We are not called to be stupid or imprudent. What they lacked was a sense of the immediacy of God's fatherly concern. How apposite to this situation are the later words of exhortation. "Humble yourselves under the powerful hand of God and God will lift you up when the moment comes. Cast all your care on God who is concerned about you" (1 Pet 5:6–7). The vital element that was lacking was the connectedness of their faith with experienced reality. Yes, the disciples had some faith, and it shaped many of their daily choices. But when they found themselves with their backs to the wall, it was a deep instinctual fear that seized control.

Jesus uses the words: "Do you still have no faith?" The

idea of "not yet" is a softening of the accusation. Even after so many signs and wonders, the disciples' faith is rudimentary. But faith is a process: there is still scope for its development. Throughout the Gospel of Mark, Jesus will keep goading the disciples with their lack of faith, even while slowly it struggles forward. In them as in us, faith and unbelief coexist. We are in two minds, "like the waves of the sea blown about and whipped up by the wind" (Jas 1:6). It is clear that, in Jesus' mind, the faith that moves mountains and calms storms does not flounder about like this (Mk 11:23).

The disciples are not completely beyond salvage. There was still a tiny skerrick of implicit faith embodied in their conviction that even in such a desperate situation Jesus could do something to improve their chances. And so, quivering with terror, they did the only thing that seemed likely to change things for the better; they turned to Jesus. Even before the miracle, they had glimpsed in Jesus something beyond the ordinary. Like Jonah or Saint Paul, he was a mere passenger, yet it seems that the crew recognized in him the key to their survival. Their appeal to him is abrupt and familiar, as if it were demanding that he do his share of whatever is necessary to ensure their safety. It is an appeal of the last resort: better late than never. We could learn something from the "faithless" disciples here: when all else fails turn to prayer. Of course it would be better if we did not wait until all seemed lost, but until we learn by experience that whatever we might be afraid of is ultimately subject to the power of Christ, this panicky recourse to prayer is probably as much as we can realistically expect of ourselves.

Saint Augustine understood that disturbances occur because faith becomes dormant. In times of crisis, we are compelled to return to the foundational reality of faith and to find there the strength and stability necessary to withstand the storm.

It is necessary to waken faith in the heart as if to awaken Christ in the boat. This is done if we believe, if we arouse faith. For we are uselessly upset. Why are we uselessly upset? Because when Christ is asleep in the boat the disciples are nearly shipwrecked. When Jesus slept the disciples were upset. The winds raged, the waves became agitated, and the boat was sinking. Why? Because Jesus was sleeping. So it is with you when the storms of temptation rage in this world; your heart is upset, as if it were you in the boat. Why? Is it not because your faith is dormant? Now the apostle Paul says that Christ dwells by faith in our hearts. So, rouse Christ in your heart, let your faith be awake and your conscience will be quieted and your ship will be freed.[7]

In the same vein, Isaac of Stella applied the narrative to the situation of his monks.

And so, brothers, as often as persecution assails us let us follow the example of the holy apostles and seek help from Christ. Let us arouse the faith in Christ within us by being mindful of the sleep of his passion, for perhaps this is what his sleeping [in the boat] well signifies. By ourselves we are weak and timid on the one hand, or inappropriately fearless on the other. In Christ we find an example of patience and from him we derive the strength to endure and we acquire the habit of constancy. Without Christ we are never capable of anything but in him we can do everything, as the blessed apostle said, "I can do all things in him who strengthens me."[8]

After the boat safely reaches the shore in the region of Gerasa, Jesus is confronted by another storm. Not a matter of winds and waves, but the tempestuous condition of a man so inhabited by thousands of demons that his humanity seems to be in remission—he had become "demonized" (Mk 5:18). The man lives among the tombs, naked (according to Luke), howling like a wild animal and doing violence to himself. Once liberated by Jesus he becomes a disciple, while the legion of demons impels a hated herd of pigs over the cliffs into a watery grave. Again, there is a sudden calm following the intervention of Jesus. In Luke's account (Lk 8:35), the former demoniac returns to his senses and quietly sits at Jesus' feet, now wearing clothes—he has become human again. Jesus is the bringer of calm to a chaotic and troubled world.

Mark's story of the stilling of the storm has a clear Christological purpose. The narrative is intended to present Jesus to the eyes of faith as one to whom are obedient not only to the demons but also the forces of the natural world. But there is more. The evangelist sets out to remind us that we need to have faith if the power of Jesus is to be exercised for our benefit. He means not only a nominal faith, or a faith for which we reach when all else is lost, but a faith that is embedded in our everyday awareness, and is expressed by a buoyant confidence, trust in Providence, and a willing obedience to all the manifestations of God's will.

Humanity at its purest and finest is transparent. The saints become icons of God for us because in them we see revealed something that is otherwise hidden from our gaze.[9] We know also that God acts through them, calling us to conversion, encouraging us in goodness, and sometimes working miracles. Let us take this a step further. The humanity of Jesus was so open to the divine that it became a permanent point of access between earth and heaven. "In Christ dwelt embodied the fullness of divinity" (Col 1:19, 2:9), so that "God was in Christ reconciling the world to himself" (2 Cor 5:19). As a result, anything was possible: authoritative teaching, healings, invitations to life, and wondrous acts of divine power. In him "the kindness and philanthropy of God our savior has been made manifest" (Titus 3:4). Jesus, fully divine and fully human, is the point where human history intersects with the creative and sustaining hand of God; at this point of meeting nothing is impossible.

CHAPTER TWELVE

A Quiet Mind

And so if you sigh for peace, if you desire to be nurtured by unbroken tranquillity, then do not love the world nor the things that are in the world (1 Jn 2:15). Those who love the world are either corrupted by pleasure or worn out by the pursuit of delights, or made blind by the ambition for a particular honor, or suffocated by two or all of these things working together. There is no rest in such things, no tranquillity at all. They yield to so many filthy affections and are scourged by so many suspicions. They burn with the flames of envy. They are wearied by their labors. Those whose love of money takes precedence over integrity are like the wicked in their treadmill (Ps 42:9), moving from nation to nation and from one kingdom to another. In the hope of financial gain they do not shrink back from the perils of floods, bandits, the dangers of the sea, and the violence of tempests. Envy tortures the ambitious and they burn with an indescribable heat of desire. In the hope of attaining glory, they shun nothing however unworthy, however filthy, however dishonorable, however reprehensible. The foundation of peace and tranquillity is laid as soon as these passions are expelled from the soul as it progresses: when the world is valued less, when libido loses its appeal, when avarice gives up and every honor becomes detestable.

AELRED OF RIEVAULX, *SERMONES INEDITI*, 20

The gift of peace is an effect of the indwelling of the Holy Spirit. As such it is much to be desired and sought. But there is also the discipline of peace, or the art of peace, which is our graced effort to make room for peace to expand in the heart. From there, we need to let it grow further so that we express what we have received in the way that we live and, perhaps, communicate our own peace to others. The discipline of peace is learned only through deliberate and long-term submission to the grace we have received. It is easy enough to be at peace when externally everything goes the way we want it. The art of peace, however, is acquired only by contending with disturbances both internal and external, and by designing our lives in such a way that there is a deep consistency between what we are and how we act. "We preserve peace within ourselves when the flesh does not oppose itself to the spirit, nor the spirit to the flesh, but sensuality obeys reason, and reason obeys its Creator."[1]

When you follow your own will there will always be interior turmoil even if you seem to avoid external trouble. When the will is opposed to the reason so that you will one thing and desire something else, how can you possess peace, since you do not even possess yourself? This turmoil of fleshly desires, this turmoil of self-will, cannot cease in you unless this fleshly love is changed and you find satisfaction in God. Moreover, the wicked are said, in the light of wisdom, to cease from turmoil (Job 3:17). This occurs when they serve the Creator instead of creatures; when they turn away from self-will, they leave behind turmoil and unrest. Having left behind the turmoil of such loves and the clamor of such thoughts there will be peace deep within you; and God, whose dwelling place is in peace, will dwell within you. Where God is, there is joyfulness.

Where God is, there is tranquillity. Where God is, there is happiness.[2]

The recipe for peace which Bernard and Aelred and many other monastic writers offer us is simple. Conform your life and your behavior to what you are by nature and by grace, and turmoil will cease. The inner flurry of conflicting thoughts can be substantially reduced by channeling desires away from self-indulgence in the direction of conformity to the will of God. Such a prescription strikes us as curious, since we tend to think that a state of peace is the result of things going well for us. We are quiet and content when our life runs smoothly. We become upset only when things go wrong and we are unable to fix them, when we lose control of the direction of our life and storms rage.

At the heart of the monastic approach is a distinction between the sort of peace that we enjoy when everything is calm, and the peace we are forced to find when things go badly. Bernard distinguishes three levels of peace, those who are peaceful because they are not hassled, those who find peace in the midst of disturbance, and those who overflow with peace so that they share their gift with others.

First, there is a peaceful person who merely renders good for good as far as possible and wishes to harm nobody. Then, there is another who is patient, who does not render evil for evil and is able to endure being harmed. Finally, there is the peacemaker who renders good for evil and is willing to be of service to the one who harms....The first, as far as possible, *has peace*; the second *holds fast to peace*; the third *makes peace*.[3]

We learn peace by our struggles to regain peace after it has deserted us. In other words, the way to a more permanent peace is patience.[4] At a first level, this search asks of us a certain measure of endurance. "Affliction gives rise to endurance, endurance to character, character to hope" (Rom 5:3–4).[5] The sort of person I am is largely determined by how I handle the negative situations in which I find myself. Sometimes I am like an infant for whom the slightest delay in gratification or the merest murmur of contradiction sends me spinning into a tantrum. I then try to reduce the pain by offloading it onto others. They become upset and vent their emotion on us or others. In this way, a deadly cycle of trouble begins that may draw many into its vortex and will certainly not assuage the inner turmoil that started the process.

As we grow older, we begin to learn from experience what sort of things upset us. If we have progressed to the stage where it is possible to be reflective and somewhat self-critical, we might begin to recognize that the upsetting events we previously blamed are not alone in destroying our equanimity. There is a fifth column within, aiding and abetting potential disturbances. This is where it is useful sometimes to make an inventory of all the situations that threaten our peace of mind and lead us to a state of upheaval. If we are honest with ourselves, we will then be able to set down beside each one of them the interior failing that has given the exterior event power over us. We find several likely items in the sermon of Saint Aelred quoted at the head of this chapter.

(a) Disordered desires
(b) suspicion
(c) envy
(d) overwork
(e) love of money, and
(f) ambition.[6]

These are thoughts and desires which almost always unleash a storm within the soul. We say to ourselves that we are upset by what our neighbors do to frustrate our wishes, but our troubles are caused primarily by our own disordinate desires and only secondarily by the actions or omissions of others. When we are upset, we need to sit ourselves down and ask, "What is troubling you?" Why are you so angry? No doubt the first answer will be a catalog of external events to which we readily assign the blame for our condition. We cannot allow ourselves to be satisfied with that answer; we must push harder. "Why are these things upsetting you?" Perhaps these incidents have been exaggerated and taken out of context. "But why? Are you afraid of what they reveal not about others but about yourself?" What seems to be an appropriate concern about a hell-raising teenager may be in reality the fear of being judged an inadequate parent. Irritation at another's behavior may cloak my fear of expedient confrontation and conflict. Suspicions may be the result of projecting my own repressed desires. I can never be at peace if I concentrate on what is outside without dealing with the emotions in me that are the proximate cause of my troubles.

What all these disturbances have in common is that they draw so much attention to themselves that we lose sight of other realities. Our world shrinks and narrows. As a result, our impulsive conclusions may lack both perspective and proportion. Each little setback begins to seem like the end of the world. We forget that, even if a thousand desires were denied us, we would still be better off than most of the earth's population. A small loss, a minor humiliation, petty squabbling over trifles or some curb on our self-indulgence, so many everyday annoyances are mere pinpricks when compared with the tragedies that are the common lot of millions. Yet we allow these small irritants to banish all sense of inward peace and all tranquillity of mind and heart. Others face genuine disaster with fortitude and patience. We are completely flattened not only by minor setbacks, but even by the fear of them. We can be just as upset by imagined troubles as by real ones. We exaggerate the dangers and so allow them to overwhelm us. It looks as though there is something inside us that does not want us to live in peace, but is perpetually agitating our souls and making us miserable.

Living in peace is a matter of controlling our reactions to potentially disturbing thoughts whether these are generated internally or are our interpretations of external events. This means, in minor matters, taking a moment to check the appropriateness of our impulses and leaving room for other considerations to emerge. In major matters, I will need much more than a moment for quiet reflection if I am to find peace. A wounding insult, an alarming medical report, the death of a loved one, or a serious personal failure cannot be denied or thought away. But we can allow alternative thoughts to come to the surface of our minds. In the midst of our anguish, these can offer some respite. The heavier the affliction, the more time and effort we need to expend in trying to go beneath the surface to find a deeper meaning. It is not denial of our pain, nor the facile dismissal of our sense of grievance, but a faith-filled exploration of the ways of God in our life. It may be a matter of accepting a share of the responsibility for what has happened, or coming to see things from another's viewpoint, or simply accepting that no human life is without its quantum of suffering. If our faith is strong, we may find solace in balancing present pain with the reassertion of trust in a loving God. Some, like Job, will remain in the darkness for many years, called to accept a high level of incomprehension and frustration. If such be our lot, it is all the more important that we consciously abandon ourselves to the mysterious plans of God and not wear ourselves out either by denial of our pain or by refusing to go beyond or beneath it.

To write a book, to develop a new vaccine, to deepen a relationship, to carve a statue, to resolve a problem, or to satisfy any all-consuming passion, we need a measure of exterior silence and solitude so that we can concentrate on the task we wish to accomplish and devote all our energies to its successful completion. Continual interruption fragments our attention and prevents us from feeling or expressing anything beyond the superficial. The same is true when troubles come. We need to take time to confront them directly in a prayer-filled environment. The Old Testament psalms of lament are good examples of how mental confusion can be brought before God and expressed in prayer. Mostly this leads to acceptance and peace, because it takes us into a different space, where issues can be evaluated differently. The only place we are going to find peace is at the level of the heart. Sometimes it is by returning to our own heart that we find the resources we need to regain our equanimity, and sometimes it is by having a heart-to-heart talk with a trusted friend that peace revives.

Sometimes a strategic withdrawal is called for—we need to pull back from an indefensible front line to a position from which a realistic resistance is possible. There are certain things that upset us disproportionately and, if we are sensible, we try to avoid them as far as possible. There is not much point, for example, in getting stirred up about matters which we cannot change for the better. We are better off husbanding our limited energies and limiting our concern to issues where we can make a difference. It is a little like triage. When some disaster overwhelms the medical resources, a division has to be made between patients so that medical assistance is given first to those who need it most and who are most likely to profit from it. Those who are beyond helping and those whose injuries are relatively minor are deferred. In the same way, we need to limit our deliberate concern to realities over which we have some control and not allow ourselves to be led up the garden

path of ersatz emotion which has no possibility of being translated into action. The question we have to keep asking ourselves is a practical one. "What can I do now to improve the
situation?" Sometimes damage control is as much as we can
do; on other occasions quiet pondering may open up pathways to a more creative resolution.

Vigilance is an important element of strategy that bears
emphasis. In some, but not all, situations it is prudent to engage in border protection, deliberately and preemptively refusing admittance to whatever uselessly upsets us. This may
mean, for example, blocking certain input from the mass media, avoiding an encounter which will be fruitlessly conflictual,
letting provocation pass unanswered, refusing to feed our suspicions, choosing not to act indignantly when our judgment is
questioned. In this way, we are preventing disturbance by denying access to potential triggers. A little bit of prudence can
save us a great deal of trouble. We may not know exactly
what it is within us that reacts to these stimuli, but by keeping
away from them we avoid an allergic reaction. In this way, we
are using our sense of inward peace as a guide to behavior. We
continually monitor the state of our soul. Unless there is a
proportionate benefit to be obtained, we opt for that course
of action that allows us to concentrate on the main game,
rather than letting ourselves be drawn into useless diversions.
Perhaps when we are stronger and have attained a solid measure of peace, we may find it helpful to confront directly whatever provokes a negative reaction in us. Until then it is better
not to bite off more than we can chew.

Being like Martha, anxious and concerned about many
things, is a surefire recipe for inner turmoil (see Lk 10:41–42).
Jesus is quite clear on this issue. "First be zealous for the Kingdom and its righteousness, and all these things will be given
you as well" (Mt 6:33). We need to keep before our minds the
great realities of life, and not allow ourselves to be sidetracked.

As Winston Churchill once wrote, we need to "watch the tides and not the eddies." This is to say that in the trials and turmoils of life we need to return to simple basic questions about the meaning of human existence in the light of God's Providence and mercy. With such a focus, there is scope for storms to cease and a great calm to ensue.

Later in this book we will reflect on Saint Mark's account of events in the garden of Gethsemane. There Jesus offers us an example of how to act when our inner peace is lost and our whole being cringes in revulsion before the future that awaits us. The way to a resolution of the crisis is so simple that we often overlook it. Faith-filled prayer is the best response to troubled times. It may not cause mountains to be moved, but heartfelt prayer can bring about such a powerful change in our dispositions that even the most ugly situation is invested with meaning and ultimate value. By turning our attention to the unseen realities of the spiritual world, we allow ourselves to be energized by them and so are more able to bear with the suffering inflicted on us in this world of space and time, where human error and malice sometimes reign supreme.

It is the virtue of hope which is the great standby when things go wrong—a hope not based on what God is perceived to have done for us in the past, nor on the prospects inherent in the present situation, but a hope based on the reality of God's love and mercy. Such assurance finds its origin in the fidelity of God and the truth of the divine promises. Nothing better stills a troubled heart than ongoing reflection on God's steadfast love to which all the Scriptures give eloquent testimony.

A quiet mind is the effect of strong faith. It is not a mere byproduct of tranquil times. Just as fear is less when we are in the presence of a friend, so our awareness of Christ's presence in our life will be the road to a more profound freedom from disturbance. Christ is our peace, not in the future but in the present, not held back but freely given, not hoped for but obtained.[7] Like the apostles in the boat, we need to turn to Jesus when storms rage.

CHAPTER THIRTEEN

Jesus the Learner

From there he rose and went away into the area around Tyre. Not wanting anyone to know, he entered a house, but he was unable to remain hidden. Immediately a woman whose young daughter had an unclean spirit heard about him. She came and fell at his feet. The woman was a Greek, of Syrophoenician origin. She asked him to drive out the demon from her daughter. Jesus said to her, "Let the children be fed first. It is not fair to take the children's bread and throw it to dogs." The woman replied thus: "Indeed, Lord, but the dogs under the table eat the children's crumbs." Jesus said to her: "For this saying, go your way; the demon has come out of your daughter." And the woman went to her house and found the child lying on the bed and the demon gone.

MARK 7:24–30

I was irritated and a little scandalized when I first came into contact with Max Ernst's 1928 painting of Mary spanking Jesus.[1] In rich Renaissance colors, the scene is set in a typical courtyard. The boy is spread over her lap, his bottom red, his halo tumbled to the ground. Her hand is poised for another smack. Although it was probably intended as a bit of irreverent humor, the image may well have something to offer to theological reflection. The scene demonstrates graphically what

Luke merely hints at when he says that the boy Jesus was under the tutelage of his parents. It is reasonable to suppose that Jesus was trained by them using methods common in their culture.

Nor is it unworthy to consider the possibility that the boy Jesus may have indulged in childish mischief-making, continually expanding the boundaries of behavior and, in the process, wearing out the patience of adults. In the folkloric tradition conveyed to us by the apocryphal Gospels, such naughtiness is often associated with the inappropriate use of divine power. Childish mischief and spite are mingled with an adult awareness of divinity.

> And after some days as Jesus walked with Joseph through the city, one of the children ran up and knocked Jesus on the arms. Jesus was angry and said to him: "This is the end of the road for you." And immediately the child fell to earth and died….But when Joseph saw what Jesus had done he harshly pulled his ear in anger. Jesus was vexed and said to Joseph: "It is enough for you to see me: do not touch me. For you do not know who I am. If you did know you would not give me a hard time. I may be with you now, yet I was made before you."[2]

In this perspective, the reluctant boy Jesus had to be trained vigorously to use his miraculous gifts with moderation. Such quaint stories are not a denial of Jesus' divinity but a strong affirmation of the reality of the incarnation. The humanity assumed by the Word began earthly life at the beginning. There was much learning ahead.

The only incident from these early days that is recounted in the canonical Gospels is the story of Jesus at twelve years of age, separating himself from his family and going off in search of knowledge (Lk 2:41–52). Two distinct themes are inter-woven. First, we notice a certain tension between Jesus' self-assertion in obedience to an interior sense of mission and due submission to his parents; this strain also appears in Mark 3:31–35 and elsewhere. Second, Jesus seems to have been aware that the training given him by his parents needed to be supple-mented by a higher learning—which could only be found among those appointed to occupy the chair of Moses (Mt 23:2). Jesus is already moving beyond the confines of the family of Nazareth.

Perhaps our interpretation of this event is too much influ-enced by the conventions of Christian art. More often than not, Jesus seems to be teaching rather than learning—a radi-ant and youthful figure dazzling with his knowledge the grizzled purveyors of bookish tradition. It is as though he were conducting a master class for the teachers of the Law. The text is quite clear: Jesus was there to learn.[3] He was listening to the teachers and asking them questions—not examining them, but seeking answers to what puzzled him. Far from giv-ing a lecture, Jesus was a full participant in the interactive dialogue characteristic of Jewish schools. The teachers, for their part, were astonished at his intelligence and his answers. Later his fellow villagers would express the same amazement: "Where do these things come from and what is the wisdom given to this man that powerful deeds come about by his hands?" (Mk 6:2).[4]

It seems likely that Luke is retrojecting into Jesus' child-hood a trait characteristic of his adult years—the gift of being able to listen and learn. This feature of Jesus' personal style is essential. God's Son, the Second Person of the Trinity, is dif-ferentiated from the Father only in that he is a listener or re-ceiver. The Word completely receives and expresses what the Father is. The fullness of divinity coexists in Father and in Son, the only difference is that the Father is the source and the

Son the recipient of godhead. Jesus is the perfect listener. "A son can do nothing on his own, but only what he sees his father doing; whatever the father does thus, likewise, the son does. The Father loves the Son and has made a demonstration to the Son of what he does" (Jn 5:19–20).[5] God's Son learns from the Father; in his human nature he continues to learn from all who have something to teach him.

Jesus certainly learned from his parents—whether by the means portrayed by Max Ernst is irrelevant. He was sufficiently knowledgeable about the Hebrew Scriptures and traditional interpretations to be able to hold his own in theological controversy. Most characteristic of all was his capacity to learn from the world around him. The parables of Jesus reveal an incisive intelligence, able to learn lessons from the most everyday occurrences. The sowing of seed, the rhythms of nature, and the devious politics of the powerful opened his mind to understand the dynamics of God's coming kingdom. Seeing the widow deposit her coins in the treasury led him to pass beyond quantitative judgments and to perceive the substantial nature of her offering. So willing a learner was he that almost anyone could become his teacher. Nor was it only a matter of gaining information about the external world. Others were able to lead him to a truer perception of himself and his mission. The Syrophoenician woman was one such teacher.

At the beginning of the episode, Jesus has a narrow conception of the extent of his mission. In pagan territory, he does not want to be known. So he attempts to hide inside a house. Even when the woman bursts through his isolation with her plaintive appeal, he is abrupt to the point of rudeness. Her trust in his powers and her humility are counted as nothing. Priority is to be given to his own people. Matthew 15:24 adds a saying modeled perhaps on Jesus' earlier instruction to the disciples (Mt 10:6): "I was sent only to the lost sheep of the house of Israel." Jesus saw his mission as calling back God's people from their erring ways, not bringing the Gentiles in from the cold.

The woman is unabashed. She points to the current wastage—the children are not such enthusiastic receivers of his mission that there is nothing left over. Jesus was already amazed at his own people's lack of faith (Mk 6:6) but had rationalized their response as typical of the reception given to a prophet. Now he is, for the first time in Mark, confronted with the lively faith of a Gentile. Maybe Jesus experienced some sense that as one door closes another opens. This is what Paul and Barnabas later expressed: "We were obliged to speak God's word first to you, but since you reject it and do not judge yourselves worthy of eternal life: see we will turn to the Gentiles" (Acts 13:46). Perhaps Jesus is beginning to realize that waiting for the children to be fed will take a long time.

Jesus appreciates the woman's feisty rejoinder and is won over by her boldness. She has held a mirror up to him and, as it were, for the first time he has seen himself and his mission more clearly. She has perceived in him more than a parochial savior; it was from her that Jesus began to consider the universality of the Good News. In an incident not included in Mark, Matthew records a similar reaction when he recounts Jesus' admiration for the faith of a centurion: "Hearing this Jesus was amazed and said to his followers, 'Amen I say to you that I have not found faith such as this in Israel. I am telling you that many will come from east and west to recline at table with Abraham, Isaac, and Jacob in the kingdom of heaven, while the sons [and daughters] of the kingdom will be thrown out into the darkness outside, where there will be wailing, and the gnashing of teeth'" (Mt 8:10–12). By his contact with the Syrophoenician woman, Jesus learned that his mission went far beyond the nationalistic boundaries that he had taken for granted. In this, she was his teacher. It is not merely a learning of new facts that resulted, but the acquiring of new attitudes, an opening of the heart to those previously excluded. In a sense, this is a moment of conversion for Jesus, a changing of his perceptual horizons and the certainties by which he operated. The Syrophoenican women has held up a mirror to him and in it Jesus has come to understand better himself and his mission.

There is something very attractive about the picture of Jesus gradually distilling his wisdom from the experience of encounter with others. It is as though the goodness of so many little people is recapitulated in him. Not a walking encyclopedia of religion, but one who, like his mother, pondered and cherished much in his heart. Perhaps this is why so many were drawn by his words; his teaching was not hollow like that of many others, but it had a power to touch and energize, a certain "authority" about it (Mk 1:27). Part of the reason they felt an affinity with the wisdom of Jesus was simply due to the fact that it had evolved in dialogue with the experience of people like themselves, and not in elitist isolation.

The immediate effect of this meeting with the Syrophoenician woman is that Jesus plunges more deeply into the Gentile world, thus taking to a new level the process of universalizing the Good News. We are the beneficiaries of this change in direction.

CHAPTER FOURTEEN

An Open Heart

In the same way do not ponder what you have to do if you have no one from whom you may seek [counsel]. God will not abandon any who wholeheartedly seek to know God's will in truth. God will in everything show them the way according to his will. For those who turn their heart to God's will God will enlighten a little child to speak the will of God.

DOROTHEOS OF GAZA, *INSTRUCTION 5* #68, SCHR 92, P. 264

Growth is one of those most characteristic features of living organisms. In different ways according to their particular mode of existence, plants and animals draw from their environment what they need to maintain themselves and to develop. Human beings have to do this too, and so much of our energy is employed procuring what we require to cater to our basic physiological needs: food, clothing, shelter. In a manner unknown to the animals, we have, in addition, the responsibility of providing for the development of our mental and spiritual gifts. To remain intellectually and affectively at the level of a child is an affront to our innate capabilities. We are designed not only to grow, but to grow up; and our human potential cannot be realized unless we leave our subjective world and develop ourselves by interaction with a wider reality.

This means education, in the sense of continually broadening our horizons, so that we see issues from an ever wider and wiser standpoint. Development continues throughout life as we leave behind the self-centeredness typical of the immature and begin to move towards an other-centeredness or altruism, and beyond that to some form of global compassion and concern that is coterminous with a dark awareness of the invisible realities of the spiritual world. Such a progression suggests that in the course of a lifetime there are substantial shifts in the network of beliefs and values by which our actions are governed. A philosophy of life that supports the practice of a purely parochial philanthropy needs to be supplemented by new perspectives if it is to embrace issues of universal concern. For this to happen we need to see things more clearly—it is this sharpened vision that enables us to evaluate possibilities differently.

There is a need for moments of conversion in which it becomes possible for us to make the transition to a higher state of awareness. This change in perceptual horizons occurs in many different ways: it can be as dramatic as Saint Paul's vision on the Damascus road or, as in the case of Saint Augustine, it can be a movement made up of many small steps, like a great ship changing course. In most cases, conversion is the result of a combination of factors: many significant incidents coalesce under the impact of some catalytic event and a window of opportunity opens that is simultaneously a surprise and yet not unanticipated.

In the course of a lifetime, most of us need to undergo several conversions—not necessarily from "bad" to "good"; more likely from "good" to "better" or from "good then" to "good now." It happens in our careers, our relationships, even our hobbies. We become aware that we are no longer satisfied by past options: we have grown out of one set of needs only to discover other demands clamoring for attention. The same elements predominate, perhaps, but we combine them in different proportions as we evolve.

Our spiritual lives develop too. We may find, at important junctures of our lives, that the religious or spiritual attitudes we have adopted in the past no longer serve as creative means of energizing us for interacting with the real world. Many people's religious knowledge, practice, and culture has not gone beyond what they acquired as schoolchildren. Such remnants of childish devotion are no longer suitable for the expanded inner and outer worlds in which life is now lived. In an emergency, when they instinctively reach out for the support of religion, they find nothing that can bear their weight. Faded memories and long-lost certainties do not have enough vigor or continuity to be transposed to a new situation. As a result, the dissonance we feel at this point may drive us into unbelief. Alternatively, if our religious instinct is persistent, the crisis may have the effect of motivating us to take up again the question of religion, and to try to reestablish a foundation for a spiritual life in the new situation in which we find ourselves. Even though we may feel aggrieved at being wrong-footed, our awkward efforts to regain our balance may well signal the beginning of a new stage in life, a step forward into the unsurveyed future.

Once we become aware that we seem to have negotiated a transition, the challenge consists in consolidating the gains. We have allowed ourselves to become involved in a process of attitudinal change, but we are now confronted by the need to break the hold of old habits and develop new ways of acting and reacting. Conversion does not bring with it a prepackaged set of beliefs, values, and behaviors. All of these have to be started from the beginning. This means devoting precious time and energy to the enterprise. We have to keep testing our assessment of what to do against the reality of the total environment in which we are operating. Sometimes we read ourselves and the external situation well, and we are pleased that our actions concord with our newfound vision. On other occasions there is dissonance, either because we don't put enough effort into the task or because we make a mistake, and then we lose heart. What we do not realize, perhaps, is that the struggle itself is formative. It is in the rhythm of everyday falling and rising that we begin to see clearly what is to be embraced and what eschewed.

In the school of Christ we are, as the first disciples were, always learning. There is no prescribed course that we may follow diligently and so graduate. Our learning is not directed to absorbing a body of knowledge so much as to making our own a distinctive way of life that is based on the Gospel. This is not book learning, but an apprenticeship under grace. Our call is to be attentive to the world around us and to all whom we meet, and to allow ourselves to be constantly reformed in the likeness of Christ: we are never the same: yesterday, today, or forever. The Second Vatican Council enshrined this principle of ongoing renewal in insisting that our task of returning to the sources must include the complementary work of paying attention to the "signs of the times."[1]

There is something in us that does not want to keep adapting to changing circumstances and wants everything to be left pretty much as it was. To make this false stability possible we erect vast defensive networks. In this way we hope to prevent our being compelled to modify anything. We deny the facts either by shutting out feedback or discrediting any who might comment unfavorably on our fantasy world. We excuse our failures by pointing to the failures of others. We rationalize, project, blame, and bluster. We succeed in making our neighbors as miserable as ourselves, all the while overlooking the fact that the principal cause of our unhappiness is our entrenched resistance to the threat and inconvenience of change.

Such defensiveness has no inherent limits, so it keeps expanding—constantly identifying new threats and blocking out more and more of reality in the process.[2] Fear begins to inspire many of the choices that we make. Instead of welcoming whatever happens as a messenger bearing news of God's love, we immure ourselves behind barricades of suspicion and rejection. In this situation we are frightened at the thought of not having absolute control over our lives.

Living in a controlled world behind high walls is scarcely living at all, and it is certainly not a situation that encourages genuine growth. Think back over your own life and you may find many examples of unexpected encounters yielding happy outcomes and precious guidance about the way ahead. Rarely does God intervene directly in our life. Usually, as in the parable of the defaulting tenants (Mk 12:1–12), others come to do God's work. Each morning as we rise from sleep we can say, "This day God will send me whatever support, whatever guidance, whatever forgiveness I need." It is only a matter of remaining alert, watching for God's agents. "Do not forget hospitality since in being hospitable some have unknowingly entertained angels" (Heb 13:2). What a difference it would make if I were to welcome everything that happens as good news. It may require some extra digging in some situations to get beneath the surface affront to discover the pleasant surprise, but what a different person I would be if I were to jettison my readiness to qualify everything unexpected as bad news. What an incredible sense of lightness would infuse my heart and mind, and thus modify the way I present to others.

This buoyant sense that every person I encounter can serve as an interface between me and God is expressed strongly in the ancient Irish poem *Faed Fiada,* sometimes titled "St. Patrick's Breastplate."

Christ in the heart of every man who thinks of me.
Christ in the mouth of every man who speaks to me.
Christ in every eye that sees me.
Christ in every ear that hears me.[3]

One who passes through life possessed by the confidence that nothing can separate us from the love of Christ greets every new situation with a childlike expectancy that is the diametric opposite of the dread and anguish that many feel in facing the future. However unsavory the appearances, a hope exists that in some hidden way God is working through such unlikely events to bring about good. This is trust in Providence brought to bear on the simple occurrences that constitute our everyday existence. Something happens. We meet somebody. Two paths intersect. Whether we like it or not, our life can be changed suddenly and permanently. Every day there is the potential to begin a new chapter.

I suppose that most of us accept this in theory, but it is not so easy to live as though it were true. If the archangel Gabriel were to make an appearance in our lives, we would probably have a fair degree of confidence in the communication, but we are a bit reluctant to give credence to less splendid messengers. Here it is helpful to reflect on the biblical incident of Balaam and his donkey (Num 22:15–35). The narrative is a little complicated but it goes like this. Balaam the seer is commissioned to curse the people of the LORD. Against the divine will he sets out on his task, but unknown to him an angel with a sword blocks his progress. Three times he is saved by his donkey who sees the danger and takes evasive action. Three times he beats the donkey. Eventually the donkey begins to speak and reveals to the seer the folly of his ways. And so Balaam changes his tune and blesses Israel instead. The point of the story in our present context is that God can provide guidance and correction by donkeys if necessary, even if we consider ourselves like Balaam to have "an eye that is clear" and thus in no need of asinine wisdom.

We are not always aware that we are "kicking against the goad" (Acts 26:14) when we defend our entrenched convictions; we are zealous perhaps, but our zeal is unreasonable

(Rom 10:2). Willy-nilly we are being led up the garden path of self-will, forgetful that our ways are often not God's ways. So God sends an unlikely messenger to turn us aside. We remember how Saint Augustine's mother was prevented from developing a more serious drinking problem by the angry retort of a serving maid.[4] It is not only our friends who can offer enlightenment about the way ahead; often enough a salutary word of correction will come from one who means us no good.

If we live our daily lives with all the windows open, it becomes possible for the Spirit's gentle breeze to penetrate our resistance and bring us relief from the tightness we impose on ourselves. We consent to live on the brink of the unexpected, alert for any indication of where inspiration may prompt us to go. This means, of course, laying aside the blueprints we have drawn up for the rest of our lives, and learning to live in the carefree insecurity that characterizes the birds of the air and the lilies in the field. We become people ready for a mission—without ever knowing what it is that we will be asked to do. We give up the self-satisfied passivity of routines and ironclad guarantees and revel in the freedom of God's children. This is not to say that we are butterflies, flitting from one perch to another without obligations or commitments. It means simply that whatever we do, wherever we are, we keep an ear cocked for the call of God and a heart open enough to be somewhat detached from our private perceptions, prejudices, and plans.

Faith is a mode of listening; it is the ability to distinguish God's call from a multitude of other summonses, to discern God's voice in the midst of so many other sounds. Sometimes the recognition is instantaneous. In other situations we have to work industriously, using our reason and consulting with others in order to establish with certainty the way that leads to a more abundant life. There is a certain romantic glamour about instantly responding to "inspirations," even in situations where the decision seems more inspired by instability and a desire for novelty rather than on a solid commitment to the truth. Most often the work of discernment requires of us a painstaking patience that is suspicious of bursts of enthusiasm lest they be no more than alternative expressions of self-will and not indications of what God wants.

The life of a disciple is insecure because it is a life lived at the behest of a master. Those who attach themselves to an earthly *guru* or *gurina* have an easier task than Christians, despite the rigor of the regimen and the severity of total obedience. We are disciples of an invisible Master who has no voice, but the voices of those around us; who teaches us by the words and actions and needs of others. "As long as you did it to one of these, the least of my brothers [or sisters] you did it to me" (Mt 25:40). If we are truly disciples of Jesus, we need to live as those who are yearning for instruction: "As the eyes of servants are on the hands of their lords" (Ps 123:2), waiting for some indication of what is to be done. This is no independent life with self-defined parameters and purposes, but it is a life lived at the behest of an invisible Other. Being a disciple of Jesus denotes a lifelong willingness to be formed and reformed without total certainty regarding the channels by which such formation will come. As a result, discipleship demands of us a certain openness of mind and heart that is the opposite of individualism.

We are familiar with many stories of those who, in retrospect, are able to perceive that it was in time of hardship and challenge that dramatic growth occurred. In a crisis, many discover interior resources of which previously we had been unaware. The point is, however, that most of us readily rise to the occasion when tragedy strikes. Far more difficult is unremitting heroism when faced with the humdrum trivialities of everyday existence. We lose our concentration at such moments and are often engulfed by events which automatically dictate our actions without much reflection on our part. Somehow or other, we think ordinary life is not the real thing—it is only a drill or a rehearsal—and so we save ourselves for major incidents. Meanwhile a thousand small opportunities to do good slip by unnoticed. We are too busy waiting for "the big one" to pay much attention to anything less. It seems incredible to us that a cup of cold water could be a channel of salvation.

Most of us have been brainwashed into thinking that only big things matter; small things have no significance. It is as though we believe that meaning resides in things, events, and external realities; and hence major affairs have major significance and minor matters are meaningless. On the contrary, meaning is a subjective reality. Something may have a meaning for me and not for you. Meaning may be qualitatively or quantitatively different from one person to another. A course of action is meaningful to me if it accords with the beliefs and values by which I shape my life. In such behavior, I express myself: the actions bear the imprint of my personality. So it is that a customary gesture of politeness may be an act of respect and love when it is performed by one person and no more than an unreflective gesture when it is done by another. I should never say "That is meaningless" but rather "That is meaningless *for me.*" Such a statement conveys something about me; it says virtually nothing about whatever it is that I find meaningless.

The Christian meaning of life is an interpretation of what happens in the context of Christ's presence and action in the world. It is the result of our responding to the call to read daily events in the light of Gospel principles. This interpretation will not always be compatible with that given by our unbelieving contemporaries and so we may arrive at different evaluations of moral issues or philosophical premises. This is only to be expected. There is no need to become involved in useless controversy about which opinion is "right." We will not be able to convince anyone unless they accept the foundational principles from which our conclusions derive. When Saint Thomas Aquinas discussed the question of God's existence, he did no more than provide "five ways" by which believers could be assured that their faith was reasonable. He did not attempt to propose a watertight chain of irrefutable logic that would send atheists scurrying for their prayer books.

What we find meaningful depends on our chosen philosophy of life. Notice the word "chosen." Meaning depends on the values I freely embrace. Let us reflect on a single instance. If imitation of Christ is for me an ideal to be followed, then otherwise meaningless events become meaningful. Patience in suffering may become a means of participating in Christ's passion and so the pain becomes more tolerable and maybe even something to be loved and pursued. We see a clear example of this in Saint Ignatius of Antioch, who was martyred under the Emperor Trajan in the early years of the second century, and saw his impending death in this light.

> I beseech you, do not exercise towards me an inappropriate kindness. Let me be food for the wild animals by whose help I may encounter God. I am the wheat of God and I must be ground by the teeth of the wild animals so that I may be found as the pure bread of Christ. Rather, charm the beasts so that they may become a tomb for me, so that nothing is left of my body so that once I am dead I will be a burden to no one. Then I shall truly be a disciple of Jesus Christ when the world no longer sees my body....

> There is no advantage for me in the attractions of the world nor in the kingdoms of this age. It is better for me to die into Christ Jesus that to rule over the ends of

the earth. It is Christ whom I seek who died for our sake. It is Christ who is the object of my willing, who rose for us. My labor pains are at hand. Spare me, brothers, do not prevent me from living, do not will my death. Do not make a gift to the world of one who loves God, nor let him be seized by matter. Allow me to receive the pure light; when I come to that place I shall be a human being. Permit me to imitate the suffering of my God....

While I am still alive, I write to you, but my passionate desire is to die. For my passionate desire [ἔρως] has been crucified and there is in me no fiery love of material things. Living water speaks in me and inwardly says: "Come to the Father." I take no pleasure in corruptible food nor in the pleasures of this life. What I want is the bread of God which is the flesh of Jesus Christ, born of David's line. For drink I want his blood, which is incorruptible love.[5]

This lyrical anticipation of a gruesome death is beyond the imagination of most of us. To be the victim of the animal savagery of the Coliseum seems to us an irredeemable tragedy. For Ignatius, even though he was familiar with the hideous reality of such spectacles, there was no cause for fear. This suffering would be for him—though it may not have been for many who suffered the same fate—a proactive means of imitating the passion of Christ and, thereby, the doorway to eternal life. This was the faith that made the prospect of an ugly death both meaningful and attractive. His belief in the reality of Christ's promises conferred meaning on an otherwise repugnant future. The faith and hope of Ignatius changed the meaning of his death. It was a similar disposition that sustained Saint Maximilian Kolbe as he starved to death in a

Nazi hunger bunker, voluntarily giving his life for the sake of a neighbor. The attitude of both is similar to that expressed by Saint Paul.

> Whatever profits I had, I regard as loss because of Christ. Moreover, I regard all things as loss because of the superiority of knowing Christ Jesus my Lord. For his sake I have lost everything. I regard them as rubbish, to gain Christ and be found in him, not having my own righteousness coming from the Law, but a righteousness that comes from faith in Christ, a righteousness from God through faith, knowing Christ and the power of his resurrection, and participating in his sufferings, being conformed to his death, so that I may arrive at the resurrection from the dead (Phil 3:7–11).

If we are true disciples of Christ, we are expected to have a philosophy of life that turns events upside down, that perceives life-giving meaning where others see only folly or scandal. This means everything is assessed and evaluated in the light of the paschal mystery. The result is that we are aware of a meaning that is hidden from those who have no faith. When we are attuned to the voice of Christ and willing to hear what he says, we hear events whispering a different message and thus dictating a different response in us. This is why the actions of the saints are greeted with stunned incomprehension by those who witness them. The saints are not mad, though they may appear so. In the words of a contemporary commonplace, they simply "march to the beat of a different drum."

There is no way that any program of catechesis can provide us with a fixed body of doctrine that will be sufficient to guide us throughout the anticipated seventy or eighty years of a normal life span. It follows that what we need to receive in this initial period of formation is aptitude to keep learning from our experiences. We need to confront reality with an unprejudiced eye, seeking to learn from it. It may be that our experience causes us to doubt what we have hitherto received, and stirs up awkward questions. This is not such a bad thing; it is a good way of finding the answers. Experience propels us into the world of reflection, study, consultation with those wiser with us, and frank conversation with fellow believers. In such ways is our learning from life achieved. Our journey through life will take us to many strange and unexpected destinations. Most of the time we will have to make the path by walking, doing most of our learning on our feet. What should give us great confidence despite the precariousness of such a process is our faith that God will never leave us bereft of guidance. Any situation assessed by the eye of faith will yield the guidance and encouragement necessary for us to continue our onward march with a lighter step.

CHAPTER FIFTEEN

Jesus Moves Around

Then Jesus went out from the area around Tyre and came via Sidon to the Sea of Galilee, up through the middle of the area of the Decapolis.

MARK 7:31

Mark's account of the public life of Jesus is the story of his comings and goings. At first these movements seem to be merely the means by which the different settings of his activities can be linked together in a continuous chronicle. There is more than this. The impression is created that the constant journeying of Jesus is part of his personal style. Already in Mark, but more strongly in Luke, is the suggestion that the wayfaring of Jesus has a theological significance. It is not aimless wandering but a directed progression towards Jerusalem and the Cross.

Most of us don't pay much attention to the itinerary outlined in the verse that provides the opening for this chapter. The place names may be familiar to us, but we are probably not too sure of their exact location; in which case the roundabout nature of the journey eludes us. Three pieces of information may be gleaned from Mark's brief statement. First, Jesus was mobile; he did not concentrate his efforts in a single town, but circulated widely. Mark notes this explicitly in 1:38. Second, as already noted, after his eyes were opened by the Syrophoenician woman's faith, he began to move more boldly into predominantly non-Jewish areas. Third, the route he followed was not simply the most direct means of traversing the distance, but was dictated by other unknown factors.

Mobility does not involve large investments in infrastructure. We are familiar with agencies of charity or service that become identified with their real estate. Long before the first meal is served or the first medicine is distributed, humanitarian organizations set up a building to house staff responsible for gathering and distributing funds. This is usually built according to professional standards and would seem like a palace to those on whose account it exists. There is a danger that those who work in such a building will soon begin to think like the rich, to attach themselves more closely to the affluent from whom they receive their resources than to the poor to whom they minister. Even while they give their services generously, they may yet be tempted to hold back something of themselves. The lifestyle generated by the building forces them to live in two worlds; in time they may forget what it is like to be needy.

There are similar hazards involved in religious building. Contrary to its original usage, the words "church" and "synagogue" in common parlance now refer to a building rather than to a gathering of people. Once you have a building, you need doors that selectively open and close, admitting some and excluding others. Security is necessary to protect the investment, and compromises have to be made in the name of practicality. A beautiful building is a great benefit in serving the people, but it can easily become a liability, taking the focus off the gathering of people and transferring it to the building. Look at all those marvelous medieval cathedrals dotted over the surface of the European continent. How expensive it is to maintain them! How easily they become tourist locales and not gathering places of those with "one heart and one mind"! How can a World Heritage edifice be adapted to suit the needs of a changing congregation?

Solid buildings easily lead to stodgy thinking. How often the Church has failed to respond quickly to conscientious needs because so much financial investment was dependent on the preservation of the status quo—its schools, hospitals, and church buildings? Just as the necessity of long-term planning can lead us to overlook immediate imperatives, so buildings can begin to dictate the form of those who inhabit them instead of vice versa.

Stability of place can easily lead to an abiding reluctance to change anything. Travel, if undertaken in a spirit of adventure, not only provides us with new experience of the world out there, it also leads to a fuller appreciation of hitherto undisclosed elements of our inner world. There is a Japanese saying: "Away from home no shame." This reminds us that in a foreign environment we may feel free to act in a way we would never allow at home. It is as though we discover in ourselves drives and tendencies that are normally repressed or suppressed, but assert themselves vigorously when the constraints and expectations of our customary situation are left behind. Whether the emerging impulses are viewed as positive or negative, they are still ours—and we deny them at our peril. It is dangerous to travel; we are liable to encounter aspects of ourselves that we would prefer to continue dormant.

The mobility of Jesus meant that he was not locked into the constraints of a physical edifice with its compelling ethos and etiquette. Jesus' temperament was not that of the stereotypical bureaucrat; he was, in the best sense of the expression, a free spirit, open to all around him and able to adapt himself to their needs and dispositions. As Jesus moved around, he developed a spirituality that drew many of its features from his state of journeying. The demands of the Gospel often seem unrealistic to us because we have not made our own this image of journeying. We tend too easily to think in institutional terms.

As Jesus continued his journey, his preaching about the Kingdom echoed his experiences on the road. The ancient Israelites wandered in the desert for four decades and thereby learned to rely on God alone, as the Deuteronomist kept reminding a later generation who seem to have changed their tune once they settled down, built a capital, and created a king. But Jesus, once commissioned, never settled down. He spent several years moving around unfamiliar territory, adapting himself to different circumstances and reframing his message to suit the different levels of receptivity that he encountered. Gospel spirituality was not thought out logically in a static situation but evolved through interaction with a variety of people and situations. We can learn something of Jesus' inner life by reading back from his teaching.

Here are eight motifs of the journey theme that may repay pondering. They tell us something about Jesus on the basis of the lifestyle that he chose. They show how his own mind and heart were formed by the experiences of an itinerant preacher traveling around with a core group of disciples. And they can indicate what measures we need to introduce into our own lives if we wish to make our following of Jesus more complete.

(a) Flexibility: Anyone who travels learns quickly that plans are made to be broken. We are precipitated into a world of contingencies, where the unexpected happens more often than not. Each situation is modified by the people we meet there—people from a world we do not know, who summon us to leave behind the world we carry with us and dare to experience something new. Somehow the fixed ideas we had on departure are stretched, expectations are modified, and our previous self-definition and discipline seem no longer fully relevant. To interact creatively with what is around us we have to become more aware of the new situation we are in, read it more closely,

and humbly ask for guidance from those who know it better than we do.

Jesus does not enclose his teaching in the hard carapace of systematic thought, but sends it forth vulnerable in images and stories, told in plain everyday language. He makes moral demands that are severe to the point of extremity, and therefore easily interpreted out of existence, if we are so inclined. His doctrine was not propounded in a single ordered discourse, but offered in bits and pieces in different places and with different people in mind. This fluidity is what makes the Gospels so untidy; they each combine into a single sequential narrative all sorts of preexisting units that sometimes seem at variance with one another. On the positive side, this plurality is why the Gospel message as a whole is so readily adaptable to different cultures, and we applaud it for this. But such a spirituality challenges us constantly to keep reintroducing the Gospel into the situation where we are and reading it afresh with a willingness to change anything in our lives that is dissonant with Jesus' teaching as it resounds at this time and in this place. We need to keep freshening up our contact with the words of Jesus, lest our discipleship become stale and meaningless, a mere formality safely confined to its own corner. As Saint John Cassian says, in the text already quoted, each day and at every moment we need to keep opening up the soil of our heart with the plow of the Gospel.[1]

(b) Frugality: The story of the pious rich man who refused Jesus' call (Mk 10:17–22) is a powerful reminder that discipleship is impossible without substantial detachment from material goods and from all the benefits they confer. People on a journey cannot hope to carry with them everything they own; they need to learn to do without some of their home conveniences. I am reminded of the poignant footage one sees of refugees fleeing a war zone. The roads are littered with

objects that have become too heavy to carry; at first what is discarded is the inessential, the sentimental, or decorative, but, progressively, even the pitiful utensils necessary to sustain life are left behind. Like the nude youth in Gethsemane, those who survive escape with nothing but their skin (Mk 14:51–52).

To continue the journey with Jesus we must be unencumbered. We do not hear much about renunciation nowadays—but the ancient monks were convinced that it was not only the necessary beginning of all spiritual progress, but an effective gauge of how far along the road we have traveled. The more free we are of an urgency to surround ourselves with material goods and to possess them, the further we have traveled along the road to God.

We need to learn to free ourselves of the emotional tyranny of material goods, and even of our fearful dependence on the more fundamental assets that are the basis of our ongoing security. This letting-go seems easier for some than for others, but for everyone some kind of juggling act is needed, trying to balance common sense and prudence with the Gospel summons to depend on God alone. Radical as it may appear, there is a clear choice between God and Mammon: we cannot serve both (Lk 16:13). Love of money, we are reminded, is equivalent to idolatry (Col 3:5). The trap is, as one of John Steinbeck's characters remarks, "You can never have enough money; you either have no money or not enough."

Of course, discipleship is not primarily a matter of having no money. The poverty that Jesus declared blessed calls for a heartfelt and joy-filled reliance on an all-provident Father. This necessarily involves a certain detachment from all alternative sources of security, gratification, prestige, and affirmation. Above all, those who choose "to follow the naked Christ naked"[2] soon find themselves gratuitously enrolled among the ranks of the insignificant. Without the power base that money affords, we are considered as nothing.

(c) Powerlessness: Even in the most modest of dwellings, when we are at home we feel comfortable and we exercise a certain power. We choose who and what comes into the house, what happens within its four walls and how things are done. Our home has its own rules and conventions. We imprint our style on its ambience and are gratified to see ourselves somehow reflected in its ethos. It is to such familiar space that we willingly return when tired or exasperated and from which, sometimes, we set forth so reluctantly.

It is a wild world out there, but it can be exciting to move beyond the comforting hug of home space, but only so long as we can return there when we wish. The Gospel asks more of us than an occasional foray into the unknown. The spirituality of the journey makes nomads of us. The journey is all. There is nowhere into which we can slink back and breathe again. "Foxes have holes and the birds in the sky make nests, but the Son of Man has nowhere to lay down his head" (Mt 8:20). This spiritual homelessness exposes us to all the negative discrimination that the dispossessed habitually experience. What influence can be exercised by one without a passport, a bank balance, and a home address? Being on a lifelong journey means we belong nowhere. We feel alienated and anxious, never quite knowing what will be required of us tomorrow. Those who speak glowingly of life as a journey and revel in the idea of a pilgrim people, sometimes forget to mention the negative aspect inherent in this image.

(d) Weariness: The theme of spiritual pilgrimage, although implicit in the Hebrew Scriptures and apparent in the New Testament, was taken up strongly by the colonial Church in North Africa during the fourth and fifth centuries. Being located at some remove from the Empire's center, Roman Africans had plenty of experience of what life on the fringes was like, and of the tediousness of repeated traveling. We will never fully

understand certain beautiful passages of Saint Augustine, for
instance, unless we appreciate that, in those times, journeys
were long, hazardous, and uncomfortable, and that Augustine personally detested travel. Even the cramped confinement
of transcontinental air travel would have seemed luxurious to
him.

Journeys derive their meaning from arrival at their destination; retrospectively, they appear worthwhile. On the road
it is different, especially if there is some uncertainty about reaching the goal. The hope which impels us forward is a hope that
cannot yet see its own object (Rom 8:24)—we are traveling
blind. We must expect that the length and hardship of the
journey will sometimes seem impossible to bear. We will be
tempted to be disheartened, to allow ourselves to lose the sharp
focus of our discipleship and drift into distracting diversions.
Inevitably, given the complex demands discipleship places upon
us, there will be failures, misjudgments, and periods of stagnation. In the context of the whole journey and from the standpoint of eternity these are trifling, whatever their magnitude.
Locked in time and space, we cannot see this and so we are
tempted to lose our nerve and give up our search for God.
"This saying is [too] hard; who can hear it?" (Jn 6:60). It is
easy to rationalize such apostasy; but there is danger that something in our own spirits dies when we settle for second best.
Those who remain become plodders, perhaps. They no longer
trust in their own virtuosity, but let go to allow God brilliantly
to bring to perfection the work begun, but in a manner that
transcends human assessment or intelligence.

The promise Jesus made of rest for the weary wayfarer
(Mt 11:28) is given cogency by the picture of Jesus himself in
John 4:6, worn out from the journey through hostile Samaria.
Travel is a heavy burden, but it becomes lighter when we are
with others sharing the same journey.

(e) Companionship: A solitary journey is always harder than one made in congenial company. We will never arrive at our destination if we attempt to make it alone. This is a difficult lesson for latter-day individualists to assimilate. As social animals, it is not good for us to be alone. Consider your own experience of travel. Is it not easier when you can leave your luggage with a companion while unencumbered you attend to some other matter? Is it not true that two people or a group can go into many places one would hesitate to enter alone? Are there not stories, observations, and tokens of friendship that fill the vacant hours of waiting? When prolonged travel is a pleasure, it is often because we are among friends.

Jesus traveled with a band of disciples, among whom the Twelve had a special place. Peter, James, and John were singled out for particular intimacy. (Mark 9:2, 14:33; 13:3 adds Andrew to the trio.) Mark gives us an additional detail about Jesus' companions on the road; they included many women. "These women were his followers in Galilee and looked after him, and many others accompanied him as he went up to Jerusalem" (Mk 15:41). Jesus was not a loner. He reached out to the estranged by having a meal with them and for this he was criticized (Mk 2:16). He sent out his disciples in twos (Mk 6:7): to many a clear indication that evangelization is a collective activity. At the last he left behind a church as the sacrament of his continuing presence among believers. Community is part of the message and method of Jesus.

Our spiritual journey needs a communal context if we are to sustain the radicality of the Kingdom's demands. At times, we need to receive encouragement, support, guidance, and correction. At other times, we are expected to minister these gifts to others. "Bear one another's burdens and so you will fulfill the law of Christ" (Gal 6:2). It is mutual presence and help that makes even such a long and difficult journey tolerable.

Such unity of heart and mind among believers does not

happen without effort. We are all making the same journey through time and space to God, but that is not the same thing as making the journey together. An airliner is not a community, even though all have the same trajectory. There must be the will to community and there must be something that binds all members to one another. In our case, this unitive force is the Holy Spirit who enrolls us in the school of Christ and causes us to be reformed in Christ's likeness. We cannot ourselves create community; what is needed is a corporate openness to the work of the Spirit who provides us with "the glue of love" that binds together otherwise disparate personalities.

In the fluidity of the journey situation, our perceptions of others lose some of their rigidity. We begin to appreciate hitherto unsuspected qualities in our companions and, as well, our stance to strangers becomes less threatened and more welcoming. We begin to enjoy giving and receiving hospitality. We are more inclined to be accepting of others who are different. We are less fearful in approaching others and asking their help.

(f) Trust: It is surprising how easy it is to feel insecure while traveling. Sometimes we are fearful that, outside our own territory, events and persons may make demands on us that we cannot meet, and so we withdraw into ourselves, like a frightened child hoping to become invisible by diving under the blankets. If we value our independence too highly, the prospect of having to seek help from another is daunting. And everybody knows that even the best-planned excursions habitually throw up something unexpected, and therefore unwelcome.

Curiously enough, many of us are surprised to find that when disaster strikes, there are people who are more than willing to help us: to go out of their way to help us. We begin to be grateful for Providence and for our guardian angels. More importantly, perhaps, we learn to view with less suspicion others who are different. Slowly, perhaps only after years of learning, the message gets through: there are many people in the world who are worthy of our trust. And there are many more who will become worthy if we give our trust to them. If, at some point of our journey, we begin to operate at this level of mutual solidarity, we are indeed well on the way to becoming other Christs.

Our tolerances have been stretched and will never shrink all the way back to where they were before we traveled. The result of this increasing capacity to trust others is that we (and perhaps our neighbors) notice changes in ourselves. It may be more accurate to say that we are becoming aware of aspects of our deep personality that have been long hidden. Finally, after so many years, dormant gifts have become active and are ready to erupt in deeds that reflect the compassion of Christ.

(g) Self-discovery: Every journey can also be an inner journey, if we permit. To the extent that we genuinely interact with changing environments, new aspects of self continually come to the fore. We are continually re-created, not according to any private blueprint of self-improvement but by the apparently fortuitous hand of accident.

It is interesting to consider how Jesus was formed in this school of chance encounter, even though the Gospels habitually present him as the teacher. Good teachers are those who are willing to learn from their students and, surely, Jesus was no exception.

Rainer Maria Rilke speaks in his poem, *Dove that wandered afar*, about how after a journey we carry with us a residue of the places we have been. This is a very beautiful image to apply to Christ. During his lifetime the people who entered briefly into his life made a lasting impression. He carried them with him as he continued on his way. When he spoke, they were invisibly among the ranks of those to whom his words

were directed. When he died it was for them, the ordinary
people of the land who had found access to his heart and who
would never be excluded. Even after his glorification Jesus
has not shaken the dust of earth from his feet (see Mk 6:11),
but has carried into eternity the active memory of so many
encounters that variously reflected back to him who he was.
In his face they saw themselves, and it was because of this that
they desired to follow him.

(h) Perceptiveness: Habituation dulls our capacity to see. Moving into an unaccustomed environment often reveals things
we could never perceive at home. This is especially true when
we move from one situation for which we have some responsibility into another where we are on the fringe. We have more
leisure to observe and ponder, more objectivity to make an
assessment, and we are not burdened by an obligation to intervene. So we see things more clearly. The same is regularly
true of many marginal people who read a situation more accurately than those in the thick of it; they have to because
often their survival depends on it. I suppose that is why in
really difficult situations we call in an outsider to act as a
troubleshooter.

Being on a journey can, as we have said, be a means to
greater self-awareness. Not unconnected with this are the insights we gain into others. We might see it as the effect of a
wider experience, a certain distance from immediate involvement and, thereby, an enhanced opportunity for reflection.
Günther Bornkamm sees such perceptiveness as a salient feature of the Gospel portrait of Jesus. "The passages in the Gospels which deal with Jesus' perception and penetrating insight
ought to be assembled without fear that this would be a merely
sentimental undertaking."[3]

The journey metaphor used by the Synoptic Gospels is
very rich. By reflecting on it, we can understand something of

the totality of the spiritual path that Jesus proposes to us and, taking it a step further, we can begin to know a little about the mind and heart from which this teaching came. But there is something else beyond this tangible journey through space and time. Jesus was certainly the product of many this-worldly influences, but more than anything else he was formed by his unseen and transcendent intimacy with the Father. It was into this relationship that he wished by word and example to initiate his disciples. Before this change could happen, however, they had to enter into a dynamic situation in which interaction could arise between positive and negative elements within them. And so they had to endure a period in which journeying seemed more like wandering confused in a wilderness.

CHAPTER SIXTEEN

Ambiguity

He showed me many trees. They had no leaves and they seemed to me to be dried up. They were all in the same condition. He said to me, "Do you see these trees?" I said, "I see them, Lord; they are all in the same dried up condition." In response he said to me: "These trees which you see are those who dwell in this age." I said, "Why then, O Lord, are they in the same dried up condition?" He said: "Because in this age the righteous and sinners are indistinguishable; they are in the same condition. For the just, this age is winter and they are indistinguishable from the sinners among whom they live. In winter, trees have cast off their leaves; and living trees are indistinguishable from those that are dried out. In the same way, in this age the righteous are indistinguishable from sinners; they are all in the same condition.

THE SHEPHERD OF HERMAS 52, SCHR 53, PP. 218–220

Scientists generally insist on performing their experiments in a controlled environment. In that way they aim to reduce the possibility of extraneous factors influencing the outcome of the processes they are observing. We don't have to live long to come to the conclusion that laboratory conditions do not exist in real life. We have no alternative but to pass our days in the wild, where anything can happen. This means that the lives of even the simplest people are extremely complex and also that there is little certainty or predictability in human behavior or experience. Who among us can say with certainty how life will be for us in ten years, or five, or one? There is even an element of uncertainty about tomorrow. As individuals, we change according to the influences into whose ambit we come; and meanwhile the world around us and human society are both constantly changing.

The journey we make through life is not a military march along a straight Roman road. It is more like sailing a small ship amid the swirling surges of a stormy sea. We are continually conditioned by the contrary currents that draw us now in one direction, now in another. Our strongest and most deliberate commitments can be weakened by changing circumstances, undermined, abandoned, and even forgotten. "It was all so different," we say, "before everything changed." Inconsistency and inconstancy are inevitable concomitants of human life both for individuals and for the race as a whole. It is no easy task to hold a course in the midst of a ferment of change.

Paradoxically, such external instability is essential for us if we are to continue growing because it exposes us to new elements that we can integrate with our current resources to arrive at a fuller synthesis which enables us better to deal with reality. We may yearn to be always the same, but this is a delusion. We are elements of a changing universe; from it we draw sustenance and being; from it is derived the challenge to ongoing renewal, just as the skin which forms our interface with the external world is constantly flaking off and being replaced. This is not to say that we allow ourselves to be blown around like fallen leaves in a gale, but we need to remind ourselves that steering a straight course demands much vigilance. We have to read the situations through which we pass and constantly make adjustments so that we continue moving in the desired direction.

No matter at what point we are on the spiritual journey (unless we are at the very end), we will have to deal with inner division and our susceptibility to being swept away by forces independent of our will. Because we are still on the way and have not reached our destination, we are unfinished. There is still more work to be done on us before we attain that unique beauty and perfection for which we were created. In more pragmatic terms, this means that right up until the last hours of our life we will be plagued by blemishes that irritate and discourage us. Some defects will be more serious than others, but all of them seem to be intransigently resistant to any campaign on our part to eliminate them.

Saint Bernard recognizes that traveling is a dirty business. Perhaps this is less so nowadays than in antiquity, but even today the first thing that many travelers want to do on arrival is to wash away some of the grit of their journey. If we, as individuals, see our lives as a journey towards God and if we recognize that the Church also is a pilgrim, we will be less dismayed when our eyes are opened to the inevitable grime that inhibits the outshining of holiness.

Saint Bernard comments in this way:

> What are these "tents" [of Kedar] if not our bodies in which we make our pilgrim way?... The dwelling place which is our body is not a citizen's residence or the home of one belonging to this country. It is, rather, a tent for a soldier or a shelter for one on a journey. This bodily tent, I say, is a tent of Kedar insofar as it cheats the soul of the sight of boundless light—its proper object—for the time that it remains here below. It permits the soul to see the light only indirectly and obscurely and never face to face.
>
> Do you not now see the source of the Church's dark hue and of the blemishes that cling even to souls

most endowed with beauty? Such defects are due to their having to dwell in the tents of Kedar, to their being laboriously engaged in warfare, to the length of their unhappy sojourn, to the troublesome restraints of being out of their own country and, finally, to the fact of the body itself which is so fragile and yet so heavy to bear. "For this corruptible body weighs down the soul, and living on earth inhibits one's powers of thought" (Wis 9:15).

Because of all this, such persons long to be dissolved so that, having put aside the body, they may fly to the embrace of Christ. So we hear the lament of one so unhappy, "Miserable man that I am, who will liberate me from the body of this death?" (Rom 7:24). Such a one knows that there is no possibility, while dwelling in the tents of Kedar, of preventing the sullying, wrinkling, and staining of purity. This is why he longs to depart and have done with the body.[1]

We are disappointed at our habitual low-level living. We have a tendency to feel guiltier about this than we should, because secretly we believe that we could do better if we tried harder. Curiously, our own failure to live up to our ideals does not make us more sympathetic to similar deficiencies in others. Instead, we become embittered and harsh when confronted with the human weakness of those around us, and we are hugely disedified when we are made aware of the general failing of the Church to attain the level of holiness that is its calling.

In recent decades the mass media have done us the service of making us aware of just how far distant the Church has become from the manner of life set forth in the Gospels. Reading the newspapers, we are exposed to allegations of sexual abuse, injustice at all levels of ecclesiastical government, unaccountable wealth, dubious political and financial alliances, unevangelical discrimination, lack of honesty and transparency, and many other ways of acting which, to the extent that they are true, should not only be deplored but actively condemned. How are we to respond to this information, such as it is?

It is no use burying our heads in the sand. As responsible and adult members of the Church, we have to admit that there is much in the behavior of some that is reprehensible and, perhaps, none of us is wholly innocent. It is not enough to say, "We are a Church of sinners, but yet we are saved by the grace of Christ." Such slick appeals to theology will only entrench us further in denial and complacency. Instead let us use our theology to energize our efforts to improve the situation. It is time for us to start thinking reform. Perhaps, at the time of the Second Vatican Council, we were too generous in claiming that the Church did not need reforming, only updating and renewal. It is now quite evident that we need reformation. The place to start is our own lives because, whether we intend it or not, "none of us lives for ourselves and none of us dies for ourselves" (Rom 14:7). The way that we express ourselves in actions has a profound impact on everyone else. A simultaneous awareness of our responsibility and of the sum of our liabilities should not depress or paralyze us but, by God's grace, should energize us to exert ourselves more vigorously. We are far from perfect, and that is to be accepted without excessive lamentation. It does not mean that we should give up trying. What it means is that we need to keep going forward on the road God has laid out before us.

> Let those who are imperfect not be afraid—all they have to do is to make progress. Let them not love their imperfection just because I said, "Let them not be afraid"; in that case they would remain where they are. Let them make progress, as far as it depends on

them. Each day let them add something. Each day let
them draw nearer—but let them not withdraw from
Christ's body.[2]

Three realities will motivate our efforts to upgrade the
situation: our clear perception of the need to do something,
our love for the Church that will not allow us to slide into an
easy despair, and our faith that God will supply whatever we
need to accomplish the work that has to be done. It quickly
becomes evident that to cope with individual and collective
ambiguity and to respond creatively to the ordinary messiness
of life are tasks that exceed our ordinary resources. We need
to switch to the level of faith and to begin operating with the
energy that comes from God's grace.

When we feel discouraged about the slowness with which
the holiness of God has been realized in our days, it is good to
see that those whom Jesus gathered around him were burdened with a similar resistance to life-giving grace. What is
especially noteworthy in the Gospel of Mark is the emphasis
the evangelist places on the obtuseness of the disciples. Even
with such a teacher and leader, they were unable to shake themselves free of the heaviness of spirit that renders us all unre-
sponsive. What is remarkable is that Jesus did not lose faith in
these frail men. He continued to teach them, to scold and encourage them, despite their recidivist tendencies. Perhaps, as
the Fourth Gospel asserts, he had some sense that they would
never make the grade in his lifetime. Only with the coming of
the Pentecost Spirit would the seeds that he sowed reach fruition. Meanwhile, Jesus sometimes showed exasperation at their
inability to comprehend the meaning of what was happening
before their eyes.

[The disciples] had forgotten to take bread. There was
not a single loaf in the boat with them. Jesus admon-

ished them saying, "Keep your eyes open and watch out for the leaven of the Pharisees and the leaven of Herod." The disciples said to one another, "It is because we have no bread." Knowing this, Jesus said to them, "Why are you saying that you have no bread? Do you still not perceive or understand? Are your hearts hardened? Do you have eyes and cannot see, ears and cannot hear? When I broke five loaves for the five thousand, how many baskets of fragments did you fill?" They said to him, "Twelve." "And for the seven loaves for the four thousand, how many containers did you fill with fragments?" And they said "Seven." And Jesus said to them, "Do you still not understand?" (Mk 8:14–21).

It is evident that Jesus' most intimate followers had made little progress in the inward journey to which he called them. Much resistance remained. Even at a relatively late stage in the Gospel, after so many signs and so much teaching, the disciples manifested a certain imperviousness to the reality of Jesus. Their hearts seem to have become hardened; they were no better than the fickle crowds or the stiff-necked religious authorities. So much time, so much care, so much affection— and with such a slight result. A quick transit through the earliest Gospel leaves us in no doubt that the Twelve were deficient not only in their attitudes and priorities but also in their understanding of the things of God (Mk 8:33) and sometimes in a basic sense of decency. When it came to operating in the spiritual world, they were out of their depth. The skills and resources they had garnered in their previous professions could not equip them for performance at the level which Jesus expected. To the attentive reader of Mark, their final betrayals come as no surprise.

As it is for us and for the Twelve so it is for humanity as a whole. Jesus' parable of the weeds in the wheat (Mt 13:24–30 and 36–43) takes up the idea of mixity and applies it on a global scale. It is not always possible in this age to distinguish between those who are contributing to the progress of God's Kingdom and those who are resisting and obstructing it. It is only from the standpoint of God that such a discernment is possible. Any attempt on our part to make a determination will be premature and risk disaster. Jesus bids us wait. It is only God's final judgment that will be able to distinguish weeds from wheat, sheep from goats, the saved from the reprobate.

> How many of those who do not yet belong to us are, as it were, inside? How many of those who do belong to us are now outside? "The Lord knows those who belong to him" (2 Tim 2:19). Those who do not belong to us who are inside go outside as soon as an occasion offers. Those who do not belong[3] to us who are now outside return when an occasion offers.

The mixity of good and evil results in a certain ambiguity in the lives of us all that is often experienced interpersonally as friction and contentiousness between good people. Such quarrels come from one or both parties operating out of their areas of weakness and woundedness, instead of letting their conduct be shaped by their strengths and virtues. The Church of the Apostles was said to be "of one heart and one soul" (Acts 4:32), yet there are in the New Testament many instances of serious division among believers; and the fracturing of the unity of the Church has been continuing ever since. Every human society—even down to the family—is sometimes threatened by factions. When we are caught in the midst of the maelstrom, it is easy to believe that it is a difference between the good and the bad, the right and the wrong, the wise and the stupid, the faithful and the false. This assumption quickly propels us into the world of prejudicial judgments and the summary exclusion of others from the circle of our affection.

The harsh criticisms we make of one another generally have a basis in reality. There is not a human being on earth who is beyond reproach when judged according to the subjective scales of others. The Gospels testify abundantly that many found aspects of Jesus' behavior and teaching unacceptable and that their rejection quickly reached murderous proportions. Early in the Galilean ministry, Jesus so angered his opponents by besting them in argument and consolidating his victory with a miracle that they were prepared to lay aside existing animosities in order to do away with him. "And the Pharisees went out and immediately began to reach agreement with the Herodians about how they might destroy him" (Mk 3:6). Likewise, given the incentive, I can always work up a case against any other human being. There are thousands of reasons for not liking a particular person and once I have assigned persons to this category, I tend to absolve myself of any blame no matter how I treat them. Think of the Holocaust at one end of the continuum and, at the other, the countless acts of petty spitefulness by which daily we try to make miserable the lives of those whom we do not like. First, I demonize those I do not like, after that I judge my behavior towards them according to different moral standards. Actions I would not countenance towards my friends become guilt free when directed at those labeled "enemies." I quench their spirits with as little compunction as I would swat a mosquito. Meanwhile, my sense of moral probity is undented.

Sometimes my rancor is directed against others because they belong to a different group, have a particular profession, occupy a particular official position, or exercise a particular function. An example of this is the rage we reserve for supporters of a rival football team, the members of another political party or faction, people of different race, religion, or culture. In particular, many of us have a deep-seated antipathy towards persons in authority. In such cases, we dismiss any claims that the other might have on us because of shared humanity or some other bond and regard them merely as legitimate targets for any sort of negative behavior. Those involved in football riots, dirty politics, or racial and religious vituperation are not, in their own view, violent or abusive people—if there is any fault it lies with their targets, who deserve punishment just for existing.

Often the processes by which we arrive at such dehumanizing behavior are completely hidden from us. As soon as the "enemy" comes into our purview, we experience an anger that we allow to be translated into an aggressive reaction. No questions are asked, the transition is immediate. If queried after the event, we usually say that the other person "made us angry." In this way the blame is seen to rest entirely with the one who, in our thinking, caused the upset; we are blameless. Alternatively, the other person may occasion a spasm of envy in us which precipitates us into a self-righteous flurry of detraction or calumny, and we are almost unaware of what we are saying, so automatic is our hatred.

The preferred mode of aggression for good people is what psychologists term "passive aggression." There is no impolite shouting or violence. We achieve our goal of hurting the other person by less visible means. We sulk, withdraw our services, and refuse to cooperate. The signs of passive aggression are inappropriate disengagement, nonparticipation, and silent subversion. Often our body language says it all. We come late to meetings, look at our watch frequently, yawn and act bored (making sure our doodling is visible to all); there is no eye contact and no attempt to follow the flow of conversation. We try to inflict death on our target by a thousand pinpricks. Nobody can challenge our unhelpful conduct because no rules have been broken and our habitual defense is "I did not do anything." In some cases, passive aggression can be a masterpiece of cumulative nonevents that create misery for others without soiling the consciences of the perpetrators. Most parents, teachers, and employers have been the victims of such behavior at some stage in their careers.

Unmasking the hidden causes of both active and passive aggression is often a job for psychotherapists. At a more pedestrian level, however, we can lessen our tendencies to act in this way if we try to hold in awareness the fundamental ambiguity of our moral status. We are an abiding mixture of good and evil, and our actions are stamped with the same duality. For instance, we can be for a prolonged period loving, generous, and self-forgetful in what we do and then, suddenly, begin to do something mean, spiteful, and exploitative. The sincerely moral person is disappointed and ashamed when this happens. The morally blind deny complicity in their own actions and project the blame onto somebody else. Until we arrive at the point of not being surprised by such moral reversals, we are not going to do much in the way of damage control.

We have to set up some sort of conversation between the different tendencies in our heart so that we can use our strengths to minimize the influence of our weaknesses. Certainly, the precise strategy will vary from one person to another. In most cases, we will need a lot of humility to break away from the habit of automatically excusing or blaming, and learn to live in the twilight zone where there is no black and white but only deepening shades of gray. Those of us who have a tendency to embody our opinions in absolute statements will probably need to learn how to qualify more carefully what we say so that it reflects reality a little more truthfully.

Of course, all this is a lot of bother. It is easier to assume that I am always good and right and that others correspondingly are bad and wrong insofar as they discord with me.

Being somewhat more reserved in my claims to infallibility and innocence will not only render me easier to live with, it will increase my own sense of well-being, since inward peace is built on truthfulness with myself. Delusion, denial, and deceit cause me more trouble than I realize.

Our onward journey is always an uphill struggle with many defeats and frequent discouragement. Emotionally, we may have to grapple with an inward surge of resentment that draws its force from an unexamined belief that somehow the good life should be easier and the false hope in us that if we do nothing then everything will settle down so that we can drift happily towards our destination. Not so. In this life, everything exists in a state of mixity: good and evil, truth and falsehood, birth and death, progression and regression. Worse than that, because we do not have the capacity to view our life in its entirety, we cannot immediately discern whether particular elements are desirable or not. A moment's reflection will remind us how often we have changed our initial evaluation of persons or events: what was sweet in the mouth becomes sour in the stomach. We need some capacity to take life as it comes and leave to God the task of assessing the ultimate value of our actions.

Important as it is not to rush into judgment about the events of our own life, it is vital that we do not attempt to pass judgment on the behavior of others. Especially negative judgment. So much depends on whether my assessment is based on a one-eyed view of their faults or an equally purblind appreciation of their virtues. Experience of life and the teaching of many religious traditions caution us against confusing reality with appearances. When we condemn others, it is often because we do not know the whole story. Without denying the possibility of malign choices and brutishness, we have to recognize that many who commit crimes are themselves victims of their own upbringing and experience. Perhaps there is also a genetic component that contributes to their aberrant behavior. When we stop the film and freeze the action at one moment, everything may seem straightforward, but it is not. We have to rewind and sit through many hours before the whole truth begins to emerge. Even in trivial instances there is more to most actions than meets the eye. The wide world of intention and motivation is concealed from us, we have to make a guess; yet so often it is precisely these hidden elements that determine the moral character of the action. Because we do not see them, we are not fit to judge. "Not as human beings view things does the LORD see; they look upon appearances but the LORD sees the heart" (1 Sam 16:7).

Jesus exhorts us to avoid judging the lives of others (Mt 7:1 = Lk 6:37). Although there are situations in which it is appropriate for the Church to make a determination, such as that envisaged in 1 Corinthians 6:1–6, mostly we have to recognize the dimness of our vision and suspend all evaluation. This is more than naivete or innate optimism. It is a stance that derives from faith. I choose to believe that no one is beyond the mercy of God and I am prepared to grant the possibility that one whom I condemn as a sinner may well be holier than I. My personal experience of mercy and forgiveness should lead me to be confident in God's power to convert even those who seem to be farthest from righteousness. "Let us not forget what we were once and then we will not lose hope for those who are now what we used to be."[4]

It is this same theocentric hope that enables us to continue to affirm the holiness of the Church without being blind to the sinfulness of its members. Saint Augustine, conscious of the elitist tendencies of the Donatist sect, was very sensitive to the importance of suspending judgment when faced with others whose lives do not conform to our ideals or expectations. His vision of the Church is very realistic. Its essential holiness is not compromised by the habitual wickedness of some or the occasional wickedness of all. What is good and holy in the Church not only outweighs what is negative, but is in the process of converting what is malign into holiness. The presence of wickedness may never serve as a pretext for withholding love, because it is only love that can change what is ugly into something beautiful.

> Brothers, let no one deceive you. If you do not wish to be deceived and you wish to go on loving the brothers then understand that every profession in the Church includes phonies. I am not saying that everyone is phoney, but every profession includes persons who are phoney. There are bad Christians—but there are also good ones.[5]

Augustine gives several examples of ecclesial communities in which good and evil coexist and which potentially scandalize those who expect the Church to be uncompromised. Here is his account of a man who is disedified by the imperfection of a monastic community that he unrealistically idealized.

> Take, as an example, a monastery where brothers live the common life. They are great men and holy, every day is passed in hymns and prayers and in the praise of God. Reading is important in their lives, they work with their hands to gain their livelihood. They do not greedily seek anything and what they receive through the kindness of their brothers they use moderately and with charity. Nobody insists on having as his own what another does not have. They all love one another and support one another. You praise them. Yes, you praise them.
> Here is a man who does not know what goes on inside. He does not know how a wind entering into a

harbor can cause ships to collide. So, he enters the community, hoping for security, and thinking that no one there would need to be tolerated. He finds brothers there who are bad, but who would not have been found to have been bad if they had not been admitted. (It is necessary that first they be tolerated so that maybe they will be corrected; they cannot be easily excluded unless they first be tolerated.) He experiences an impatience that is beyond tolerance. "Who asked me to come here? I was thinking that there was charity here." Thus while he becomes irritated at a few nuisances, he himself does not persevere in the fulfillment of what he vowed. He deserts his holy endeavor and becomes guilty of not rendering what he vowed. And when he departs from that place, he curses it, and speaks badly of it. He speaks only of what he endured and insists that he was unable to carry on. Sometimes these [difficulties] are real. However the real difficulties caused by the evil ought to be tolerated for the sake of association with the good. Scripture says to him, "Woe to those who lose endurance" (Sir 2:16). Furthermore, he belches forth the evil odor of his anger with the result that others about to enter are dissuaded, simply because he himself when he entered was not able to persevere. What are they like in his opinion? They are envious, contentious, nonsupportive, mean. This one did such a thing and this other one did that. Wicked man, why are you silent about the good? Why do you speak loudly about those for whom you had no tolerance, and keep quiet about what they had to tolerate because you were bad?[6]

Because the Church preaches high morality, it is satisfying for those hostile to it to be able to point the finger of blame at the misdemeanors (and worse) of its own members. In this way, we can excuse ourselves for our failure to be guided by the moral principles the Church proclaims. It is easy to mutter about pastors not practicing what they preach. Yet we all sin in many ways; if we silenced sinners, who would proclaim the Gospel? Those whom Jesus sent forth to announce the demands of God's kingdom were sinners like ourselves and sometimes failed in what was expected of them. No matter how much we hate the manifestations of human weakness, blindness, and malice, we cannot realistically expect the Church of today to be any better than that of the Apostles. Weeds grow among the wheat. While we are yet on our journey we are weary and begrimed. That is part of the story, but it is not the whole story.

CHAPTER SEVENTEEN

Jesus Transfigured

And after six days, Jesus took Peter and James and John and brought them up to a lofty mountain, alone by themselves, and he was transformed in their presence. His clothes became gleaming white, such as no fuller on earth could bleach them. And Moses and Elijah appeared to them and they were in conversation with Jesus. Peter responded by saying to Jesus: "Rabbi, it is good that we are here. We shall make three shelters, one for you and one for Moses and one for Elijah." He did not know what response to make because they had become frightened. Then it happened that a cloud overshadowed them and there was a voice from the cloud: "This is my Son whom I love. Listen to him." Then suddenly, looking around, they no longer saw anybody, but only Jesus was with them.

And as they came down from the mountain, Jesus instructed them that they were to tell no one what they had seen until the Son of man would rise from the dead. They kept this word, asking themselves what it meant to rise from the dead.

MARK 9:2–10

Twenty centuries after the events took place, we read the Gospels to discover more about the earthly career of God's Son. For Jesus' contemporaries, including the disciples, the exterior facts of his life were too well-known to generate much interest. Is not this the builder, the son of Mary, whose family lives among us? The early Church, likewise, without the benefit of the theological sophistication achieved through many centuries of dire controversy, had to explain what was so special about Jesus of Nazareth—beyond his words of wisdom and miraculous powers. There were two realities that disclosed the core of Jesus' identity and set him apart from all others: He was still alive, notwithstanding the fact of having died; and he would come again in that cataclysmic moment in which time would fold in on itself to reveal eternity.

Resurrection and the Second Coming or *parousía*: these are the two essential elements in the Church's primitive preaching which elevate Jesus above the level of mere prophet or holy man. These are realities, however, that belong to the luminous sphere of faith: unconstrained by space and time they cannot be seen, touched, or known otherwise. As these truths became clear, the Church began to search its collective memory for intimations of the unique status of Jesus. "When Jesus rose from the dead, the disciples remembered that he had said this, and they came to have faith in the Scripture and in the word that Jesus had spoken" (Jn 2:22). This clearer perception was the work of the Holy Spirit, as Jesus had predicted. "The Paraclete, the Holy Spirit whom the Father will send in my name will teach you everything and will remind you of all that I have said to you" (Jn 14:26).

It was by the Spirit's prompting that the disciples "remembered" the anticipation of resurrection they had witnessed and which hitherto had been sealed under a veil of silence. They came to realize that it was because they had been privileged "observers of his greatness" that they were qualified to proclaim his power and *parousía* (2 Pet 1:16). "We have seen his glory, glory as of the only-begotten of the Father, full of grace and truth" (Jn 1:14). The veiled divinity began to be revealed to them as they pondered the signs or miracles which Jesus worked (Jn 2:11) and the underlying dynamism of a career that continued to unfold its mystery long after it had finished. For Saint John even the very humanity of Jesus—what was seen and observed and touched—was a means of access to the invisible world and a promise of entering into communion with God (1 Jn 1:1–3). This is why in the Fourth Gospel even the passion and death of Jesus testify to the fact that there were aspects of Jesus that were not "of this world" (Jn 18:36).

The accounts of the Transfiguration in the first three Gospels give tranquil testimony to the unseen status of Jesus during his lifetime. Mark's account of Jesus' baptism describes events reserved to Jesus alone: the heavenly voice addresses Jesus, using the second person pronoun in the singular. They are intimate words between Father and Son. An almost identical expression occurs in Mark 9:7, but it is couched in the third person. This is a message not for Jesus, but for the disciples, with the added rider, "Listen to him."

All that transpires on the mountain is meant for the instruction of the three disciples whom Jesus had set apart for this purpose. They are given an insight into the divine mystery which underlies the ordinary, obscure, and everyday appearance of the man Jesus. It was, in fact, the unexceptional public face of Jesus that made such a revelation necessary. Jesus was a man of the people with nothing to distinguish him externally from the common throng. He was able to slip up to Jerusalem and attend the festival *incognito*; even though many were looking for him, his presence went undetected (Jn 7:10–11).

The three Gospels agree in locating the Transfiguration after Jesus' first prediction of his eventual passion, death, and resurrection. The function of the narrative is to provide some buttressing—for both disciples and readers—against the horrendous storms that will soon break upon them. Just as there is more to Jesus than meets the common observer's eye, so hope need not perish when, on a human plane, all seems lost.

Before the disciples' wondering eyes the hidden nature of Jesus is revealed. Mark speaks only of the unearthly radiance of his garments whereas Matthew and Luke indicate that Jesus' face was transfigured, as Moses' was when he encountered God. The point being made is that in the seclusion of the place and the security of the company, Jesus is able to be more fully himself. Here the evangelist is alluding to a theme which will be much more strongly emphasized in the Fourth Gospel: Jesus belongs to the spiritual world, the sphere of God. "You are from below; I am from above. You are from this world; I am not from this world" (Jn 8:23).

At this point, Moses and Elijah appeared to the disciples. Not Abraham, Isaac, and Jacob, as we might have expected if Mark had merely wished to emphasize Jesus' affiliation with the people of God. But the two prototypical teachers of Israel, symbolizing the twin streams of formation: the Law and the prophets. Jesus is being presented as the one towards whom all ancient teaching pointed. "We have found the one of whom Moses wrote in the Law and the prophets: Jesus, son of Joseph, from Nazareth" (Jn 1:45). Luke specifies that they were "speaking about his exodus that he was going to accomplish in Jerusalem"—preparing him, as it were, for what was about to happen. It is in this same rereading of the Old Testament that the risen Lord guides the disciples. To the disciples on the way to Emmaus he expostulates:

> "O unintelligent and slow to believe all that the prophets have spoken! Was it not necessary that the Messiah should suffer and so enter into his glory?" Then beginning with Moses and all the prophets he interpreted to them what had been said about him in all the Scriptures (Lk 24:25–27).

And to the Twelve he speaks in like vein.

> "These are my words that I have spoken to you while I was still with you, that it is necessary to fulfill all that has been written in the Law of Moses, the prophets, and the Psalms about me." Then he opened their mind to the understanding of the Scriptures (Lk 24:44–45).

The early Church came to realize that a more profound understanding of the Old Testament would prepare the way for intellectually grasping the significance of the rejection and death of Jesus. From there, it was but a short step to inferring that Jesus himself had been sustained in his agony by his familiarity with the Law and the prophets. In this perspective, in the Transfiguration, Moses and Elijah are seen briefing him as a preparation for the ordeal to come.

Peter is conscious that he is privy to a great mystery and, like all of us in such a situation, is uncertain how to respond. His babbled offer of hospitality goes unheeded—the disciples, clearly, are privileged observers of the scene and not participants. Like the women who discovered the empty tomb and are cast into silence (Mk 16:8), they are overcome by awe and are completely at a loss to know what must be done.

Then begins the theophany. The disciples are enveloped by the cloud and witness something of the internal dynamic of Jesus' being. By being instructed to listen to Jesus, the disciples are being informed that he is God's voice on earth because this man is, in reality, the Son of God's love.

The various elements of mystical experience are multiplied in the account: separation from the mundane, ascending the mountain, the vision, the cloud, the voice; and for the disciples feelings of awe, delight, unknowing, confusion. As sudden as is the scene which unfolds before them is the abrupt return to

normality. Looking around, the disciples find nothing unusual—just the familiar figure of Jesus of Nazareth, and the
need to come down from the mountain to the lower world.

For a moment Peter, James, and John have stepped out of
space and time and visited eternity. The "transfiguration" is
not so much a temporary event in the life of God's Son—it is
his permanent status—but it is a special moment in the lives
of the disciples. Their eyes are opened to the invisible connections of the man Jesus with the spiritual world. Their finite
minds are unable fully to comprehend what they have seen
and they can find no language adequate to convey what they
have experienced. Only in the context of resurrection and
parousía will they begin to have the interpretative tools to
grasp what they have witnessed.

In Jesus of Nazareth there is both continuity with the past,
embodied in his relationship with the revealing tradition of
Israel, and something radically unique and new. To casual acquaintances, as to many in subsequent centuries, Jesus seemed
only quantitatively different from anyone else—outstanding
in many ways but still just a man. What the three disciples
glimpsed in the incident and wished to share with other believers throughout the ages was their discovery of a qualitative difference in him. In a unique manner that human language stumbles to express, Jesus is not merely a true being of
earth but he belongs also and even principally to the sphere of
God; he is God's Son. "None of the rulers of this aeon knew
this. If they had known it, they would not have crucified the
Lord of glory" (1 Cor 2:8).

This disclosure of the hidden dignity of the man Jesus dra-
matically demonstrates to us that there is nothing essentially
incompatible between humanity and divinity. Although he was
truly one of us, Jesus lived wholly in God. This paradox raises
the question of our own latent potential. If it is true that "of
his fullness we have all received" (Jn 1:16), then we too are

destined to become not only bearers of divinity, but sharers in the divine nature (2 Pet 1:4). Only sin and time impede our divinization. For most of us, the leaching out of sin, such as no fuller's alkali could accomplish, is spread over a lifetime, "seventy years or eighty for the vigorous" (Ps 90:10). Slowly we are transformed; eventually we will become radiant. "My friends, we are God's children now. It is not yet apparent what we shall be [in the future]. We know that when he appears we will be like him because we shall see him as he is" (1 Jn 3:2). This is the goal of our existence. It is towards this that our journey leads.

In the days before Christmas, the Latin liturgy turns its gaze to various individuals in salvation history that embody this faith-filled expectation of Jesus' *parousía*. A beautiful prayer for December 20, illustrates the truth that what was effected in the incarnation of the Word is made available to all people of good will, of whom the Mother of the Lord is the prototype and example.

> O God,
> at the angel's message
> the untarnished Virgin welcomed
> your Word that is beyond all human language.
> She became the dwelling place of the divinity
> and so was filled with the light of the Holy Spirit.
> Grant that we, following her example
> may have the strength humbly to adhere to your will.[1]

What is this prayer saying? It portrays Mary as the archetypal "hearer of the Word"[2] who has consented to God's action on her, in accordance with the word that it was her habit to ponder in her heart. She was a hearer and keeper of God's word. By some divine alchemy, the word of God expressed in human language becomes the person of the Word that is beyond all human power of conception: *verbum ineffabile*. In this way, Mary becomes "a dwelling place of divinity," the Word-made-flesh has pitched his tent within her; she is the site of the new divine Presence, *shekinah*. As a result, she is filled with the light of the Holy Spirit. The transformative Spirit that was seen to descend on Jesus at his baptism and remain with him (Jn 1:32) is communicated to the one in whose womb the Word-made-flesh is contained. Although Jesus was later to affirm that physical motherhood was of lesser importance than obedience to God's word (Lk 11:27–28), it is not unreasonable to conclude that the bonding between mother and child would have formed Mary in the likeness of her Son. Listen to what Bernard of Clairvaux says:

> Is it not true that someone who handles apples for half a day will keep the fragrance of the apples for the rest of the day? How great an effect, therefore, would the power and tenderness of love have had on the womb in which it rested during nine months.[3]

Welcoming the Word and being filled with the Holy Spirit had a profound, if hidden, effect on the Mother of the Lord. The same is true for us. That is why the liturgical prayer we are considering concludes by asking that we may follow the pattern she has traced out: in humility, we accept the strength from on high to adhere to the divine will. The word "adhere" that is used in this context is related to the text of 1 Corinthians 6:17: "The one who adheres to God becomes one spirit with God." This is no fearful conformity to the whims of a capricious God nor slavish obedience to external commandments. It is the profound and heartfelt union of hearts to which we give the name "love." By staying close to God at the level of will, though we still live lives fragmented in space and time, we begin to advance to eternity. The process of transformation begun at baptism takes effect in the course of a lifetime; we, too, are undergoing transfiguration. "We all, with faces unveiled, gaze upon the reflected glory of the Lord, and so from glory to glory we are transfigured in his image by the Spirit of the Lord" (2 Cor 3:18).

CHAPTER EIGHTEEN

Meta-Experience

Thus does she come in spirit beyond time into the eternity of love which is timeless. In love she is lifted up above the human mode and, in her desire for transcendence, above her own nature. That is her being and her will, her desire and her love, in certain truth and in pure clarity, in noble loftiness, in splendid beauty, and in the sweet companionship of the supernal spirits who all abound with overflowing love and who live in the clear knowledge and possession and enjoyment of their love.

BEATRICE OF NAZARETH, *THE SEVEN MODES OF LOVE*

Writing a decade or so after the end of the Second Vatican Council, the theologian Karl Rahner suggested that the Christian of the future will be a mystic. The reason he gives for this proposition is that, increasingly, the faithful will be deprived of the support of a Christian ambience. Like the ancient martyrs, they will not have much external support and so they will need some deep inner experience to sustain their courage in the lonely decisions required to follow their consciences.[1]

The Christian perspective on life depends on experience of grace, vocation, and faith. Perhaps it would be more accurate to speak of such realities in terms of "meta-experience," since our being touched by God does not coincide with what we normally term experience. To hear, understand, and be persuaded by the words of a preacher is an experience; to be touched inwardly, energized, and brought to conversion is the invisible work of grace accessible only at the level of meta-experience. It is possible for any literate person to read the Bible; to find in its pages words of eternal life is something that flesh and blood cannot reveal. It is a question of adding something that bare human effort cannot achieve. Many years' fidelity to the dark prayer of silence can be unpredictably trans-formed by a moment of intensity that rewrites previous experi-ence and injects into our life something radically new. Beyond our mundane experience lies another world. When the door opens and we pass into it, the meaning of our life changes, and we experience everything against a different horizon. The act of contemplation, although it occurs within a spatio-temporal shell, is not of this world. It is like a glimpse into eternity.[2]

It is, as we have already remarked, too easy to reduce Chris-tian existence to its cognitive and ethical components. These are important because they provide the kindling and fuel by which the fire of devotion is initiated and sustained; but it is the flame that is the irreplaceable heart of religion. Without ongoing access to the invisible world where God dwells, all the other aspects of Christian discipleship lose their savor. Con-trary arguments seem more convincing and the attractions of loose living more powerful. Rebellion seethes. Without personal experience of the divine, there is a danger that our spiritual life will become mere semblance without substance, keeping up appearances.

Most of us are a little frightened of what may happen in our lives if we give an unconditional assent to God's grace. Like Saint Peter, we are inclined to want God to remain at a safe distance. "Depart from me, Lord, I am a sinner" (Lk 5:8). As a result, there is a tendency to assign religion or spirituality to a particular compartment in our lives, lock the door, and live the remainder of the time as if there were no God. Even when we enter the locked chamber, we are careful not to give

God too much freedom; we do not want any surprises. We are prepared to pay our dues, but we do not want to be challenged to change our attitudes and behavior.

In attempting thus to straitjacket God, we succeed only in straitjacketing ourselves. The human being, as understood in ancient Christian tradition, differs from the animals in having the capacity to transcend the world of space and time and thus, by grace, to enter into a relationship with God. Created in the image and likeness of God, there remains even in the human being deformed by sin, a sufficient residue of that original integrity to trigger in us a desire for the God whom we cannot find in the world of the senses. By nature we are God-seekers. Our heart's desire finds fulfillment only in God. It follows that if I build God out of my life I am condemning myself to a very dim level of existence. Yes, I may join the ranks of the rich and famous; I may live a life of comfort and even reach high levels of philanthropy. Even so, there is a profound aspect of my being that has been forced into dormancy.

Consider this example. When someone close to us passes away, we become aware that part of us has also died. There is a corner of our hearts to which no one else has access, a part of us that came alive in the presence of the deceased that nobody else can reanimate, which now exists only in shadowy memory. What this common experience illustrates is that human personalities do not come into existence through spontaneous generation: they are drawn forth and shaped by scores of relationships with other persons. We guess that most people would be different if they had grown up without the benefit of mother, father, siblings, or extended family. These others have, to a large extent, made them what they are, for better or for worse. They have helped them to activate aspects of their personality that would otherwise have lain dormant. A similar process continues throughout our entire life: "Tell me your friends, and I will tell you what you are."

If it is true that God has made us for himself, then without God we will be no more than a shadow of what otherwise we could have become. The necessary conclusion is that God's absence in our life will result in our being stunted in our growth as human beings. We can never reach our full potential. Here, however, it important to make some distinctions. We are referring to people who do or do not allow God access to their lives and who are familiar or unfamiliar with the invisible world beyond sense and self-interest. We are not merely talking about the flagrantly religious as opposed to a secular majority. The reality is that many unbelievers serve God under another name, although they feel insulted when we say this. They are what Karl Rahner has termed "anonymous Christians." Because we are discussing meta-experience, it follows that this mystery is not accessible to ordinary observation or measurable by ordinary standards. It does not coincide perfectly with membership of a particular church, adherence to a particular system of belief, or the practice of ethical behavior. It is not the prerogative of the overtly religious nor do such people have any guarantees. There are many church-going persons who exclude themselves from a more intense encounter with the divine otherness, and do not allow their religion to influence their behavior. In such cases, it eventually becomes evident that outward observance, however holy, cannot take the place of personal encounter with the living God. Rituals are no more than lifeless superstitions unless something is happening at the deep center of personal being. It is this dark intrapersonal bonding with the Unseen that is the basis of genuine religion, and the spark by which our spiritual faculties are activated. Christians call this mysterious reality "faith." It is gift and not achievement; nor is it merely a cognitive event; we perceive that it is the work of God deep in our souls.

There is a certain utility in recalling our own experiences

of faith; how they came about, what we were feeling, and
what was their effect in our lives. Perhaps we tend to deny
that anything extraordinary has happened in our lives. I doubt
that this is so. Why, if that is the case, are you reading a book
like this? Where did the questions come from for which you
are seeking answers? There is no smoke without fire. Listen to
how Bernard of Clairvaux challenged his monks to stop denying their own inner experience and, instead, to affirm it in all
humility and to return to it as a source of energy and guidance.

> It is clear that each one of you has knowledge of God.
> If anyone says, "I know him not" (Mt 26:72 = Lk
> 22:57), he is a liar like worldly people. If you have no
> knowledge of God, who is it that led you here? How
> else could you have been persuaded freely to renounce
> the affection of your friends, the pleasures of the body,
> and the vanities of the world? How else could you
> have been led to cast all your thoughts on the Lord
> and to make over to him all your concerns since, as
> your consciences testify, you merited nothing good but
> only punishment? I repeat, who could have persuaded
> you of all this unless you know that the Lord is good
> to all who hope in him, to the heart who seeks him,
> unless you had recognized for yourself that the Lord is
> gentle, kind, and full of mercy and faithfulness? How
> else could you know these things unless the Lord had
> come not only to you but into you?[3]

The words used are cognitive, but their meaning is experi-
ential. Bernard is saying, in effect, that our interest in the spiritual life, especially if it leads us in the direction of sacrifice, is an
indication that something has happened deep within us. There
has been an attraction, a stirring, an invitation, a leading or

drawing, an awakening. We do not always have the vocabulary to describe these events and so sometimes they slip from
consciousness and memory, even though they continue to influence the choices that we make. It is important, as Bernard
insists, to return to these moments of light, especially when
we find ourselves in darkness. They can help us to reframe
our present situation. Reflection on them can motivate us to
call God back into the chaos which through our inattention
has descended on us.

If we ask ourselves to describe how we felt when we were
under the influence of meta-experience, we will often find ourselves saying something like this: "I felt alive." It is true. Meta-
experience liberates and engages our spirits in a way that nothing
else does. We hear examples of child prodigies who suddenly
discover a vast musical talent that needs only a short apprenticeship before attaining the level of genius. The gift was always there, waiting to be aroused. It can be the same with us.
We have an innate spiritual latency that needs only a little
external prompting before it bursts into flower. When it does,
we feel like new persons. We feel alive. We experience a freedom to be ourselves. This is how the Cistercian mystic Beatrice
of Nazareth (d. 1267) described this moment.

> She is like a fish that swims in the breadth of the ocean
> and rests in the depths. She is like a bird that flies in
> the spaciousness and height of the sky. Thus she expe-
> riences her spirit as walking unbound in the depth and
> spaciousness and height of love.[4]

Thoroughly earthy creatures that we are, it surprises us
that we feel so at home in the spiritual world—free to be fully
ourselves. Julian of Norwich attempts to capture the moment
by referring to the "homeliness" of God. God is not like those
who need to assert their superiority. The "courtesy" of God is

such that when we are welcomed we feel welcome, and our awkward self-consciousness disappears. We are made to feel at home with God, allowed to be ourselves without pretense—welcomed, accepted, loved just as we are. Mystical experience is not so much a matter of being catapulted into metaphysical abstraction as being drawn to meet God present in the lowliest and loveliest speck of creation. Maybe even within the self.

Our spirits were created as windows into the reality of God. The problem is that we allow them to become begrimed, so that they lose their transparency. In that condition whenever we look inward we see only ourselves. God seems absent. Whenever we try to project ourselves outward to other people, the impediments that block the outshining of our inward light interpose themselves. To attain a state in which we see and are seen without distortion we have need of that inner simplicity that Jesus called "purity of heart." "Blessed are the pure of heart for they shall see God" (Mt 5:8). Such simplicity is difficult to attain—it demands almost a lifetime's channeling of our energies away from self. It demands a certain level of detachment from self-indulgence and a disciplined way of life. In the words of Saint Gertrude the Great, the transparent person is one "with a pure heart, a chaste body, and a love that draws ever closer."[5] The best preparations for contemplative experience are not esoteric, even though they are demanding. Bernard of Clairvaux sees the "ecstasy of contemplation" as finding its foundations in "the labor of self-knowledge" and in the "felt compassion" for the sufferings of others.[6] Contemplation is the fruit both of radical self-honesty and of kindness to others.

The call for detachment seems a grim prelude to the happy fulfillment of our innate potentialities. Is there not another way? Perhaps the way of love and sweetness? Alas, the gate is narrow, and the road that leads to God is hard and rough. This is not an arbitrary imposition intended to restrict access

to an elite. The difficulty of the journey derives from the nature of the destination. The gift of contemplation seeks an
empty space, or it creates one. The very nature of meta-experience requires this detachment. It is necessarily an act of self-
transcendence; we go beyond the frontiers of our comfort zone
and are drawn into the dark desert beyond. Usually there is
hesitation, there is resistance, there is dread.[7] That is because
the call to experience something of the reality of God is an
absolute. Everything else must be relegated to a subordinate
place in our hearts and in our lives. "Love for fleshly things
breaks up the concentration of the mind and blunts its cutting
edge."[8] No wonder that along with the joy of being drawn
towards God there is anguish. As the poet Francis Thompson
(d. 1907) wrote, "Yet I was sore adread / Lest having Him, I
must have naught beside."[9]

Detachment can sometimes be rough and violent, as when
events abruptly rob us of one whom we love or something
that brings us joy. More often, there is a gradual loosening of
alternative attachments over a period of time—not, however
without occasional tugs and twinges. Our being attracted to
God is complemented by a loss of interest in pursuits that
previously served as substitutes for spirituality. There may not
be a dramatic change in our scale of values, except in retrospect. What happens is that we become aware that some of
our previous gratifications have lost their charm, and we willingly set them aside. Exaggerating a little, as spiritual writers
often do, Gregory the Great concludes: "What previously
brought pleasure to the soul subsequently becomes an intolerable burden."[10]

> Those who experience fully the sweetness of the heav-
> enly life happily leave behind everything they previously
> loved on earth. In comparison with this, everything
> else is devalued. They abandon their possessions and

scatter what they had amassed because their souls are on fire for heavenly things and they have no pleasure in the things of earth.[11]

Intense experience of spiritual reality demands a reversal in our mental fragmentation. It is the concentration of our thoughts in a single direction until they are fixed on a single point. Drawn into mystery by love we become intent. For the while nothing else matters. Listen to the way Saint Bernard describes that moment in which all life's energies are brought into a laserlike beam and concentrated on God.

There is, now and then, an experience of ecstasy and a recession from bodily senses so that the soul is so aware of the Word that it is no longer aware of itself. This happens when the mind, enticed by the unimaginable sweetness of the Word, is somehow stolen from itself. It is seized and snatched away from itself so that it may find pleasure in the Word.[12]

In this text, Bernard is speaking of the way in which our soul, or *anima*, is conjoined by a deep and intimate spiritual love to the Second Person of the Trinity. Years of truthful living and unfeigned love of neighbor have cleansed the soul of its impurities so that its inward gaze no longer stops at a mirror image of self, but passes through the self to be connected to God. There is a duality of experience. On the one hand, the world of sense and reason does not intrude: there are no concepts, no pictures, no messages to take home—only a brilliant darkness and a resounding silence. Time ceases: an instant may seem like a whole season of celebration or, alternatively, clock hours may pass in what seems like a few seconds. This apparent emptiness is so full of activity that mind and heart suffer overload and turn off. It is as though all skills and resources have been voided. "The mind, enticed by the unimaginable sweetness of the Word, is somehow stolen from itself. It is seized and snatched away from itself." Ecstasy is not lunacy; it occurs when persons are so intent and transfixed in the acts of looking and seeing that anything else has no power to seize or hold the attention. "The soul is so aware of the Word that it is no longer aware of itself." Meanwhile, the cavalcade of desires, anxieties, and preoccupations trundles past unnoticed. For a moment our love for God is our whole being. To everything else we are blind and deaf.

What is happening here is that after many years of faithful discipleship,[13] great slabs of willful selfishness have been worn down or have fallen away. What remains at the level of consciousness is an unshakable faith in God's mercy and an abiding conviction of one's great need for that mercy. Need becomes desire, desire moves towards love, and sometimes this love becomes overpowering. The soul is like bushland at the end of a long hot summer; the merest spark will trigger a conflagration. One who has loved God well, but hiddenly, needs only a break from external occupation or preoccupation together with the slightest prompting in order to step through the door into eternity. But, as Bernard notes, "the relationship may be sweet, but the moment is short and the experience rare."[14] More often than not, we are too anxious and concerned about many things for this to happen.

Our spiritual experiences always seem complete in the sense they totally fill our awareness and more. Yet, without our doing anything directly to change matters, there is an imperceptible increase in our capacity to enjoy God. If we are caught in a rain shower, we are wet; but we are a long way from being sodden. Sometimes we may be so wet that we feel saturated, as though the division between body and water has been blurred. Even though the experience of God fills every crevice of our heart, it admits of an infinite capacity to go deeper and deeper, beyond anything we may imagine. Sometimes we may begin to experience in ourselves the truth of that saying of Saint Paul so often quoted by the mystics: "The one who adheres to God becomes one spirit with God" (1 Cor 6:17).

There is a kind of progression in contemplative experience. At first, the incarnate Word is the focus of our attention. We begin to be attentive disciples of Jesus, inviting him into our life and experiences and keeping before our eyes his words and example as they are conveyed to us in the Gospels. Already we are moving beyond the everyday world of sense experience and positioning ourselves in an inward world, formed by the Scriptures. From outward teaching and actions, the mind is drawn inward to the heart of Jesus. Instead of prayer being merely engagement with Jesus as an object of meditation, a real relationship develops. This intersubjective stage is characterized by a new sense of freedom to be oneself. I no longer need to invest most of my effort in being good, because I have a sense of being known, accepted, and loved as I am and, in turn, "I know the one in whom I have placed my trust" (2 Tim 1:12). This relationship changes the way that we live and how we relate to other people and, over the years, it grows ever stronger.

At some point, an unexpected change occurs. The visible, comprehensible Jesus whom we have followed and to whom we have given our loyalty and love recedes into the background. It is as though Christ is ascended into heaven and we are left bereft. This is the conclusion of the first phase of spiritual life; we are being invited to go higher: "If we had once known Christ according to the flesh we know him thus no longer" (2 Cor 5:16). For some, this is a painful transition, but it is the only road to deeper union with God.[15]

At this stage, we are being drawn towards the glorified humanity of Jesus, no longer subject to the limitations of space and time but everywhere present at the level of spirit. In other words, our prayer is operating out of a different region of our being. It is not merely at the level of sense and imagination; it has passed through the zone where affectivity comes into play and now it has penetrated the frontiers of the spirit. In the language of ancient monasticism, this is "the prayer of the heart"—it belongs at the inmost core of our being. This state is to pass beyond sentiment and beyond will power to a deep level where it is hard to distinguish what we do from what is done to us. Doing and being done to coincide. Yet we are never so alert, active, and alive as when this work is being accomplished in us. Listen to the fourteenth-century English classic, *The Cloud of Unknowing.*

> To express myself briefly: let this thing deal with you and lead you wherever it likes. Let it be the worker and you but the sufferer; look at it briefly, then leave it alone. Meddle not with it as though to help it for fear of spilling all. Be the tree and let it be the carpenter. Be the house and let it be the householder dwelling inside. Be blind in this time and cut away all desire for knowledge, for that will hinder you more than it will help. It suffices that you feel yourself stirred pleasantly with something you do not know—except in this stirring you have no specific thought of anything under God, and that all your desire is nakedly directed towards God.[16]

Meanwhile nothing is happening that is externally observable, and the state of the more outer zones, reason and sensibility, is one of such deep restedness that it is close to sleep.

> Your bodily wits may find there nothing to feed on. They think that you are doing nothing. Still keep on doing this nothing—provided you do it for the love of

God. Cease not. Travail busily in that nothing with a
conscious desire to want to have God whom no human being can know. I tell you truly, I would rather be
in this nowhere place, blindly wrestling with nothing,
than to be some great Lord who could go where he
wanted and amuse himself with anything he liked.[17]

Thus the soul begins to find its feet in the spiritual world,
where landmarks are none and precedents rare. It is a period
of learning not only to live in the absence of discernible light
but, progressively, to love the darkness. What a spiritual di-
rector looks for at this stage is a certain alacrity for prayer,
which makes the person willing to dedicate more and more
time to it, with little apparent result—except one's daily battle
against disruptive thoughts and the uprising of dormant desires. The effort involved in continuing to "travail busily in
that nothing" can be considerable. There is always the possibility of losing heart and giving up. To people in this situation
the words of Julian of Norwich can be encouraging.

Pray with your whole being, even though you think
that it has no savor for you. For such prayer is very
profitable even though you feel nothing. Pray with your
whole being, though you feel nothing, though you see
nothing, even though it seems impossible to you. It is
in dryness and in barrenness, in sickness and in feeble-
ness, that your prayer is most pleasing to me, even
though you think that it has little savor for you.[18]

The active emptiness of this stage of prayer has the effect
of hollowing out the heart. Although certain imperfections
and vices may still run rampant during the rest of the day, the
time of prayer is progressively free of their influence. It is a
zone of deep quiet, even though sometimes it may be a still

center surrounded by a raging tempest. Entering this sacred space, we are obliged to release our grip on everything, our weaknesses as well as our strengths. Here we appear naked before God "before whom no creature is hidden" (Heb 4:13). We experience our utter lack of skills or resources so that the dominant theme of the encounter, whether expressed verbally or not, is a cry for mercy.

Prolonged immersion in this form of prayer completely voids our spiritual self-reliance. We are forced, as it were, to trust in the merits of Christ. We seek to pray with the voice of Christ, since our own voice seems unable for the task. We desire to enter into Christ's relationship with the Father—to journey with Christ in the Spirit into the depths of God. What is happening is that we are being drawn into the subjectivity of Christ, beginning a process which will lead to our being able to say with Saint Paul, "I live, now not I, but Christ lives in me" (Gal 2:20). The glorified Christ prays within us, we become participant in a prayer that is beyond our competence to frame.

> The Spirit comes to the aid of our weakness. For we do not know what to pray as is necessary, but the Spirit mediates with sighs that are beyond language. The One who searches hearts understands the Spirit's meaning, because the Spirit mediates for the saints as God [wills] (Rom 8:26–27).

This prayer is not a means to an end. It is the goal of all human existence and a foretaste, as we have already said, of eternity. It is a moment of transcendent life. There is no content for us to share with others; the only effect is that we advance more speedily on the road of transformation. But this is not something that is apparent to us. There is a sense of having fed well. We come out of prayer almost as spotty as we entered it. Bernard, who speaks about this experience in terms of a visit from the Word, writes thus: "When the Word departs, it is as though you were to remove the fire from beneath a burning pot. Immediately the water becomes lifeless and begins to cool."[19] All is not lost, however; there is a lightness in our steps and perhaps a fire in our hearts.

> One who is granted to experience in prayer this overflowing of the mind with regard to the mysterious divine reality returns from that experience burning with most vehement love and boiling with a zeal for holiness. Such a one is extremely fervent in his zeal for spiritual occupations and duties so that he well might say "My heart grew hot within me, and in my meditation a fire blazed out."[20]

As we look upon the Father with the eyes of Christ we are rapt in contemplation. As we look on people through the same eyes, we find that we are drawn into compassion. Contemplation and compassion are inseparable. Love is indivisible. The love poured into our hearts by the Spirit not only joins us to God, it also increases our solidarity with those around us through recognizing their lovableness and bearing their burdens with equanimity and even a measure of joy.

Meta-experience is the dynamism by which ordinary people become holy. It is not commonly chronicled because, in the final analysis, there is little to write about. It is the simplest of all human events, since by it all life and consciousness are concentrated in a single point which then disappears. It is often hidden even from those who experience it. Meta-experience is not communicable to others, nor do we ever possess it securely. It is more like a lightning flash than the enduring illumination of the noonday sun. Isaac of Stella sees it as comparable to the disciples' experience at the Transfiguration; the chosen trio experienced something extraordinary but were yet unable to speak about it.

> Peter, James, and John heard the Father but did not see him. Coming down [from the mountain] they told no one about what they had seen and heard. Dearest brothers, so it happens with spiritual persons whose sensibility has been refined by long practice. In their prayer and contemplation they see, taste, and feel wonderfully sweet and pleasing realities that are over-flowing with light so that they are suddenly seized by ecstasy of mind. When they return to themselves, they cannot say anything of this—they can scarcely even remember it.[21]

Let us pause at this point to reflect on one of the most beautiful descriptions of meta-experience from the pen of Bernard of Clairvaux. He is speaking about how the soul that thirsts for God often experiences a "visitation" from the Word, which rekindles its fervor and does for the soul whatever needs to be done.

> But now you must bear with my foolishness for a moment. As I promised, I wish to speak of how this happens in my own case. It is for your benefit that I speak about myself even though it is not good to do so. If you derive some profit from my foolishness then I shall feel better about it, if not, then I shall plead guilty to foolishness.
>
> I admit, in all foolishness, that the Word has visited me many times. When he enters I do not usually advert to his coming. I sense that he is present and I remember that he had been absent. Sometimes I have been able to anticipate his entry, but I have never been

able directly to experience either his arrival or departure. I confess that I am ignorant of where he comes from when he enters my soul, and where he goes when he departs. I do not know the manner of his entry, nor how he leaves. This is in accordance with the text of Scripture: "Nobody knows whence he comes or where he goes to." This should occasion no surprise since he is the one of whom it is said: "Your footprints shall not be known." He does not come in through the eyes, for he has no color; nor through the ears, since he makes no sound. It is not through the nose that he comes: he does not mingle with the air, but with the mind, to the atmosphere he gives being not odor. Nor does he gain entry through the mouth, because he is not food or drink. He cannot be experienced by touch, since he is impalpable. How then does he find entrance? Perhaps he does not enter at all, as he does not come from outside and is not to be identified with any external object. On the other hand, he does not come from inside me: he is good and I know there is nothing good within me.

I ascended to what was highest in me and, behold, the Word loomed loftier. Earnestly I explored the depths of my being and he was found to be yet deeper. If I looked outside, I saw him beyond myself. If I gazed within, he was even more inward. It was then that I realized the truth of what I had read: "In him we live and move and have our being." Happy are they in whom dwells the one by whom they live; happy they who live for him and are moved by him!

You might ask how it is that I know the Word has arrived, since all his ways are beyond scrutiny. I know because the Word is living and active. As soon as he arrives within, he shakes to life my sleepy soul. He moves, softens, and wounds my heart which previously had been hard, stony, and unhealthily intact. The Word begins to root up and destroy, to build and to plant. He waters the arid lands and brings light to the gloom; he opens up what was closed and sets fire to what was frigid. The twisted roads he makes straight and the rough ways smooth. All this is done so that my soul may bless the Lord, and all that is within me may bless his holy name.

When the bridegroom comes to me, as he does sometimes, he never signals his presence by any indicator: not by voice or vision or the sound of his step. By no such movement do I become aware of him. He does not enter the depths of my being through my senses. It is only by the movement of my heart, as I have already said, that I perceive his presence. It is by the expulsion of my vices and the suppression of carnal desires that I recognize the power of his might. I am lost in wonderment at the depth of his wisdom when he subjects my secret life to scrutiny and correction. It is from some slight improvement in my behavior that I experience his gentle goodness. It is from the reformation and renewal of the spirit of my mind, that is, of my deepest humanity, that I perceive his beauty and attractiveness. From the consideration of all these taken together, I am overwhelmed by his abundant goodness.[22]

It is erroneous to think that such experiences are reserved to elite spiritual athletes. On the contrary, it is the little people who seem to have privileged access, even though they may not have the concepts or vocabulary to describe what has happened to them. Anyone who has visited a church in time of distress and found there solace and strength has tasted something of this. Persons who have prayed doggedly over many decades are sustained in their practice by more than a sense of duty. Many of us find our lamps lit unexpectedly by events and encounters. Children often see things that are invisible to adults. Sometimes dreams can serve as a funnel for the inpouring of light. Mystical experience in all its forms and at all its levels is an integral component of human life, but strangely we have banished it from awareness and discourse. In the process we have lost sight of an important element in what it is to be human.

The beginnings and endings of meta-experience are hard to track; and while the Word is present there is no room in the awareness for anything else, even though what we "see" is, as Saint Paul says "through a glass, darkly" (1 Cor 13:12). The genuineness of the experience can be verified only in its effects: "by the expulsion of my vices and the suppression of carnal desire...from some slight improvement in my behavior." Such effects are, however, only the outermost reflections of what has taken place. Bernard uses a phrase based on Ephesians 4:23 to describe what is happening—"the reformation and renewal of the spirit of my mind, that is, of my deepest humanity." It is in meta-experience that I am being most fully human, most fully myself. This is the pinnacle of all human experiences; it was for this that I was created, it will be in this that I will enjoy eternal life.

> This is freedom of conscience, sweetness of heart, goodness of mind, nobility of soul, lightness of spirit, and the beginning of eternal life. This is already an angelic life and after it follows eternal life. May God in his goodness give it to us all.[23]

At the end of the transfiguration narrative, there is a sense of moving onwards to the Passion. The radiant experience on the mountain is meant to offset the grueling days ahead—certainly for Peter, James, and John, and possibly for Jesus himself.

CHAPTER NINETEEN

Jesus the Prophet

And when they were coming near to Jerusalem, at Bethphage and Bethany towards the Mount of Olives [Jesus] sent forth two of his disciples saying, "Go into the village ahead of you. When you enter it, immediately you will find a colt tied up, upon which nobody has ever sat. Untie it and bring it. And if someone should say to you, 'Why are you doing this?' say, 'The Lord needs it and will send it back here immediately.'" [The disciples] went off and found the colt, tied up near a doorway, outside in the street, and they untied it. And some of those standing there said, "What are you doing untying the colt?" [The disciples] replied to them as Jesus had instructed and they let them proceed. They took the colt to Jesus and placed their cloaks over it, and Jesus sat on it. And many people strewed their cloaks on the road; others greenery cut in the fields. Those who went ahead and those who followed were crying out: "Hosanna! A blessing on the coming kingdom of David our father! Hosanna in the highest!" And [Jesus] entered Jerusalem and the Temple; and he was looking around at everything. It was already evening and he went out to Bethany with the Twelve.

MARK 11:1–11

Mark has long delayed the moment of Jesus' entry into Jerusalem—using Jesus' circuitous southbound progression from Galilee with all its detours and side trips as the occasion for a deeper initiation of his closest disciples into "the mystery of the Kingdom" (Mk 4:11). Three times the procession halts, as it were, and Jesus soberly reminds his disciples of the outcome awaiting him in the capital. Three times the journey is resumed without the disciples understanding what he is saying; even towards the end of the progression, James and John are conspiring to secure the best seats for themselves on the day of his glory. Jesus alone seems to understand the nature of the "cup" that awaits him (Mk 10:39, 14:36).

Because Mark is writing a Gospel for believers and not simply telling a story, he knows that his readers are fully aware of what happened as a result of Jesus' coming to Jerusalem. Accordingly, there is a strong sense of irony about the narrative. In the light of what happened subsequently, there is an aura of unreality about the events surrounding Jesus' arrival at Jerusalem. "In the same city, by the same populace, and at the same season now he is honored with a glorious procession and divine praises, and afterwards interrogated with insults and torture, and numbered among the sinners."[1] The most curious aspect of the whole incident is that Jesus seemed not only to acquiesce in the public adulation of his followers, but actively planned the whole scenario.

The events, as Mark describes them, have been considerably amplified by the later Gospels, so we have to be careful in reading Mark's account that we restrict our attention to what he says and not interpolate material from elsewhere. We know that Jesus was traveling south with a group of disciples that included the Twelve and many women (Mk 15:41). It seems that they may have been in the habit of picking up extra disciples as they went along (Mk 10:21, 10:52). Mark says simply that "many" accompanied him, shouting messianic slogans and paving his way with garments and greenery.[2] Perhaps in reality it was no more than a ragtag invasion of rural enthusiasts noisily arriving in the capital for the first time, but there is an undertone in the narrative that indicates that something singular is occurring.

The role which Jesus seems to have assumed for his confrontation with the hard core of religious authority was that of a prophet, similar to those known from the Old Testament: thus Matthew 21:10, Luke 24:19, and John 4:19. Instead of being "himself" as he was in the home territory of Galilee and letting himself be seen simply as one who "has done all things well" (Mk 7:37), Jesus feels the need of a more recognizable identity if he is to make an impact on the more sophisticated inhabitants of Jerusalem. It is not as though Jesus were unaware of the danger of taking up the prophet's mantle: "A prophet is not without honor except in his own country and among his own kinsfolk and in his own house" (Mk 6:4). A different Jesus emerges in this part of the Gospel, a far more decisive, adversarial, and "dangerous" man—one who certainly qualifies for Simeon's description as "a sign of contradiction" (Lk 2:34). Let us look at some of the manifestations of the new attitude in the account of his entry.

(a) The narrative begins with Jesus using the prophetic device of foreknowledge, command, and fulfillment, repeated later in Mark 14:12–15. Two disciples are dispatched on a mission, the details of which are described to them before they depart. In a dreamlike sequence, everything unfolds exactly as Jesus predicts.

(b) Jesus exercises an arbitrary authority in borrowing a colt; no resistance is offered.

(c) The point about riding on a donkey's colt may be that the action was considered to have messianic overtones. Matthew makes explicit a reference to Zechariah 9:9 which refers to the arrival of an unwarlike king, riding on a donkey's colt.

(d) Mark increases the aura of mystery by insisting that it is a colt that had never been ridden, thus signaling that something unprecedented is about to take place. It is hard to know exactly what message he intends to convey by this item of information. There may be an oblique reference to ancient ritual prescriptions. See Numbers 19:2, Deuteronomy 21:3, and 1 Samuel 6:7.

(e) The solemnity of what is happening is increased by Mark's singular and uncharacteristic usage of the title κύριος (the Lord) for Jesus. Theoretically, it could mean simply "the boss" or even "the owner," but in Christian ears it could refer only to the title of honor given liturgically to the risen Jesus (Phil 2:11), and in the other Gospels retrojected into Jesus' lifetime.

(f) In the days before ticker tape and streamers, throwing greenery and bits of clothing was the way to turn a walk into a gala occasion. The Second Book of Kings 9:13 is often cited as a literary precedent for using clothing to dress up an occasion. Greenery is mentioned in the processional Psalm 118. It was carried in procession at the Feast of Tabernacles and, in 1 Maccabees 13:51, music and palm branches are mentioned in the context of a victory parade.

(g) The acclamations attributed to the crowd have definite "messianic" connotations. "Hosanna!" is found in Psalm 118:25 and means something like "God save the king!" This is one of several Hebrew or Aramaic words embedded in the Marcan tradition, perhaps reflecting either an element of a typical storyteller's technique or liturgical practice. Using the words of the next verse of the same psalm, blessings are called down on "the One who is to come (perhaps a messianic title even on its own) in the Lord's name." Following the celebration of the coming of God's envoy is the evocation of the establishment of a messianic kingdom—politically a more dangerous proposition.

(h) The procession does not discreetly dawdle around the outskirts of the city but proceeds directly to its heart: the Temple. This would, of course, mean coming into the vicinity of the Roman headquarters in the Fortress Antonia. No doubt the occupation forces were watching events closely from behind the battlements.

(i) Mark concludes his account efficiently. Jesus looks around at everything but does nothing. He then beats a retreat to Bethany, accompanied by the Twelve. Is there here, as at Mk 13:1, some indication that Jesus and his followers were coming to Jerusalem for the first time—country boys impressed by the grandeur of the city?

We find the same pattern repeated in the period following. No longer is Jesus content to heal and to teach in general terms about the Kingdom of God. Let us recall some of the other features of this phase of Jesus' career that give the "Judean ministry" a flavor quite distinct from what we witnessed during his activities in Galilee and on the road. A stronger note of stridency can be heard. The Gospel tells of a number of symbolic and prophetic gestures by which Jesus drew attention to himself and heightened the hostility of the religious authorities. The very ambiguity of some of these actions must have been a source of additional confusion to his uncomprehending followers. Notice that there is no indication that all these events took place within the space of a week—from "Palm Sunday" to the Passover.

(a) The day after the entry into Jerusalem, there is another dramatic incident. Jesus is hungry. He looks for some fruit on a fig tree and finding none he curses it. Mark adds the information that it was not the season for figs; Matthew and Luke omit this clarification. The next morning the tree, previously in full leaf, has withered to its roots.

(b) Sandwiched between the two scenes of the cursing of the fig tree, Jesus goes back to the Temple and drives out both buyers and sellers, scatters the moneychangers' coins, and kicks over the booths of the vendors of doves needed for the ritual. There is a tinge of fanaticism here. He denies passage to persons carrying anything and begins to teach "day after day within the temple precinct" (Mk 14:49). His message seamlessly blends the words of Isaiah 56:7 and Jeremiah 7:11: God's house is a consecrated place, not to be profaned by mundane activities.

(c) Jesus thus denies the Temple to the religious ascendancy and, inevitably, incurs their wrath. Jesus does nothing to appease them. As Mark recounts matters, Jesus exposes their lack of integrity in dealing with John the Baptist (Mk 11:29–33), he tells "against them" the parable of the murderous tenants (Mk 12:1–12), he evades their trap on the question of taxes (Mk 12:13–17), he robustly debates theology and ends by telling the Sadducees that they are "quite wrong" concerning resurrection (Mk 12:18–27), and to the crowd's delight he poses questions that baffle the experts (Mk 12:35–37). Notwithstanding the fact that one of the scribes was "not far from God's kingdom" (Mk 12:34), Jesus denounces the scribes in general as pompous, greedy, and hypocritical (Mk 12:38–40), worthy of condemnation and of less merit in the eyes of God than a poor widow (Mk 12:41–44). Jesus is here doing battle not so much with the unimaginative country practitioners of the law, as with the slick big-city experts who were adept at interpreting the ancient texts to suit their own purposes. In this series of controversies, Galilean Pharisees have given way to Jerusalem scribes and Sadducees, with their connections through the priestly families with the various levels of indigenous and occupying authority. For Jesus, this is a dangerous confrontation.

(d) What was implicit in the cursing of the fig tree, the cleansing of the Temple, and the undermining of scribal authority becomes explicit in the so-called "Apocalyptic Discourse" of Mark 13. The times are changing. History is fast reaching its culmination. The Son of Man is coming to inaugurate the reign of God (Mk 13:26, 14:62). The massive solidity of the Temple will crumble, civil society will be torn apart, while the physical world will be wracked by earthquakes. Persecutions, unprecedented suffering, and cosmic cataclysm will give rise to false messiahs and false prophets. Many, if they do not remain vigilant, will be led astray. This is teaching unlike anything that we have come to expect from the smoothed-out accounts of Jesus' Galilean ministry: it is starkly eschatological, forthright in its predictions of doom, and uncompromising in the moral stance demanded of Jesus' followers.

(e) At Bethany in the days before Passover, Jesus accepts an anticipatory anointing at the hands of an unnamed woman disciple. Perhaps, since the spikenard was poured on Jesus' head, the woman intended to reenact Samuel's consecration of David as king (1 Sam 10:1), but Jesus deflects this purpose and sees it rather as a farewell rite for one who is dead (Mk 14:3–9). The prospect of death begins to loom large in Jesus' thoughts.

(f) The apostasy of Judas, the dribbling away of the disciples, the flight of the naked youth, and the "betrayal" of Peter thread their way through the Passion narrative as an anticipation of the mass apostasy expected when the eschatological troubles fall upon the earth. Jesus predicts that these desertions will occur (Mk 14:17–21, 26–31) and stands aloof from them. His destiny is a singular one in which the disciples cannot share. The Fourth Gospel understands this (Jn 13:36).

(g) Jesus' last meal with the Twelve is full of mystery. Jesus again sends two disciples ahead of him to make preparations—predicting accurately what they will find. During the meal, in actions that no Christian reader could fail to see as prefiguring the liturgy of the Eucharist, Jesus breaks bread and pours out wine—identifying these elements with his body, about to be broken, and his blood, about to be poured out—not wasted but shared by all. A covenant is made whereby those who share the meal are firmly bonded. (The best manuscripts of Mark do not speak of a *new* covenant.) The idea of a redemptive act is suggested by the phrase "for many" (see Isa 53:12). Jesus announces that this is his last meal in this temporal sphere—the kingdom of God is truly at hand (Mk 1:15). How much mystery, symbolism, and theology Mark has managed to pack into these four verses (Mk 14:22–25).

How did these events impact on the consciousness of Jesus? He would not have been human if the thought did not occur to him, even momentarily, that perhaps there still was some hope of a happy outcome to his ministry. Perhaps popular enthusiasm might outweigh the entrenched opposition of the religious authorities, or more scribes would come forward who were "not far from God's Kingdom." In either eventuality, all would be well. Those who have experienced it tell me that it is difficult not to become intoxicated by a crowd's roared approval. It washes over one like a giddying moment of empowerment in which nothing is impossible. Unfortunately, as celebrities, athletes, and politicians often discover to their grief, this heady sense of euphoria can be hollow and even delusional. It can inspire an excess of optimism which obscures the data that stares us in the face.

Is it possible that Jesus became an accomplice in the mob's hankering after a political solution to their troubles? Or, at least, was he tempted to do so? Was it a case that a simple prophetic gesture was hijacked by the mob and turned into a potentially revolutionary ferment? We know that Jesus seems successfully to have evaded their king-making schemes up to this point. But has a false hope germinated in his heart as he comes closer to the hideous fate that he had so often predicted would be his? Is it such an affront to suggest that, like ourselves, Jesus' first impulse on the brink of tragedy was to be lured into believing in the possibility of a more optimistic scenario? When, earlier on, Peter pointed out this possibility to him, Jesus rebuked him with sufficient severity to indicate that what Peter was proposing was, in fact, a real temptation and not just a stupid suggestion. Remember that the name by which Jesus addressed Peter was that of the tempter (Mk 8:33, 1:13). Now, later in the story, is Jesus bedeviled by the thought and the hope of an easier way? The most we can say is that it is not impossible.

We all know that mistakes are a necessary part of the human condition, as the poet Alexander Pope wrote, "To err is human."[3] Our mistakes can be due to errors of fact, deriving from inattention or insufficient knowledge. We can also make errors of judgment. The sensory data on which we base our assessments can be misshapen by the interpretative matrix in which it is processed, by unrepresentative sampling, or by emotion-based resistance to objective evidence. Such errors get us into a lot of trouble and make our lives and those of others more miserable, but *in themselves* they are not sinful. They are part of the burden we bear as human beings. If it is

true that "the one who never made a mistake never made anything," then perhaps as members of the human community
we will find that the magic phrase "I was wrong" is one that
may be usefully learned. We find it so hard to say because we
do not want to admit to being mistaken, yet so often such an
admission is the beginning of a healing process that repairs
the rifts caused by thoughtless and ignorant actions.

Jesus was not immune from making mistakes, and we do
him no favor in claiming that his life was totally error free. As
we have mentioned earlier, there is no doubt that Jesus' knowledge of the natural world was that of a first-century Palestinian: much of which he took as certain is unacceptable to us
who have the benefit of centuries of science. But we need not
be afraid of taking the matter further. He slips up in his biblical knowledge when he speaks about Abiathar instead of
Ahimelech in Mark 2:26.[4] Some of the apocalyptic expectations that he shared with many of his contemporaries were
misplaced (Mk 9:1, 13:30). Even his usually astute judgments
about people were not necessarily infallible. His choice of Judas Iscariot is an obvious example, and he must sometimes
have wondered about the other disciples, especially Peter. It
seems almost heretical to deny to Jesus the inborn fragility we
all experience in matters of knowing and judging. It looks like
an effort to protect his divinity by watering down the effects
of his being human, limited to one point in space and time,
without continual access to the overarching knowledge proper
to God. The precise wonder of the incarnation is that the Second Person of the Trinity was able to exist and operate through
a human nature, like unto ours in all things except sin.

Did Jesus rejoice inwardly at the rowdy welcome he received and the impact he was making on the people? Did he,
as we would say, "against his better judgment" allow himself
to be carried along by the enthusiasm of those around him
towards a role that was easier and, perhaps, more gratifying

than the "cup" prepared for him? We know that at this point the Fourth Gospel pictures Jesus as suffering a fit of revulsion at the prospect of the Hour that he had hitherto embraced with serenity (Jn 12:27). Was there a temptation to slip into the role of an all-conquering prophet-king instead of the pain, disgrace, and rejection of public execution?

In these incidents, Jesus is clearly presenting himself as a prophet, enjoying some of the immunity granted to the ancient bearers of God's messages, partly because of the fickle favor of the crowd. From the taunts of the midnight assembly that condemned him, it is clear that his adversaries understood that Jesus was presenting himself as a prophet; now they mocked his impotence to substantiate that claim (Mk 14:65). Later, his supposed claim is expanded and perhaps distorted to include kingship (Mk 15:2, 15:9, 15:18, 15:26) and messiahship (Mk 15:32).

Why is it worth considering the possibility that Jesus may have been buoyed up by a false optimism as he entered this final phase of his public ministry? One reason is that it makes more comprehensible the supreme agony he experienced in the garden of Gethsemane as he came to realize the inevitability of his death and the apparent failure of his mission. Furthermore, he would scarcely have been human if initially he had not entertained hopes that, despite appearances, things would work out if not well, at least not badly.

The prospect of personal extinction is so shocking that we cannot cope with it. No matter how strong our faith in an afterlife, it is almost impossible to look death squarely in the face without having passed through an exhausting series of stages. In her book *On Death and Dying*, Elisabeth Kübler-Ross has formulated a plausible sequence through which many pass on their way to accepting the imminent reality of death. These are the stages she distinguishes:

(a) Denial and isolation: "Denial functions as a buffer after unexpected shocking news, allows the patient to collect himself, and with time to mobilize other, less radical defenses."[5] It is a case of temporary withdrawal into oneself and that means excluding any data that might jolt one back into reality and the avoidance of any who might be the carriers of such information.

(b) Anger: "When the first stage of denial cannot be maintained any longer, it is replaced by feelings of anger, rage, envy, and resentment."[6] This seething rage may be directed not at death itself, but projected on those around. The dying person is impotent before the inevitability of death, frustrated by being deprived of a future. Imminent mortality is no temporary discomfort endured for the sake of better prospects; this is the end of the road.

(c) Bargaining: Because negotiation is the stuff of adult life, we quickly learn to make concessions in order to achieve our major goals. In a life-threatening situation we tend to look for something to appease a vengeful God—to repair damage done by past choices, to reform our lives, to discontinue practices about which we feel guilty. Objectively speaking it seems like a pitiable tactic, but this phase is often an important one in the journey towards acceptance. Finally one admits that death is round the corner.

(d) Depression: When bargaining fails to yield the desired miracle, depression sets in. This is not yet the gradual closing down of a life that is soon to end. It is more like a reaction to the shock of death's imminence. Lost opportunities, unfaced issues, and past failures loom large, and the possibilities for corrective actions steadily diminish. Cruel though it seems, such disheartenment seems as inevitable as death itself, at least for a time.

(e) Acceptance: When the reality of death is finally accepted, the lights in the building are turned off one by one. Interests drop away, energy declines, conversation lags, and the struggling is over. A quiet serenity may be achieved and a sense of life's closure may slowly seep into one's being.

Jesus was not dying of a terminal illness, but he was facing the prospect of certain death. Despite his confident predictions of resurrection, the unknown still threatened. Is it so unlikely that he would have been tempted to dream of an outcome less horrible than crucifixion? Must we deny to Jesus the recalcitrance typical of humanity at the prospect of its own extinction? Can we read into the anger directed at the fig tree and the religious authorities a projection of the inner rebellion he experienced when pondering his fate? Reflecting on these questions can help us to understand Jesus in his passion. He was not a man so elevated by religious conviction that he felt nothing of the dread and anguish that we experience in the face of death. He was one "like us in all things except sin," who recoiled instinctively from the act that would complete the self-emptying which was the hallmark of his life. The agony he experienced in Gethsemane and on the cross is comprehensible only in terms of a huge interior struggle that continued even until his last breath.

The piety of the Middle Ages often conjured up for itself graphic scenes of the physical torments suffered by Jesus in his passion and to wonder at the love that accepted to undergo such suffering on our account. For a generation less familiar with physical pain at a personal level and yet daily overexposed to violent images of others' suffering, such imaginative recreations are less effective in stirring devotion. It seems to me that we can come closer to the reality of the passion by pondering more deeply the mental anguish and confusion that Jesus experienced. In this, we can begin to move towards a gentler understanding of the pain we experience when our lives are in disarray, whether this pain is the result of our own misguided actions or derives from the malice or stupidity of others.

CHAPTER TWENTY

Confession

The Holy Spirit is in the one who confesses. It is already a sign of the gift of the Holy Spirit that what you have done is displeasing to you. Sins please the unclean spirit and displease the Holy Spirit. Although it is pardon for which you are pleading, nevertheless you and God are one when the evil you have committed displeases you. What displeases you also displeases God. Now there are two of you contending against your fever: you and the physician. The confession and punishment of sin is not possible for a human being unaided. When one is angry with oneself, this does not happen without the gift of the Holy Spirit.

AUGUSTINE OF HIPPO, *ON PSALM 50,* 16, CCHR 38, PP. 611–612

Jesus' short-lived career as a prophet reminds us that not all avenues into which we enter sincerely are guaranteed means of permanent advancement. In God's Providence we can easily be led up a path that goes nowhere. Despite our efforts at discernment, we can misread the cues that are given us and so invest much energy and effort in an enterprise that fails. As our stalwart denials finally collapse, we face the prospect of picking up our bundles and retracing our steps. Disappointment, disenchantment, discouragement, and even desperation are the familiar companions of anyone who tries to live a fulfilling and creative life. Only vegetables know nothing of them.

It is easy to fall into the trap of thinking that human life is a matter of linear progression. Like the scientific optimists of the nineteenth century, we too readily see development in terms of ongoing forward movement. There is not much room in such a view for slowing down, stalling, veering off the path, going around in a loop, or completely reversing course. When we survey our lives and find ourselves in a dead-end street, unable to go any further, we get upset. This is not the way we planned it; this was not how it looked on the map; something has clearly gone wrong. At this stage we begin to look for someone to blame.

Most of us would be a lot happier if we were to embrace the notion that human life is necessarily a trial-and-error reality. Its goal is eternal life. That is fixed. But the ways by which we attain that goal and the objectives we pursue *en route* are relatively flexible. We do not operate in a vacuum. Our course must be chosen in the context of all sorts of things that are happening within us and around us, over which we have no control. There is no means of verifying that a particular choice is guaranteed to be the right one. Such infallibility is the prerogative of hindsight. Faced with multiple options, all we can do is to make a judgment on the available evidence and act on that. Even with all the diligence and intelligence we can muster, we will often misjudge a situation, and a negative outcome will result, with varying degrees of damage to ourselves and others.

At a first level, there is a limitation on how much we can know. We are fallible. Many mistakes are caused by ignorance. Obviously if we knew that a bridge was about to collapse, we would not cross it. Hard as it is for some people to admit, we do not know everything. If we did, we would be no better off, since we would still be obliged to make a choice between conflicting data. Add into the equation the unpredictability of human behavior and you have an impossible computation.

This is why people who know less sometimes make better choices than those who know more. The ignorant impulsively arrive at a conclusion that has a 50 percent chance of being right while the more knowledgeable are still weighing up the odds.

We must also consider the wobbliness of our wills; they are not totally committed to doing the right thing on every occasion. Sometimes we choose not to make a choice; we let things happen or we leave the decision to others. Even when we know what is right and good, we do not always want to embrace it. On some occasions, we lack the necessary freedom; on others, we perversely turn our back on what we know to be right and head off in a different direction. As a result, the possible good choices which we are willing to make may be considerably less in number than those that are available in the abstract.

Taking all these into consideration we will soon come to the conclusion that we spend most of our lives off the track. If we are honest with ourselves, we will be prepared to admit this. In the course of a lifetime we have certainly made many erroneous choices, and we are never perfectly sure that even the most significant life-shaping decisions we have taken have been free from misinformation, delusion, or distorting motivations. Such is human life.

The good news is that no decision we humans take here on earth is irreversible. We do not possess ourselves in the same way as angels do. The medieval theologians tell us that each angelic act of will is final and definitive since it is clouded by no ignorance, and the will itself is not fragmented by spatio-temporal existence. This means that, unlike the angels, we have the liberty of changing our minds as we receive new data; on the basis of later information we can alter the direction of our progress. This is to say that human life is self-corrective. Like the ancient navigators we are continually changing course, based on our calculated position relative to the destination. It does not matter that the winds and tides have caused us to veer away from our intended path; we simply take a new sighting and set a new course. It is theoretically possible to arrive at the destination despite being off course for most of the voyage.

The key element in such a happy outcome is knowing exactly where we are. Many of us are not too keen on any form of self-knowledge that might reveal that we are lost. We all know drivers who refuse to pull over and look at a map or to ask assistance, preferring to bumble on until they see a known landmark and meanwhile becoming more confused than ever. There are those also who are reluctant to take stock of their lives. If I am not to be one of these, the first thing I have to do is to admit the possibility of my going astray; then I have to take steps to verify my position. If I am not where I had hoped to be, I have to confess that I am in error and then take steps to rectify the situation. All this is mere common sense.

There is a magic mantra that keeps us sane and lubricates all social relationships. The words are simple to understand but difficult to say: "I was wrong." Think how many word games, rationalizations, and lies are employed to avoid using this simple formula. We hate admitting that we have been wrong and we will do anything to avoid it. The results of such "honorable" obstinacy are bizarre to any onlookers. A silly quarrel over trifles can easily terminate a long-standing relationship if both parties are reluctant to accept any measure of blame for what has eventuated. There are very few completely innocent parties in conflicts, as anyone who has ever been involved in the work of mediation knows. No lasting resolution of differences is possible unless everyone involved is prepared to admit that, at least in hindsight, things could have been done better.

Friendships are prone to shipwreck wherever they are

infected with the assumption of being always right. Meanwhile, the denial of guilt wreaks havoc interiorly. The memory and imagination become occupied with selectively replaying events that support the plea of innocence, a log of grievances is drawn up and frequently reviewed, stories are edited and embroidered to avoid any hint of ambiguity, and mutual acquaintances are subjected to a barrage of propaganda. In most quarrels, truth is the first victim. But beware. Untruth always does its worst harm to its advocates. It demands that they close themselves off from any evidence that does not support their claims. They begin to live more and more in the past, distorting whatever happens in the present to convince themselves that nothing has changed. It takes a lot of energy to keep up pretenses; and, as a result, potentially life-enhancing possibilities are not pursued. The stubborn refusal to admit to being wrong is cumulatively soul destroying.

Healthy human living demands of us the capacity to regret, to apologize, and to admit to being and doing wrong. This needs to be more than a private gesture that leaves our public image intact. It needs to permeate all the modes of our self-presentation. I am not perfect. I have made many mistakes. I am a sinner. As for persons, so for the Church. Perhaps someone should inform some of our ecclesiastical spokespersons just how off-putting is a Church that proclaims itself infallible, especially when in the ears of outsiders the term seems to mean incapable of sin. How much more embraceable is an ecclesial body that willingly numbers itself among sinners and glories in its infirmities, secure enough to apologize for the betrayal of its trust not only in the distant past, but still today. "If we say we have no sin we deceive ourselves and the truth is not in us" (1 Jn 1:8).

Without the recognition and confession of guilt there is no integrity. To claim that we are whole and undamaged is to reveal that we still live in the thrall of delusion. The more we bluster about our righteousness, the more suspect it becomes. Conversely, genuine confession of sin is a liberating experience—we are freed from the tyranny of denial. Truth can be hard sometimes, but it is nourishing and invigorating. It enables us to read our situation accurately and to take appropriate steps to make things better.

There is a wonderful example of the power of humble confession in the biblical story of David and Bathsheba in 2 Samuel, chapters 11 through 12. When rebuked by the prophet Nathan for adultery and murder, David responds simply, "I have sinned against the LORD" (2 Sam 12:13). No evasions, no excuses, but an unvarnished avowal of guilt. How many of us are capable of such honesty? The most eloquent expression of repentance in the Book of Psalms is linked to this moment. To understand the nature of the act of confession and its role in our spiritual life, it is worth pondering Psalm 51, the *Miserere*.

Far from being a limited acceptance of blame, the *Miserere* manifests an awareness of the vast extent of sin reaching back to the moment of conception. This latest transgression is not viewed as an unexpected and isolated event; it is seen in the context of a lifetime's resistance to God. If it was not this particular sin precipitated by this particular situation it would have been some other sin, just as grave but different. "I know my malice and my sin is always before my eyes" (v. 5/3). There is here a sober sense of being alienated from God by contrary choices. There is no overdramatization; just the dull ache of recognizing that one has turned away from God. This is not just the breaking of a law or commandment: it is a personal affront to God: "Against you alone I have sinned: I have done what is evil in your eyes" (v. 6/4).

Such a global admission of guilt could well lead to gloom and despair were it not counterbalanced by another awareness—the recognition of the boundlessness of divine mercy. "Have mercy on me, O God, according to your steadfast love, and according to your great maternal pity blot out my malice" (v. 3/1). "Hide your face from my sin and blot out all my evil" (v. 11/9). It is this recognition of the active love of God that changes the whole thrust of the psalm. Instead of being simply a confession of sin it becomes a passionate plea not only for forgiveness but for restoration. The honest recognition of blameworthy conduct first brought about a sense of being crushed by guilt, the heart is broken and bruised (v. 17). There is a feeling of having been defiled from which arises the repeated cry to be washed and purified. But beyond mere neutralization of guilt the psalmist boldly asks for total transformation. "O God, create in me a pure heart and make new a steadfast spirit in my innards" (v. 12/10). "Restore to me the joy of your salvation and maintain a willing spirit" (v. 14/12). Thus saved from the effect of sinfulness by the action of God, the psalm becomes a hymn of praise. "Lord, you open my lips, and my mouth will announce your praise" (v. 17/15). The psalm concludes on a very upbeat note with a prayer for a more universal restoration and the promise of future fidelity.

This psalm has been over the centuries one of the mainstays of Christian devotion, and we could do worse than making ourselves familiar with it, even to the point of knowing it by heart. We will discover for ourselves, in using this psalm, a realistic way of growing in the consciousness that we are sinners in need of God's healing, and that this healing is permanently available to us. Instead of itemizing our sins and putting a value on each particular offense, we move towards the sense that all our misdeeds, large and small alike, are wrong primarily because they undermine our life-giving relationship with God. Sin makes us deader than we need to be.

It is in the context of our acceptance of the boundless reality of God's unconditional mercy that we find the strength to admit that we are prone to evil. It is always easier to stop denying a problem exists when we know that a solution is at hand. A person who finds a confessor or physician to be understanding and sympathetic will often append to their initial description of symptoms a new line of discussion that is closer to the heart of the matter. "By the way, there is another little problem that is bothering me." If we meet someone who seems approachable and competent, we are inclined to reveal more. In the same way, when we are permeated by the conviction that God's love for us never wavers despite our sins, we are more inclined to face up to their reality. Once the general admission is made, it becomes somewhat easier for us to admit having made mistakes in particular cases and to be ready to seek forgiveness for the harm and havoc for which we have been responsible.

There is something very healthy and liberating about sincere confession. But owning our waywardness in secrecy before God is not enough. "Confess your sins to one another and pray for one another; thus you will be healed" (Jas 5:16). There is a second commandment superimposed on the first. Confession to God needs to be supplemented by the act of expressing our guilt before another human being. It is not because we need to pass through the stages of an earthly bureaucracy in order to obtain the remission of our sins, but simply because it is only in the presence of another person that we can find the courage to face the unpleasant truths about ourselves that we prefer to leave concealed.

In the story of Adam and Eve in the Book of Genesis, the immediate effect of their rebellion against God was shame, expressed in the unwillingness to be seen as they were. A pattern of concealment was begun then that continues until today. Mostly we do not want our sins to be known—at least our real sins. We may boast of particular actions that are generally classified as "sins" if we are among like-minded friends, but we keep very quiet about those secret acts of which we are desperately ashamed: petty deeds of meanness, selfishness, lying, cheating, and hurting others, and especially we try to keep concealed those enslaving habits that lead us to act in a way contrary to what we believe ourselves to be. Concealment bedevils all we do. The most frequent cause of the breakdown of long-term relationships is the existence of a concealed non-reciprocity between the partners; a gulf that is not acknowledged cannot be bridged.[1] Many of us feel that we would have few friends if our associates knew the extent of the weakness, blindness, and malice that afflict us. And so we hide from any searching moral assessment of our behavior and hope that events will not expose our secret lives to public scrutiny.

Let it be stated without equivocation that confession is necessarily a source of embarrassment and shame. If we admitted only to those aspects of our behavior of which we are not ashamed, our confession would be very shallow indeed. If we really bring forth the sources of our genuine guilt, we cannot but be uncomfortable. We are all very dependent on the approval of others for our sense of well-being; inviting someone else to join us in gazing upon our sins is a risk—so usually we expose ourselves layer by layer, watching the other closely for any sign of rejection. It is only when we are mentally convinced that confession is good for the soul, that we are prepared to recognize the feeling of shame without allowing it to retard our self-exposure. First, we need to admit our failing to ourselves; then it must be brought to God in prayer; most difficult of all is to expose our wrongdoing to another human being. There is shame in all this, but there is also healing.

> Let it be said to one who experiences shame: "Why are you ashamed to speak of your sin, when you were not ashamed to commit it? Why do you blush to confess it to God, from whose eyes it cannot be hidden? If, perhaps, you are ashamed to reveal your sin to another human being who is also a sinner, what are you

going to do on Judgment Day when your conscience will be laid bare in the sight of all?"[2]

Confession is a moment of truth that calls us beyond a childish fear of punishment or desire for rewards. The one to whom we confess becomes a mirror in which we see ourselves without distortion; not a judge who punishes, nor a false mother who kisses away the hurt and sends us back into denial, but a stalwart friend who stands at our side and encourages us to look reality in the face. Spiritual directors and confessors have to be very restrained in their jubilation at someone's "success" in overcoming a bad habit or in being good, in case their approval becomes an incentive for the other to conceal the inevitable relapses and reverses that are part of genuine progress. Besides, as each layer is shed, another is uncovered; confessing one level of sin frees the mind to see more clearly its subtle roots. The deeper our self-knowledge penetrates, the more stinging our blushes. And there is a quiet dread that there is more to come. "Who can understand their error? From hidden faults release me" (Ps 19:13/12).

Shame notwithstanding, there is great comfort to be found in telling my story—not on television, not to everyone I meet, but just to a few or even one.[3] Perhaps we have had personal experience of how a deep heart-to-heart conversation can help in rebuilding a life that seemed to have fallen apart. As long as we feel that we are genuinely understood, we can endure much and are ready to spend a lot of energy in pursuing a goal. This is as true in the spiritual life as it is in other areas. In fact, one of the greatest benefits that the Church can offer is to provide us with someone who can accompany us through the dark and puzzling passages of life, helping us to discern the work of God amid so many contrary indications and encouraging us when difficulties seem insurmountable.

When another person's acceptance and love of us survives

the discovery of our inner ambiguity which is reflected in the inconsistency of our outward lives, we take a giant step on the road to the recovery of integrity. We remain wounded and fragile, but no longer alone. In the presence of that significant other, we see mirrored not only our weaknesses but also our strengths. Thus fortified we are more likely to go forward, spending our energy on positive progress instead of wasting it in denial and concealment.

Therapists, counselors, confessors, spiritual directors, and good friends fill this supportive role in different ways. In such a relationship the crucial factor is our willingness to trust another person with the intimate secrets of our inner life. This means ignoring our embarrassment, transcending our timidity, and going beyond the boundaries of our comfort zone into an area of heightened truthfulness. In a certain sense, this discomfort is essential; it is a sign that we really are venturing into virgin territory and not merely trotting out the same tired monologue to a new set of ears. Of course there is risk involved; our confidence may be betrayed. Most often, however, this will not be the case, especially if our choice of confidant was made with care.

For Catholics of the previous generation, the sacrament of reconciliation was the great means of manifesting their consciences and receiving spiritual direction. When pressure of time reduced the ritual to a formalized itemizing of sins and the rapid giving of a standard penance followed by absolution, many began to find receiving the sacrament meaningless. To exploit its dynamic potential, confession has to be more than offering a laundry list of the "sins" we have committed. It is exposing our whole life to the compassionate gaze of another person in the hope of receiving not only sacramental grace but also some measure of feedback that will guide and support us on our journey. Reducing the complexity of a human life to a few standardized formulae risks trivializing both sin and the person who confesses. It takes time to penetrate and describe the chaos of an individual life, and the task of listening, hearing what is said and responding appropriately, is also demanding. I doubt that the sacrament of reconciliation will ever flourish as long as it is seen as no more than a five-minute fix to sins committed. A much greater investment will be needed if it is to be the visible sign of the compassion of Christ.

Saint Bernard sees three essential qualities of genuine confession: it must be genuine, naked, and personal.[4] Confession without repentance is either narcissistic or boastful; we acknowledge what we have done without anything more than a vague sense of regret. When confession becomes merely a routine recitation of formulae, its potential benefits are correspondingly reduced. A confession driven by fear, legalism, or scrupulosity rarely generates a very energetic desire for the amendment of life. The sacrament is most fruitful when it sacralizes an already present, deeply felt repentance. There are many channels by which grace may generate such compunction: the liturgy, the Scriptures, the Church, or the voice of conscience. Genuine confession is confession accompanied by sincere sorrow.

> Confession should be naked, stripped of every concealing veil. What profit is there in speaking of some sins and concealing others, to be partly washed clean and partly to be at the service of filth? Can one and the same vessel hold both sweetness and bitterness or be a source of both palatable and tasteless? All is naked and open to God's eyes (Heb 4:13), and would you hide something from the one who holds God's place in this sacrament? Show yourself and lay bare whatever is lacerating your heart. Uncover the wound so that you may receive the physician's attention.[5]

The third quality that Bernard prescribes is that our confession may focus on our personal sinfulness and not on the manufacture of excuses by casting the blame on others. Gently exploring the circumstances of our sinfulness is important in coming to fuller self-awareness, but sometimes we can allow ourselves to be carried away by rationalization. The more we think in that way about what happened, the more we begin to see ourselves as nearly innocent victims. We blame others and so the moment of grace slips away from us.

In our confession, honesty and gentleness need to go hand in hand. We will never be totally truthful if we are afraid of violent recrimination from within or without. Honesty requires of us a certain strictness both in reviewing our past and in charting a different course for the future. "In this strictness, discretion must be observed always, lest through the desire to punish too much we destroy what is healthy, and while seeking to subdue an enemy we kill a citizen."[6] Patience is necessary because if we are too zealous in scraping off the rust the only result will be that we will end up putting a hole in the bucket.

Forgiveness of sin is one of the tenets of our faith which we rattle off whenever we say the *Nicene Creed*. So many of our prayers include a petition for forgiveness that it becomes a familiar notion, but I wonder whether we ever stop to consider what a remarkable belief this is. Sin is that which is most intimately mine. Of my talents and gifts and good deeds it can be said rightly that I have nothing that I have not received. Genes, nurturing, friendship, education, and good luck have made a massive contribution to my life. The only thing that I can claim to be solely mine is my personal tally of sins. For God to be able to liberate me from this inextricable guilt is an astonishing fact. It is, in reality, a deed of infinite gratuity and kindness that derives from the nature of God as extroverting goodness, rather than from anything I can do for myself. No wonder Jesus' words of forgiveness addressed to the paralytic caused such an affray (Mk 2:8–9). The New Testament teaches us that we are not wired into endless reincarnations until we have leached out of ourselves every tiny skerrick of malice. Instead, "the kindness and philanthropy of God our Savior have become manifest" (Titus 3:4), offering us the possibility of being reborn by the action of the Holy Spirit and not by our being good. Mercy, redemption, grace, justification—these are the words Saint Paul heaps up in an attempt to give some idea of the wonder of what God does in intervening to separate us from our sins.

In Latin and Greek, there is a happy ambiguity surrounding the word "confession." It can mean, obviously, the admission of sin. However, it has another meaning: the "confession of praise." The same word is also used of the act of professing the faith or the faithful giving of testimony, as in martyrdom. Its meaning of praise occurs often in the Psalms, many of which begin with the confession of sin and end on a note of praise and jubilation. We see it also in Saint Augustine's *Confessions* and Saint Patrick's *Confession*: in both cases, the narrative is not merely the recital of sins, but a praise-filled account of God's wonderful deeds of mercy. "We will confess our sins, we will confess your acts of goodness, for in both is God given glory."[7] In a sense, Christian joy is built on the foundation of confession. It is only to the extent that we recognize clearly the evil we have done that we can begin to move towards an appreciation of just how unconditional is God's love for us. Undeserving of human love as we have become through our blameworthy acts, we yet remain loved by God. Francis Thompson expresses this truth eloquently in *The Hound of Heaven*.

"And human love needs human meriting:
How hast thou merited—
Of all man's clotted clay the dingiest clot?
Alack, thou knowest not
How little worthy of any love thou art!
Whom wilt thou find to love ignoble thee,
Save Me, save only Me?"

Confession of sin leads to truthfulness in prayer which, in time, is transformed into an experience of God's abundant and resourceful mercy.

CHAPTER TWENTY-ONE

Gethsemane

And they come to a piece of land called Gethsemane and [Jesus] says to his disciples, "Sit here while I pray." And he takes Peter, James, and John with him and he begins to go into shock and be overcome. And he says to them, "I feel so utterly sad that I could die. Stay here and keep watch." And going on a little further he collapsed onto the ground and he prayed that if it were possible, the Hour might pass him by. He was saying, "אבבא, Father, all things are possible for you; take away this cup from me; yet not as I will, but as you will." And he comes and finds [the disciples] sleeping. And he says to Peter, "Simon, are you sleeping? Do you not have the strength to keep watch for a single hour? Keep watch and pray so that you may not enter into temptation. The spirit is eager, but the flesh is weak." And going away he prayed, using the same expression. And coming a second time he found them sleeping, for their eyes were very heavy. They did not know how to answer him. And he comes a third time and says to them, "You can sleep from now on and take your rest; it is all over. The Hour has come, and behold, the Son of Man is betrayed into the hands of the sinners. Rise. Let us go forth. Behold the one who is betraying me approaches."

MARK 14:32–42

From the memorial meal, Jesus moves on with an ever-diminishing band of disciples into the night. His intention is clearly to give himself to prayer, and he surrounds himself with two rings of disciples who are to keep watch; while he prays they are also to pray. As Jesus separates himself from his followers, panic overtakes him. The Greek words here translated as "he begins to go into shock and be overcome" are extremely strong.[1] The first word occurs only here in the New Testament. In its passive form it points to a combination of shock, anguish, and dread that stuns and immobilizes. Jesus is described as being like a person who has experienced a traumatic accident or disaster, stumbling around in a daze. The second verb reinforces this impression; Jesus is totally exhausted by what has come upon him. The description of his state quoted by the evangelist has a vaguely biblical sound, perhaps it is modeled on the Greek version of Jonah 4:9. "I feel (or "My soul is") so utterly sad that I could die." These words of Jesus, spoken not in prayer but to the disciples, give some sense of the depth of anguish that Jesus was experiencing, faced with approaching torture and death. In an astonishingly graphic moment, Jesus stumbles off and falls to the ground. The disciples do nothing to assist or comfort him. They seem almost autistically unaware of the desperation that Jesus is feeling. Their detachment could only have heightened his pain.

John of Forde insists that the mental anguish experienced by Jesus throughout his passion was as great as bodily pain and external reproach.

> I see confusion in the inner experience of humiliation which covers his face—"though it is brighter than all light"—with a red cloud of fierce shame. Even though he sets his face to be as hardest flint [Isaiah 50:8/7], it is contrary to faith, religion, and a sense of charity to think that the sword did not reach to his very soul. If

this were not true, how could he have prayed to the Father in deep trouble, "Save me, O God, for the waters have entered even to my soul" (Ps 69:2)? Finally, if a sword pierced the soul of his mother who suffered with him, with how much greater force would it have struck the soul of the suffering Son? This is truly a two-edged sword and able to cut right through; a sword of sharpest pain and boundless confusion. "Surely he has borne our weaknesses and carried our pains" [Isaiah 53:4].[2]

In this extreme Jesus turns to prayer. What we have in Mark's narrative is clearly richer than an objective historical record; there were no witnesses, since Jesus withdrew from the disciples who were, in any case, asleep. This is an exemplary account written for our instruction. Jesus is in grave distress. His options are limited. Faced with insuperable opposition he could flee, as his disciples will (Mk 14:50). He could offer armed resistance as one of them would (Mk 14:47). Or he could stand his ground, trusting in his Father's intervention to deliver him—expressed explicitly in Matthew 26:53. As we know from our own experience, the hardest thing of all when events go against us is to do nothing. Even the most futile and foolhardy schemes seem preferable to staying still and yielding the initiative to others. This is the dilemma Jesus faced and before which he shuddered. We know that, in the end, he boldly went forward entrusting everything to God's hands. But it was not without a struggle. Interestingly, Luke links this narrative with the temptation in the desert, concluding that account with the chilling words, "And the devil departed from him until the Hour" (Lk 4:13).

Jesus prays to escape his destiny. The Fourth Gospel makes explicit the ambiguity such a prayer involves. "Now I feel troubled. What do I say, 'Father save me from this Hour'?

No, for it is for this that I have come to this Hour." Then he adds a clause resonant of the Lord's Prayer: "Father, glorify your name" (Jn 12:27–28). Jesus' teaching on prayer in the Gospel of Mark is based on the premise that "for God all things are possible" (Mk 10:27), and so when we pray we ought boldly to ask for the impossible.

> If you have faith in God, Amen, I say to you, that if someone were to say to this mountain "Be lifted and thrown into the sea" and he did not try to work things out in his head but believed that what he has said would happen, so it would be for him. For this reason I say to you that you have received all that you pray for and ask, and so it will be for you.
>
> MARK 11:22–24

The phrase that I have translated a little loosely as "he did not try to work things out in his head" is usually rendered in terms of hesitation or doubt. The point, however, is that the interference to the passage of prayer is due to mental activity—the heart in Semitic thought being the source of intellect rather than the organ of affection. The verb διακρίνω means to discern (the associated noun διάκρισις became a technical term for "discernment" in later monasticism). This involves sifting through the data from all angles, separating possibilities and making distinctions. It is used also in James 1:6, "Let him ask in faith not discerning." For James such a process of weighing up the pros and cons is a sign of persons who have two souls or, as we would say "are in two minds." Faith is the bold opposite of a judicious selection. It operates by principles that cannot be reduced to logic. It has a special affinity for what human reasoning regards as impossible. The more unlikely the outcome, the more prayer is driven by faith. To pray for the almost-inevitable needs no faith at all.

Jesus prays to the Father as he taught others: forthrightly and in few words. The boldness of faith does not allow us to dissimulate our real needs or to hide our desires under a cloak of respectability. We are not to work things out in our head, as we would if we were approaching an earthly superior with a request. In that situation, we prepare a line of sound reasoning and dress it up with pleasing phrases. With God who knows the heart, our only approach must be direct and unabashed. We are to pray for what we desire, without first working things out in our head. Jesus prays from the trepidation in which he is plunged, asking in all simplicity to be delivered from the fate that looms ahead of him.

Mark gives us a formula which expresses the prayer of Jesus. The words are simple enough to understand, but perhaps it will be only when we find ourselves using them in some dire situation that we will really comprehend their trust and vigor.

> Abba, Father,
> all things are possible to you.
> Take away this cup from me.
> Yet
> not as I will
> but as you will.

Jesus is doing more than expressing the seriousness of his own plight. The prayer begins with an ecstatic moment, a standing away from self and an opening to God. It is bringing a new element into the equation, offering the possibility of reframing. Such a heartfelt invocation of God is like switching on the light in a darkened and fear-filled room. Things begin to look different. By these words, Jesus reaffirms the relationship of intimacy that exists between him and God, as it were, deliberately turning his attention away from the prospect of extinction and fixing his gaze on the One on whom his selfhood depends. "Abba," the Aramaic word embedded in the Gospel tradition, reflects Jesus' sense of being at home in the spiritual world and his family relationship with God. It is a word not lightly used. It is reserved to those who belong to the intimate circle of the family; in the mouth of outsiders it is an affront. Its use at this moment adds a tender bathos to the story. Like countless other victims of violence throughout the century, Jesus struggles to reconcile intolerable human misery with the affirmation of a compassionate God. There is no doubt that it is a cry from the heart, full of love, and yet full of the hurt that comes with incomprehension.

If all things are possible for God, no prayer is inappropriate. That Jesus prays to be saved from the cup of suffering he sees ahead of him is not an expression of wavering or moral weakness, but a clear consequence of his own teaching about the nature of prayer. There is no hiding from reality in the presence of God; it has to be confronted. At the beginning, the presence of God and the sense of desolation do not mix. There is no bridge between them. Prayer brings together the opposites—even though, like water and oil, they cannot combine. This is, however, but the beginning of prayer, not its end.

The most important word in Jesus' prayer is the "yet," which introduces an antithesis. The cry for deliverance, at first all-absorbing, becomes conditional. Juxtaposed, love and dread jostle for supremacy. If God is Abba, a loving Father, then reactivating the awareness of this relationship has the effect of regenerating in Jesus his consciousness of being a loving Son, expressed concretely in obedience. Thus, the revulsion of Jesus at the prospect of his impending death never develops into revolution; instead, it is softened into submission. In the early part of their Gospels, Matthew and Luke presented the temptation in the desert as a contrast between Israel the faithless son and Jesus the true Son of God.[3] In the desert struggle, Jesus demonstrates his Sonship by his obedience, even though this involves the acceptance of suffering. The same dynamic is at play in Gethsemane. We find a reflection on this in the Epistle to the Hebrews (5:7–8): "In the days of his flesh [Jesus] offered prayers and supplications with great cries and tears to the one that had the power to save him from death. He was heard for his reverence. Although he was a son, he learned obedience from the things he suffered." In this text which expresses a later theology, the author writes in the full awareness of the resurrection. Thus he recognizes that it was Jesus' "reverence" (translated in the NRSV as "reverent submission") that most fully expressed his Sonship; it was by this that he found favor with the Father. Jesus' victory over temptation was a matter of arriving at a disposition that could be characterized by such phrases as religious meekness, devout submissiveness, deference to his Father's will. It was this attitude of voluntary obedience that was the logical continuation of the self-emptying which had powered the act of incarnation that opened the doorway to resurrection.

As we all know by experience, coming to such a point of submission is not easy—even in relatively small matters. We tend to cling to our own will, not necessarily out of obstinacy, but mostly because it corresponds to the way that we read the situation and the knowledge we have of possible solutions. We depart from our chosen course reluctantly because it seems right to us and the alternatives are less appealing. To change our will—except in response to brute force—we need to be convinced. In some cases, this means that we need to be supplied with new data. More often, it involves our seeing existing data in a different light, perhaps allowing ourselves to become more sharply aware of known elements that had been hitherto sidelined. In order to reframe, we need to withdraw somewhat from the clangor of compelling emotions with a view to ensuring that a proposed course of action is not forgetting something very important.

In the case of Jesus, it is through returning to an aware intimacy with the Father that the situation is clarified. Note that such clarity is at the level of will, not intellect. Jesus still has to deal with the dark and incomprehensible reality of death. Of itself death has no meaning and is not directly willed. What his will embraces in an unconditional way is whatever the Father intends. This is much more than mere resignation before the inevitable. It is a consciousness so suffused by trust that there is a gradual process of conformation of Jesus' will with that of his Father.

Initially, Jesus is unnerved by the agony ahead, yet slowly, from within, his vigor returns. The dramatic construction of Mark's narrative ensures that we do not think that the prayer once uttered achieved immediate results. Two parables, "The Friend Who Came at Night" (Lk 11:5–13) and "The Woman and the Unjust Judge" (Lk 18:1–8), remind us that persistence is a necessary part of prayer. So it was with Jesus even at his hour of direst necessity. The prayer in the garden lasts a long time—so long that the disciples were unable to stay the distance and fell asleep.

Mark has no scruples about revealing how frequently Jesus reproached his disciples for their lack of faith and understanding. In the present incident, when Jesus returns from prayer to find his disciples asleep, his response to their failure is very mild, and his words to Simon are softened by being in the plural. The reason he uses to explain away their lack of vigilance must surely have come from his own predicament. "The spirit is eager but the flesh is weak." What Jesus too was experiencing was the weakness of the flesh that he had assumed. Not so much its boisterous opposition to the spirit about which Saint Paul speaks (see, for example, Galatians 5:17), but rather a natural heaviness that resists the initiatives of the spirit. It is because he feels so helpless at the level of the flesh that Jesus returns to his prayer. Surprisingly enough, the consciousness of such sluggishness, tinged as it often is with dread and self-reproach, is often the starting point for prayer. When we become aware of our compromised status, we groan to have it resolved. Thus prayer is born. "Because we are human we are weak. Because we are weak we pray."[4]

The prayer of Jesus has its origins in the ambiguity of human nature. Its outcome can be a great encouragement for us as we try to achieve some level of interior consistency in our own lives. Through prayer the situation changed. Beforehand Jesus was unmanned, in a state of deep anguish and confusion. Now, after prayer has done its work, he appears almost a new man. He stands upright and takes charge of the situation. His familiar sense of irony returns and he calls his disciples to follow him and to confront those who were seeking him. Having risen from his own incapacitating dread, Jesus calls his disciples to a resurrection from their sleep of impotence and hopelessness. "Rise," he says, using the word that will describe his own subsequent victory over death, "let us go forth" (Mk 14:42). The crisis has passed, even though the torment has yet to begin. Jesus' solemn use of the title "Son of Man" perhaps harks back to the three predictions of the passion, and may indicate that he is beginning to see his immediate future in terms of a more global mission.

It is worthwhile pondering the sea change that took place during Jesus' prayer in the garden. In this narrative, prayer serves a purpose similar to a bout of weeping. The grief, once acknowledged and expressed, has lost its power to paralyze. The affliction is contextualized within a wider framework and becomes less powerful. When the dominant priorities within a personality are allowed to reassert themselves, it becomes possible to resume living. This is not a denial of grief but a refusal to be overcome by it. It is, however, no easy victory. The instinct to deny what we hope to avoid is strong. To face up to the prospect of imminent death and not be overwhelmed by it requires great strength of character. The work of prayer is to place beside this fearful reality what has been learned in the school of lifelong experience—the Father's undeviating and effective love. Holding both realities simultaneously in one's mind takes a bit of mental juggling. Now one, now the other, seems to dominate. Prayer becomes a dialogue between two known facts: God's love and impending death. It is only by repeated assertions of love and being loved that fear is beaten down. As Saint Paul says, "If God is for us, who can be against us?" (Rom 8:31).

Jesus goes to his death not as a hapless victim of malign circumstances but as one who has arrived at the point where he is able to give free assent to the fate that has befallen him as being, in some mysterious way, the expression of his Father's will. His assent is an act of pure will; he does not understand why this has to happen to him. He is not immune from physical pain, the degradation of sensibility that goes with it, nor the mental confusion and outrage it generates. His suffering is real, profound, and intense. The only bulwark against utter hopelessness is his certainty of the faithfulness of his Father's love.

CHAPTER TWENTY-TWO

Crisis

*Every man goes through this period of crisis. For the
average man it is the point in his life when the demands
of his own fate are most at odds with his environment,
when the way ahead is most hardly won. For many it is
the only time when they experience the dying and resurrection which is our lot, during the decay and slow
collapse of childhood when we are abandoned by everything we love, and suddenly feel the loneliness and
deathly cold of the world around us. And a great many
people stay forever hanging on to this cliff and cling
desperately their whole life through to the irrevocable
past, the dream of the lost paradise which is the worst
and most ruthless of all dreams.*

HERMANN HESSE, *DEMIAN*, TRANSLATED BY W. J. STRACHAN,
LONDON: PANTHER BOOKS, 1969; PP. 46–47

The original Greek meaning of *krisis,* or crisis, is the act of
judgment, often with the negative sense of condemnation. What
is repudiated is a *krima,* or crime. We find it thus used in the
Fourth Gospel. The modern use of crisis evolved in the middle
of the sixteenth century as a medical term. It is defined thus
by the *Oxford Dictionary:* "The point in the progress of a
disease when an important development or change takes place
which is decisive of recovery or death." In this sense, an example from 1625 is quoted: "Then shall the sicke by the vertu

261

and power of a happy crisis saile forthe into the haven of health."[1] From its initial use in medicine, the term came to mean any dangerous situation whose likely outcome was uncertain. Apart from its sensationalist connotations in second-rate journalism, the key insight in a contemporary understanding of crisis is that matters have reached a turning point and the future will be qualitatively and irreversibly different. Whether this consequence is welcomed or rejected will depend on the perspective from which it is viewed.

Linked with this understanding of crisis is another concept that appeared at roughly the same period of history, the notion of development.[2] At the earliest stage (1592), it referred simply to the unrolling of a scroll; by the middle of the next century it had assumed the more abstract meaning of revealing what was hidden and, thence, bringing forth potential. In the nineteenth century, apart from its use in photography, "development" came to be associated with such concepts as growth, progression, and evolution. In 1845, more than a decade before Charles Darwin's *Origin of Species*, Cardinal Newman wrote what he termed "a sort of obscure philosophical work...with little to interest and much to disappoint," which he entitled *An Essay on the Development of Christian Doctrine*.[3]

Development implies more than perpetual expansion. Qualitative change occurs. When we consider human development we are aware that the person remains the same throughout all the stages, yet the quality of experience is different in a child from what is found in the adult. Some changes, such as puberty, are physiological and easily visible. Other developments come about because of unforeseen circumstances and may involve either a major or a minor paradigm shift. The experience that Christian theologians have termed "conversion" is a dramatic turning point in a person's life. The elements of that life remain roughly the same, but they are integrated differently because they are viewed against a different perceptual horizon.[4] One's conscious goal of life has changed and, as a consequence, there is a certain discontinuity with the past at the level of the beliefs and values by which one lives.

Crisis is the doorway to qualitative change. If, over the decades, we have built up a firm self-concept, then this will be subject to deconstruction and we will need to begin rediscovering who we are and what we are doing with our life. In so far as we have received an identity from relationships, relationships are modified. If we have been defined by our work, then we will either change our job or seek to do it in an entirely new way. Every genuine crisis is potentially empowering, because it has the capacity to lead us to a greater level of authenticity and freedom. A person who has never had a crisis is one who remains forever inhibited, repressed, entrenched in delusion, and constricted by limitations so habitual that they have become invisible. In this state of half-life, routine, convention, the expectations of others, and the sanction of those in authority assume an unnatural importance. Alongside zones of professional competence can subsist regressive attitudes so severe as to amount to infantilism.

The agony of crisis is not accidental and cannot be bypassed. Nobody wants their fundamental assumptions questioned and their integrity to be challenged. The hidden rancors underlying an apparently placid relationship can suddenly erupt so that the future of the relationship is threatened. Instinctively, we sense that such outbursts represent a make-or-break situation. They can no longer be denied or plastered over; they have to be faced and decisions have to be taken which will change the course of the future. A man or woman goaded relentlessly by professional ambition may wake up one day with the realization that the possibility of a happier life may demand a courageous leap into the unknown.

In such cases of crisis, there is the sense that the beliefs, values, and activities of the past are no longer yielding proportional fruit. Yesterday they were right; today they seem to have lost their relevance and are no longer creative. Something is lacking in the equation of my life. This feeling of itself does not constitute a crisis. Such negativity is more like an overpowering sense of meaninglessness or depression. The crisis begins when it dawns on me that there is an alternative. I have to make a practical judgment about whether I continue my half-life where I am or whether I take the risk of beginning anew. It is not always a question of pulling up stakes and moving on, abandoning all previous commitments—but it is probably necessary at least to entertain that possibility. There is no room for pretense in the resolution of crisis.

You may have seen in scientific publications models of complex molecules, composed of little differently colored balls connected by rods to form a three-dimensional structure. If we think of ourselves in such terms, we can perhaps see our lives as constituted by a network of interacting realities: family, education, work, recreation, relationships, hobbies, projects, dreams, ideals. Some are larger than others, but all of them contribute something to our sense of being who we are. When life is running smoothly, it is because there is no conflict among its principal elements. Work does not clash with family, fidelity is not threatened by friendship, and our recreational pastimes do no damage to our overall sense of responsibility. In a major crisis, this harmony is lost and things get out of kilter in a way that resists piecemeal intervention. One thing leads to another and before long we are faced with a serious breakdown, either at the level of personal identity or in our sense of social belonging. In such a situation, it is as though the rods connecting all the colored balls disappear. The elements of our life remain, but they no longer work together as a harmonious whole. Each has to be redefined without reference to its previous linkages before it becomes available to be incorporated in a new integration.

Often there is a precipitating factor that comes unexpectedly from outside, the straw that breaks the camel's back, as it were. The disproportion between the triggering event and our reaction to it signals that it is no more than a catalyst. Discontent was already fermenting within, needing only an excuse to manifest itself. A souffle that did not rise; a quarrel about trivialities; a shoplifting episode; an unforeseen infatuation; the humiliation of dismissal, failure, or a significant moral lapse. Sometimes several things happen one after the other and the effect is cumulative. On its own, the overt cause of our distress could be dealt with, as perhaps we have done previously. But in this case, our inner state is such that we are quickly propelled over the edge and our whole life falls into disarray. There seem to be no certainties because all the elements of our life are free-floating, and the old life-giving and empowering linkages are no longer operational.

A crisis is an earth-shattering event because it involves a radical rewriting of the script of one's life. Most people seem to experience no more than one or two major crises in a lifetime. Those who seem to have two or three crises every day before breakfast are probably in a codependency situation with a resident crisis manager. Part of the bathos of crisis is that it involves the disassembling of an entity that has taken many years and much effort to create. It is the sense of years wasted and labor lost that erodes self-confidence and produces a high degree of mental confusion. There is dread also at the prospect of slow rebuilding without the old certainty that the product of one's toil will last forever.

Saint John of the Cross distinguished two "obscure nights" that are experienced by those who make progress in prayer. If our primary commitment in life is to prayer, then this will probably be the sphere in which crisis will occur. It can equally occur in the area of personal commitment, vocation, art, work, relationships, or any other zone of our inner environment which means much to us. When it occurs, a crisis seems like the worst thing in the world, but this is because our perceptions are awry. In retrospect, we may be able to recognize the inherent blessing of these troubled times and, perhaps, even come to the conclusion that without the crisis we would have eventually ended up disastrously.

Let us reflect for a while on our experience of crisis, seeing them as more than times in which we struggled to stay afloat, recognizing them as seasons of grace. Strengthened by our pondering of Jesus' experience in the garden of Gethsemane, perhaps we can see how crisis has served to purge us of unrecognized inconsistencies and reoriented us to live a more intense and more focused life.

(a) Crisis isolates: Although sometimes we speak about groups undergoing crisis, it is more usual for crisis to be an intensely individual event, partly because it is compounded of particular elements of personal history and partly because it often bears directly on an individual's relationship with a significant person or group. Just as Jesus separated himself first from the twelve and then from the three disciples so that he was completely alone so, in times of crisis, we may find friends and neighbors withdrawing. "You have taken away loved ones and neighbors; now darkness is my friend" (Ps 88:18). Sometimes the distance is physical, but it may also be emotional. Perhaps there is an overt breach of a longstanding relationship over some trivial difference. It may be that others withdraw to give us space, or maybe they cannot cope with our prickly sensitivity. There are often legions of Job's comforters, ready to tell us what is wrong with us and to prescribe remedies. Others, acting out of an uncomprehending kindness, try to superimpose their own history on ours. And there will

always be some who try to jolly us out of our downcast mood, as though it were something that we can and should readily snap out of. As crisis deepens, we find ourselves alone. This overpowering sense of not being understood by those around us is really a sign of our own interior confusion both of intellect and will. Previously, it would not have mattered much. We are no longer certain who we are or what we want, and we cannot accept that others may perceive what is invisible to us. That is why we insist that nobody else knows what we are going through and often brush aside well-meaning attempts to help us. Such painful misunderstanding is an essential prelude to a new self-definition, but at the time we do not realize this.

(b) Crisis impoverishes: More often than not crisis is not solved by the vigorous deployment of all one's spiritual forces in order to achieve a victory. One of the cruelest aspects of crisis is that it often occurs precisely at a time in which our energies are low and we are left resourceless. Perhaps we have been weakened by dealing with a series of taxing events so that our capacity to cope with the unexpected has been depleted. Perhaps the unimaginable has occurred. A large measure of passivity or helplessness shatters our delusion that we have the capacity to manage our lives. This sense of being overwhelmed by a *force majeure* is coupled with a foreboding that we need to act decisively. It would be much easier to be a victim, the plaything of hostile forces. We are not allowed this luxury. If we could run away and hide, no doubt the storm could pass. The problem is that at the very time when we feel least inclined to act, we are called to make one of the momentous decisions of our life: a choice that will shape our future and perhaps impact on many people. This is where we discover our poverty of spirit: when it comes to taking the most crucial option of our life, we find ourselves at the behest of subpersonal

fears, forces, and resistances. We are crippled by our cumulative past and weighed down by present heaviness.

(c) Crisis deepens: One thing leads to another. Usually we can cope with most issues as long as they arrive singly. Crisis is horrible because so many things are falling apart simultaneously. Not unusually the initial triggering event may sail off into insignificance, but it leaves a colossal disturbance in its wake. The issues that have thus been uncovered are deep-set and substantial; they ask existential questions of us that cannot be answered quickly. We have to learn patience, allowing matters to get worse and worse until we touch bottom. For most of us, this waiting is not an easy task. There is going to be no easy turnaround.

(d) Crisis distresses: Even apart from new and old issues that have to be dealt with, the fact of being in a crisis upsets us. Because crisis leads to the questioning of the basic tenets of personal identity, it is profoundly upsetting. We may find it hard to sleep, we may lose our appetite, and our zest for life is markedly reduced. In some people, severe anxiety can disable their faculties and interrupt their normal functioning, so that they seem unlike themselves. If we move too deeply into this country, we may need professional help to extricate us. In that case, as always, it is important to "watch the tides and not the eddies." Sometimes it is easy to exaggerate the distressing data thrown up by a crisis. Too much attention given to collateral issues can have the effect of distracting from what is at the core of all that is happening: the need to reach a life-defining decision.

(e) Crisis leads to prayer: The gift of faith is not inactive during these difficult days. Without very much connection with what is going on around us, it begins subtly to invite us to sidestep our troubles and to begin to look in a new direction.

Even though our normal avenues of prayer seem closed to us, a new way of access to God begins to open out before us.[5] This new mode of prayer carries us through our troubles to the eye of the storm, where all is quiet. We begin to find peace in the very act of owning our interior malaise, in opening up our woundedness before the Lord and, in a wondrous way, feeling ourselves welcomed and loved. Nothing is changed externally and the storms still rage within, but there is a new awareness of empowerment that enables us to walk with confidence, even though the path before us is hard and rough.

(f) Crisis ends: Crisis is a transition from one mode of being to another; it makes no sense if it takes over our whole life. Its very intensity ensures that we are propelled towards a major decision. And that is the way a crisis terminates. The previous phases of the crisis have dismantled much of our assurance and have put us into contact with our own fragility so that there has been a shift in our center of gravity. No longer do we see self as the most important reality. We are more radically open to God so that we are prepared effectively to subordinate our lives to the divine will. It sounds like surrender, but in reality it is a moment of freedom previously unparalleled in our experience. Coming from the depths of our spirit, such self-abandonment is an act of love that fills us with peace and joy. It brings about a sea change in our life and sets up a decade or two of spiritual growth that leads to a happier, more fruitful, and more fulfilled life at every level.

As we ponder the stages in which genuine crisis evolves, we are struck by the reality of the issues which it raises. This is no storm in a teacup, even though it may appear so at first. Spiritual crisis is about the fundamental orientation of our life; it is an invitation to review our previous priorities and, probably, to step back a little from the unrelenting pursuit of self-enhancement. In other words, it is an invitation to allow God more freedom to act within us, without the obstruction due either to our slavish devotion to rules and expectations or to our unwillingness to submit to anything outside ourselves. Crisis itself creates in us the dispositions necessary to survive: the upheaval breaks up our complacency, gives us the solitude necessary to reach a creative decision, inculcates in us poverty of spirit and patience, and leads us to sustained and intense prayer.

The kind of prayer that begins to impose itself is different from that to which we have become accustomed. It is much emptier. In it, we are passive, and prayer is active, gradually creating new linkages that connect us with God. Meanwhile we need the grace of patience.

In fact, a movement towards deeper prayer is the ultimate meaning of crisis. For many spiritual persons changes in prayer are the first indications that something unusual is happening.[6] A crisis that generates prayer ends happily. In the backing and forthing of our dialogue with God, we gradually create a new self-definition. So much that was hitherto denied is now accepted that we perceive that our task is to integrate this new self-understanding into our general picture of ourselves and how we interact with the world. The end of crisis is not the end of growth, but the beginning of a new stage of growth. There is still much work to be done, but it is somewhat easier because we have a fuller notion of who we are.

Needless to say, not every crisis ends happily. The danger of shipwreck is ever present and never beyond possibility. There are two principal ways of subverting the creative dynamic inherent is crisis. First, we can adopt a siege attitude, continuing exactly as we have been, refusing to look more closely at issues raised or to countenance any change in self-definition. While we may sincerely believe that this stubborn resistance to new data is a form of fidelity, all that results from our effort is lost opportunity. We keep on doing the things that used to work, but the heart has gone out of them. They have lost their magic. Meanwhile, progress ceases, even though we seem to keep going forward. What happens is that we are on a loop, skirting around the challenges posed to us, until we meet them again ten years or so down the track. The pity of it all is that what seemed so threatening was really an invitation to grow. Whether we recognize it or not, our avoidance of issues has dried up our vital juices. We stagnate. No wonder there is a creeping sense of frustration and misery. It will take even more courage next time round when, by God's mercy, another crisis will attempt to catapult us back onto the road that leads to life.

Avoiding decision is one way of flunking a crisis; premature and precipitate decision is the other. Especially in the early stages of crisis, matters seem so hopeless that cutting one's losses becomes an attractive proposition. The least creative course is to withdraw from the situation in which awareness of unease is most acute. The best advice is: "Change nothing! Let the issues keep coming to the surface. Do not frighten them away, have a good look at them, and see if something can be done to integrate them. Running away does not solve anything. You simply take your difficulties to a different location where the novelty of the new situation keeps them submerged—but only temporarily."

All that is left is to allow crisis to run its course, and when the day dawns on which we feel able to begin rebuilding our life we will be ready to take the first small step. Meanwhile we cultivate serenity of heart, which means effectively reducing our trust in our own efforts and increasing our confidence in the goodness of God. For some of us, it also involves learning or relearning to trust other people, especially those nearest to us. We cannot go far wrong in extending the ambit of our trust. As the attitude develops and deepens, we ourselves are slowly transformed, though we may notice nothing.

In the Fourth Gospel, the coming of Christ into the world precipitated crisis. People could no longer sit on the fence in a state of benign noncommitment. For John, the spiritual sphere and that of human activity ruled by "the world, the flesh, and the devil" are diametric opposites. They cannot coexist and so a choice has to be made. Before Christ's coming, this incompatibility was somewhat obscured but, when the light came into the world, postponement and compromise were no longer possible. Fence sitters had to decide one way or another and, inevitably, the choice of one option excluded the other and thus involved loss and pain. Christ saves us first of all from indecision, lukewarmness, and having a double soul. His coming causes crisis, especially for the hesitant.

We will once or twice experience something similar in our own lives, though the movement seems to be in a reverse direction. First, we experience the crisis and the need to overhaul our life and decide between possibilities. It is only afterwards that we realize that this agonizing reappraisal has been a grace-filled event. It has been a new coming of Christ into our life, but a coming that was known only by the upheaval it provoked in our calm and settled existence. Christ comes not to bring peace but to cause trouble, but it is trouble that detaches us from harmful patterns of behavior, opens our hearts, leads us to greater freedom, and ultimately saves us.

CHAPTER TWENTY-THREE

Desolation

And when the sixth hour came there was darkness over the whole earth until the ninth hour. At the ninth hour Jesus cried out in a loud voice, אלהי אלהי למה שבקתני, *which means "O God, my God, why have you forsaken me?" Some of those standing round heard this and said, "See he is calling Elijah." And someone ran and filled a sponge with sour wine and putting it on a reed gave him a drink saying, "Stop. Let us see if Elijah comes to take him off." But Jesus gave a loud cry and expired. And the curtain of the Temple was torn in two from top to bottom.*

The centurion who was standing there in front of him saw him cry out thus and expire, and he said, "Truly this man was God's son."

There were also women there, watching from a distance: Mary Magdalene, Mary the mother of James the Less, the mother of Joses and Salome. These had followed him when he was in Galilee and had ministered to him. And there were many other women who had accompanied him up to Jerusalem.

MARK 15:33–41

John's Gospel, written long after the others, portrays Jesus in his passion as a figure characterized by dignity and serenity. He seems almost untouched by the flames of hatred and cruelty that rage against him. Mark's Jesus is much more vulnerable. The Marcan account of Christ's passion is an unbroken sequence of unfairness, desertion, rejection, insult, and injury, culminating in the torture of crucifixion and an agony lasting for six hours.

The image of darkness was often used to indicate the coming of divine judgment. "The sun will be darkened and the moon will not give its glow; the stars will be falling from the sky" (Mk 13:24–25). Here darkness also represents externally the dying moments of the one whom John will proclaim as "the light of the world" (Jn 8:12). Slowly Jesus' life ebbs away. Nothing remains that attaches him to this world, all bonds have been severed. The slow extinguishment of vital functions is poignantly described in the Old Testament book of Ecclesiastes (Qoheleth).

> In the days of your youth,
> remember the One who created you
> before the days of trouble draw near
> and the years when you will say
> "There is no delight for me in them."
> Before the sun and the light and the moon and the
>   stars grow dark
> and, after the rain, the clouds come back.
>
> On that day, those guarding the house tremble
> and men of strength are stooped;
> the women grinding [corn] cease because they are few
> and those looking through the window are darkened.

The doors to the street are closed
and the sound of grinding fades.
One rises at the sound of a bird
and all songs grow faint.

One is afraid of height and of dangers in the streets.
Though the almond tree blossoms
and the grasshopper drags itself along,
desire remains dormant.

At that time human beings go to their eternal home
and the mourners go about in the streets.

[Remember the One who created you]
Before the silver cord is severed
and the golden bowl is broken
and the vessel broken at the spring
and the wheel at the well is broken.

And dust returns to the earth from which it came
and the spirit return to God who gave it.

QOHELETH 12:1–8

What the Preacher thus describes may be considered as taking place gently over several years as the organism begins shutting itself down in preparation for death. The external world loses it capacity to captivate and charm; sense impressions are fainter and the inward fire is slowly reduced to ashes. In the case of Jesus, this period of withdrawal was concentrated in a few agonizing hours of torture, loneliness, and shame. The night has come in which no one can work; it is the hour in which only suffering is possible.

> Indeed, excessive pain, like a stormy winter that precedes death, allows us to think of scarcely anything except its own unremitting severity. There is no place

for being sorry because pain fully occupies the person's mind and thought. The soul bidding farewell to this life is like someone on the sabbath; not permitted to do any meritorious work but able only to do nothing. To do nothing, that is, that might be of profit, meanwhile [suffering] from whatever afflicts, upsets, and tortures.[1]

Jesus, like all victims of torture, was reduced to a state of total passivity: no action was possible. There was no means of avoiding or diminishing the physical torment which others chose to inflict on him, no answer he could make to their taunts and mockery. He had no rights, no credible comeback, no threat of vengeance. The time for action had passed; suffering was all that remained to him. Jesus on the cross expresses his humanity by the pain he endured. He was one of us. Physical torture, mental anguish, the bitter potion of rejection and hatred, radical powerlessness, and the certainty of impending death.

Julian of Norwich describes the suffering of Jesus in great and sympathetic detail. In particular she speaks of the cold he experienced as his body lost its vital moisture and began to wither.

> For at the time when our blessed Savior died upon the cross there was a dry sharp wind, that, as I saw it, was cold beyond belief. Even when the precious blood had bled out of the sweet body, I saw that there remained a certain moisture in the sweet flesh of Christ. On the inside, bloodlessness and pain met together with the blowing of the wind and the cold coming from outside to dry out the sweet body of Christ. These four dried out the flesh of Christ as time went by. And though this pain was bitter and sharp, yet I saw that it

lasted a very long time. And the pain dried up all lively spirits of Christ's flesh. Then I saw the sweet flesh dry out before my eyes, part after part drying out with extreme pain. And as long as any spirit had life in Christ's flesh, so long he suffered. It seemed to me as if he had been dying for a week, dying and on the point of passing out. When I say that it seemed to me that he had been a week in dying, it means that the sweet body was so discolored, so dry, so shriveled, so deathly, and inspiring so much pity as if he had been a week in dying, continually dying. And I thought that the drying out of Christ's flesh was the most painful and the final aspect of his passion.[2]

The external sufferings of Jesus are dramatic enough to seize our attention. The mental agony he experienced in those long hours draws us inward to a more profound meditation. Although, as we have seen, he gave his free assent to what was about to happen, once he had fallen "into the hands of sinners," no vestige of control remained. He was completely in the power of others, to hurt and humiliate as they chose. Rejected by his own people, he was thrown into an alien context of nonmeaning, where he could be mocked as "King" five times by uncomprehending Gentiles (Mk 15:2, 9, 12, 18, 26), a theme quickly picked up and expanded to include the notion of Messiah by the chief priests and scribes (Mk 15:31–32). We should not underestimate the bitter weight of such rejection.[3] If human beings long to be loved and quickly cease to flourish if love is lost, how great must be the anguish when all around is hatred. In Mark's account, there is no friendly face in the crowd; even the women stand apart at some distance. Jesus dies alone; bereft of the warmth of human solidarity that was the meaning of the Incarnation.

As the end drew near, Mark tells us of a more fearsome

loneliness. Jesus, having lost access to those sectors of experience that previously mediated the presence of his Father, now feels abandoned by God. We cannot easily comprehend the confusion, terror, and utter anguish to which this sense of dereliction gave rise. Jesus had previously declined the kindly offer of drugged wine that would have clouded his consciousness and made his sufferings less acute (Mk 15:23). Instead, he faced the full fury of his own fearful agony and was, as it were, the witness to his own diminishing vitality.

Mark transmits to us an Aramaic fragment embedded in the primitive tradition he had received. Jesus cries out in his mother-tongue the horrifying beginning of Psalm 22, "My God, my God, why have you forsaken me?" The verb used for the act of crying out is related to the noun describing cattle. The last cry of Jesus was a bellow, like that of an outraged bull: not a pretty sound. Nor did the cry shape itself in the formal words of Hebrew, but in the language first learned in the bosom of his family. These final words of Jesus carried such emotive power that they had a profound effect on the hitherto scornful bystanders, whose first impulse was to intervene. Even the hardened soldier in charge of the execution was touched.

The psalms expressing an individual's lamentation constitute about a third of the Psalter and are, accordingly, a significant segment of the Hebrew Bible. Although they are literary compositions rather than spontaneous outbursts, there is a depth of feeling contained in them which has helped many to express their misery in times of extreme suffering. Sometimes these psalms concern external sufferings caused by the actions of enemies and result in such robust curses that the pious pale, and so these are often excluded from the worship of the faithful. Other laments derive their energy from loneliness, sickness, and the imminent prospect of death. In all of them, there is sense of grievance against God. Why has this been allowed to happen? Why does God do nothing to improve the situation?

Above all, it is the sense of being abandoned by God that oppresses the sufferer. If God deserts us who can deliver? If God begins to bring our sins to judgment, who will survive?

> I cry to you, O LORD.
>> My Rock, do not be deaf to me.
> If you are silent towards me
>> I shall be like those who go down into the grave.
>
> PSALM 28:1

We hear in so many laments the pain and confusion that arises from a sense of God's absence. It seems more than a temporary loss of contact; there are moral implications. God has withdrawn in an act of rejection and condemnation. God is angry and has become my enemy. Twenty-five times in the Old Testament this is described in terms of the hiding of God's face.

> Answer me quickly, O LORD,
>> my spirit is faint.
> Do not hide your face from me
>> or I shall be like those who go down into the grave.
>
> PSALM 143:7

The absence of God gives birth to many agonizing questions: former certainties have faded and meaning is lost.

> How long, O LORD? Will you forget me forever?
>> How long will you hide your face from me?
> How long must I struggle with the thoughts of my soul?
>> How long must I bear sorrow in my heart?
> How long will my enemy triumph over me?
>
> PSALM 13:2–3

In the eighth-century prophet Micah and in Deuteronomy the hiding of God's face is a sign of divine anger occasioned by our infidelity; when this happens, we fall out of God's awareness and so can expect no response to our cries for help (Deut 31:17–18, 32:20; Mic 3:4). Our moral failure interrupts our contact with God: "Your evil deeds have been barriers between you and your God, and your sins have hidden [God's] face from you" (Isa 59:2).

The already familiar words of Psalm 22 burst forth from the mouth of the dying man weighted with this Old Testament world of meaning. It was not a desperate cry for help (although there are many in the Psalms). It expresses only an overwhelming and heartfelt sense of dereliction. And yet it is spoken in the second person: the words are not about God, but are spoken directly to God, although God was utterly hidden from Jesus' sight. They are words flung into the hostile darkness that was slowly possessing every cell of his body. Jesus died in prolonged physical agony, feeling the hatred and scorn of those around him and all the while he was comforted by no sense of the immediacy of God.

In most of the laments there is a resolution of the crisis that converts groaning into songs of gladness and celebration. Psalm 22 is no exception, but there is no indication in Mark that Jesus experienced this reversal. Closer to what the Gospel describes is Psalm 88 which climaxes its lamentation with the words, "You have taken away loved ones and neighbors; now darkness is my friend."

At the moment of his baptism by John, Jesus, who carried on his shoulders the sin of all humanity, was submerged beneath the waters of the Jordan. What was enacted ritually at the beginning of his public life is now accomplished in reality. If the act of sin is a turning away from God, then the state which results from sin is a state of being separated from and turned away from God. There the Spirit descended and the

Father's voice spoke words of love. Here there is no answer but the busy babble of the bystanders. A great sound issues forth from his mouth and Jesus breathes forth his spirit—gives up the ghost. The body remains on the cross, but he is no longer there. In a dramatic example of synchrony, Mark notes at this moment that the veil hiding the Holy of Holies from the common gaze was rent from top to bottom as if by God; human beings would presumably have torn it from the bottom up.[4] The centurion, as if struck by lightning, comes to faith. And from afar the women watched and saw.

CHAPTER TWENTY-FOUR

Nakedness

If you desire the things that are perfect, go forth with Abraham from your homeland and from your family and venture forth without knowing where. If you have property, sell it and give to the poor. If you do not have it you are freed from a great burden. Naked follow the naked Christ. It is a harsh reality and no small thing; it is difficult. But the rewards are great.

JEROME, LETTER 125, 20; PL 22, 1085

T hree times in the Gospel of Mark, Jesus predicted his rejection by his own people and his death. After each solemn warning, he drew his disciples' attention to the necessity of their enduring their own measure of hardship if they were to be true followers. He expressed this obligation in stark terms.

> Any who wish to come after me
> must deny themselves,
> take up their cross
> and follow me.
> Any who wish to save their lives
> will lose them.

MARK 8:34–35

Jesus makes it perfectly clear that self-preservation, self-exaltation, and the accumulation of material goods are incompatible with serious discipleship. This is hard teaching, but we cannot claim to be his disciples unless our everyday lifestyle falls under its influence.

(a) Renunciation: It is not so easy to embrace the principle of renunciation that Jesus teaches both by word and by example. There is an essential paradox in Christian discipleship that transcends mere morality or abstract philosophy. We follow Christ by refusing to live for ourselves, by withholding certain gratifications from ourselves, by living in the firm faith that unless the seed die it will never reach its full potential. To unbelievers, the preaching of the cross is, as Saint Paul declares, both a scandalous affront to human dignity and utter foolishness (1 Cor 1:23). What we Christians term "the paschal mystery" cannot be comprehended without the faith that enables us to pierce the spatio-temporal shell in which we live, and to perceive the meaning of human life in the radiant light of eternity. This opening to the invisible and ultimate reality is a gift that is given to us—we cannot manufacture it for ourselves. "No one can come to me," says Jesus, "unless the Father who sent me draw them" (Jn 6:44).

Yes, we believe in resurrection, even though it is at this point that smart people begin to lose interest (Acts 17:31–32; Jn 6:60). To accept diminishment in this life, however, demands that it be perceived as a condition for receiving an even greater gift. Nobody in their right mind chooses to have less for the sake of less. The Christian is somewhat detached from temporal gratification and sustained in hardship solely by the promise of "treasure in heaven." Without such assurance it makes sense to be totally preoccupied with saving one's own life and seeking every sort of gratification and enrichment. "If for this life only we have hope in Christ Jesus then of all people we are the most to be pitied" (1 Cor 15:19). If life ends with the grave, then we are foolish to deny ourselves the right to eat, drink, and be merry, or to do whatever we please, supposing we can get away with it. If, however, our faith in a future life is well-grounded, then present pain and deprivation are tolerable. "This slight and momentary affliction is making us ready for an abundance beyond measure, an eternal weight of glory. So, our attention is fixed not on things seen but on things unseen, not on what lasts for a season but what is eternal" (2 Cor 4:17–18).

It is in hope that we obey Jesus' summons to deny ourselves. This is where some clear thinking is needed, because certain definitions and distinctions need to be made. There are two different ways in which the "self" may be understood. The first and obvious "self" is the identity given to us from the outside, from our family, from where we live, from our role in social groups, and from the state that issues us with official identity papers. This is what we teach little children to remember, in case they get lost. Anybody who has access to our personal data may know who we are and become acquainted with many details about how we live, even though we may never meet. This is a first level of identity or selfhood.

There is a deeper sense of who we are that blossoms within us as we grow in years and wisdom. This is a sense of our personality, our "inner self" that is constituted by the cumulative total of our experiences. Nobody else knows everything that we have done or what has been done to us, and nobody else knows exactly how we feel as we pass through the different situations of life. Even those with whom we are intimate have no more than a partial understanding of who we are. This is a self that is deeper than that known by superficial acquaintances, a self known by God who calls us by name. It is only through a measure of withdrawing from external experience that we can begin to experience who we are at the deepest level.[1]

When we hear admonitions such as "lose yourself to find

yourself" and "give up your life in order to save your life," we are not dealing with meaningless contradictions. What they signify is that we have to let go of much of what constitutes our external identity in order first to discover and then to give priority to what is deeper and more permanent. Every scholar, athlete, artist, and self-serving politician knows about sacrifice as a means of realizing their goals. Such hard choices are a part of being human. We cannot do everything; some things have to be left aside, some possibilities must remain unrealized. Sometimes we make a selection with a heavy heart. Sometimes we later regret our choice of options. Choices are inescapable; we have no guarantee that we will decide correctly, but we cannot afford to be passive before life's opportunities.

The hard teaching of Jesus is prefixed by an important clause: "If any one wishes to come after me" (Mk 8:34). The way of utter detachment is not imposed indiscriminately on all; it has to be freely chosen as a means of following Jesus more closely. Jesus is not laying down the law but telling us in advance of the hard and difficult things to be encountered on the journey towards God. Persevering commitment is required. If you want to play the violin, you have to practice. If you want to be a rocket scientist, years of study are ahead of you. If you want to be a disciple, then you must prepare yourself for a lifetime of growing into self-forgetfulness. The same point is made to the rich man who asks the way: "If you wish to enter into life, keep the commandments...if you wish to be perfect, go and sell everything" (Mt 19:17–21).

> Once you have heard the saying of the Savior, "If you wish to be perfect, go and sell everything that you have and give to the poor and come, follow me," you must convert the words into works, and naked follow the naked cross, and you will climb Jacob's ladder more quickly and more lightly.[2]

Half a century ago the popular preaching of the Catholic Church gave a fair amount of emphasis to penance, self-denial, and mortification. Friday abstinence from meat and fasting during Lent and at other times gave a distinctive character to our religious observance. This was on top of a detailed and restrictive body of moral teaching and recommended devotional practices. Probably correctly, it was presented as the "narrow way" that leads to life.

For various reasons, many people saw these ascetical practices in a negative light and rejected them. They were said to be based on a false anthropology that undervalued the body.[3] For some they conjured up images of a God of judgment and condemnation. They became inextricably associated with exaggerated feelings of guilt and were thus viewed as punitive and vindictive. Ascetical practices were said to cover with ashes a life intended to be marked by love, peace, happiness, and joy, and so were relegated. The Age of Aquarius had no time for the practice of even the soberest self-denial.

A different generation has different perceptions. Many fervent young believers wonder why their pastors are disinclined to encourage mortification. They are aware of the dietary restrictions practiced in Judaism and the religions of East Asia; they know about Ramadan, the Islamic month of fasting. They see the rigorous tithing practiced by some evangelical Protestants. So they ask questions. Have the demands of the Gospel been watered down? Has the Church become so assimilated to the mindless hedonism of contemporary Western society that it has lost its capacity to inculcate an alternative path?

It seems strange to those of mellower years that many young people find the hard line promulgated by Pope John Paul II inspiring. Maybe such idealism needs to be tempered by experience, but perhaps we who are older need to admit the possibility that God may be showing us the way through the dissatisfaction and criticism of callow youth. If we study a bit of history, we will notice that God usually speaks through the powerless, and often reveals through the young the course to be followed.

At a scholarly level also, there is some evidence that the role of asceticism, self-denial, and mortification is beginning to be appreciated more.[4] We ourselves, if we are serious about our commitment to following Jesus, probably need to ponder how to implement in our own life the hard sayings conveyed to us by the Gospel tradition. This is not to say that we must embrace immediately the whole gamut of penitential practices. There can be no harm, however, in asking ourselves whether we have lost our sensitivity to the negative elements of Jesus' message. Taking up our cross can never be a pleasant or popular pastime, but it is what Jesus has asked us to do.

> Our leader wished to make his soldiers ready for this spiritual warfare....They ready themselves by stripping off all the concerns and riches of this world, all their emotional attachments and their self-will so that naked they may follow the naked Christ.[5]

If we are looking for a practical means by which the value of renunciation can find expression in our lives, we may find guidance in the words of the oddly named Abba Paphnutius, relayed to us by John Cassian.

> Now we must talk about the renunciations which the tradition of the Fathers and the Sacred Scriptures show us to be three in number. In the first, we despise bodily all the riches and possibilities of the world. In the second, we reject the behavior and vices and our former passions of soul and body. In the third, we call our mind away from all present and visible real-

ity and contemplate only what is future, yearning only for what is invisible.[6]

In renunciation, there are three processes that follow one another, but with some overlap. To begin with, we need to start imposing external limits on our consumption of material resources and on our attachment to such social enrichments as prestige, status, and the perquisites of office. Paphnutius adds the word "bodily" to indicate that as we begin to downgrade the importance of these realities in our life, we can renounce them simply by getting rid of them. No special interior feeling is needed, just the will to dispose of what we had previously gathered. As this process advances, we begin to turn our attention to the quality of our personal lives, to monitor our behavior, to temper our vices and progressively to order our affective self so all that we do is marked by love. In this process, we are gradually becoming detached from earth and more and more concerned with the invisible reality of heaven. Mysteriously, we begin to taste the fruits of contemplation.

(b) Detachment from possessions: The acid test of the sincerity of our religion is the level of our detachment from material goods. The first of Jesus' beatitudes declared blessed, those who are "poor in spirit" (Mt 5:3). Gregory the Great is uncompromising in seeing the stripping off of earthly attachments as the first stage of discipleship.

> The Lord has instructed us who come to him that we renounce what we own because whoever among us who comes to the contest of faith must assume the task of wrestling against the malign spirits. Now these malign spirits possess nothing as their own in this world. We must be naked to wrestle with a naked opponent. If someone is wearing clothes when wrestling

with a naked opponent, there is something to grab and so he is quickly thrown to the ground. All who hasten to wrestle with the devil must strip off their clothes or they will succumb. They may possess by love none of the delights of passing things lest the desire that covers them be grabbed and so cause them to take a fall.[7]

The same idea occurs in Bernard of Clairvaux.

Having allowed all cupidity to be dried out, all temporal things are to be held in contempt. This is not because they are given to us for our use, but because they are a cause of death for many. Those who are fully loaded cannot run well; those who are empty and unoccupied make progress more quickly and more safely. You must be naked to fight with a naked opponent, the devil, for he is not burdened with earthly possessions. See that you are wearing nothing by which he could get a grip on you. Take off from your back whatever might prevent you from hastening to the home country.[8]

Here, as often in the writings of the Church Fathers, we have to make allowances for a tendency to exaggerate. Discipleship is not a matter of making dramatic gestures, but of a lifelong commitment to growth in spirituality. Nothing happens all at once, but a long process is begun by which our priorities concern less the visible world than the unseen world of the spirit. Only in death is the truth of the human condition revealed, when we discover that we cannot take our wealth with us, and that when it comes to prestige and status, we are all equal. To "die daily" is voluntarily to anticipate some of the effects of our eventual demise because, appreciating where our treasure is, we know where to invest our energies. Jesus is uncomfortably uncompromising. "No one can be the slave of two masters...it is not possible for you to be the slave both of God and of mammon" (Mt 6:24).

Poverty is an important part of the message of Jesus, especially emphasized in the Gospel of Luke, but prominent in all the Synoptic Gospels. In the first place, it is the ecclesial community that is called to continue Jesus' practice of not relying on material wealth or temporal privilege to secure the promulgation of God's Kingdom. It is only when the Church can say "Silver and gold have I none" that it can add "Arise and walk" (Acts 3:6). The individual Christian, however, is also called to walk the path towards dispossession, knowing that it is easier for a camel to pass through the eye of a needle than for someone who is rich to enter God's kingdom" (Mk 10:25).

At the end, Jesus owned nothing, not even the clothes on his back. His friends fled, his reputation was besmirched by the taunts of those standing by, and there was no sign that the seed he had sown would ever bear fruit. In a sense, Jesus was reduced to the level of a nonperson. In most vindictive societies, prisoners are dehumanized before being executed, lest any movement of sympathy provide comfort to them and reduce the horror of a violent death. Mark's portrayal of the death of Jesus and his relaying of Jesus' message that we must embrace the cross is a sober and even fearsome challenge to us. The cross that we honor is a call to a radical program of self-emptying that may begin small, but is meant to strengthen and continue until it is brought to completion by death. The first step to be taken is to declare our independence from the thrall of material possessions. We need first to relinquish our hold on what is superfluous, then constantly to define more narrowly what is necessary, until we reach the point of being content with little and progressively indifferent to things whose value is far from permanent.

"It is not enough to relinquish our possessions if we do not relinquish ourselves as well."[9] The giving up of our reliance on property achieves nothing unless it makes us more willingly dependent on God. Here there can be no question of demonstrating how tough we are and how we can survive on almost nothing. It is a matter of learning that the horses and chariots of Assyria cannot help us realize our goals, nor can we live on mere bread. To realize our humanity means opening the doors of our heart to admit a God who is willing to shower us with every good gift. The essential element of disappropriation is emptying our hands so that we can more fully receive. This is impeded not only by the congestion caused by concern for material goods but also by the muddiness of spirit that comes about when our awareness is clouded by delusion or by intractable self-will.

(c) Uncovering our soul: We are apt to judge strangers by the things that they own: we are favorably impressed by a person with a good address, who arrives in a luxury car with impeccable grooming and designer clothing. Someone who has none of these things and, moreover, lacks the fawning deference of paid attendants has to rely on more interior qualities to make a good impression. Even more stupid than assessing the value of others by the amount of money they have is the attitude of making our own self-worth dependent on our possessions and on the privileges consequent upon them.

Human beings need relatively few things to survive, yet look how much we accumulate in a lifetime. It must be that all these things that we will rarely use and certainly not wear out have a symbolic rather than a real importance for us. We acquire them because, mysteriously, they make us feel good. Who but a millipede needs hundreds of pairs of shoes? On the other hand, when we begin to attach less importance to what we have, we become more aware of what we are. Strip away the accouterments and all that is left is a particular human being almost indistinguishable from a billion others of that race. Naked, there is more chance that we will begin to see through the disguises and distractions we had hitherto embraced.

At least a token gesture of voluntary impoverishment is necessary to begin walking the way of discipleship. Parallel to our withdrawal from wealth and all the benefits it brings is an inward journey by which we seek to come to a more honest self-appraisal. It is even more demanding to cast aside the fig leaves of rationalization and self-justification and to leave aside all our excuses and pleas of innocence and, baring everything, to confront ourselves with some measure of objectivity. How much there is of what we have become that we do not want to see! The way ahead can be broached only when we dismantle our defenses and embark on a voyage of self-discovery.

> There are many human sciences but none is better than that by which we know ourselves. For this reason I must return to my heart and stand there habitually, so that I can subject my whole life to discernment and know myself.[10]

Most of us post-Freudians are at least vaguely familiar with the mechanisms of denial, repression, and the projection of blame onto others. These are the means by which we preserve our fragile self-esteem by blocking out, or splitting off from our awareness, behavior that is reprehensible. By imposing a blanket ban on anything potentially blameworthy we prevent ourselves from ever becoming fully aware of significant actions in our lives. As a result, we do not ponder them and seek to understand why we acted in such a way. Although we seem to be self-protecting, we are really very hard on ourselves, quick to dismiss certain actions as unconscionable. If we had the courage to examine them more closely, we would discover, more often than not, that even our worst actions may have some admixture of good, just as our best deeds are sometimes tinged with imperfection. Humans are pretty mixed up creatures. We do not have the capacity to be absolutely good or absolutely bad. This means that when we act badly it is important to understand what is going on, so that we can reduce the level of vice without crippling the good intentions that may have been operative. In many cases, the main problem is inattention. We do not know exactly why we feel inclined to act the way we do, and we are too lazy to scrutinize our motives. In addition, we do not pay enough heed to the impact our behavior has on others nor to the change that will result to our relationships because of what we have done. Without a solid level of self-knowledge, there is no guarantee that our actions will have the meaning we intend.

Like politicians, we are so much in the habit of issuing favorable press releases about what we do that we lose the capacity to distinguish reality from the interpretative spin we instinctively impose on it. This protective covering of falsification, distortion, and cliché may seem to be a defense against criticism, but it also serves as a means by which the truth is concealed from ourselves so that our intelligence becomes perverted. No doubt we feel very exposed when we cast away such nonsense, but it is only by ridding ourselves of pretense that we allow our lives to be grounded in truth. In such a state, whatever efforts we invest in turning away from evil and doing good have a greater chance of producing good results.

Arriving at the truth is not usually the result of a massive program of solitary introspection. We need to be ready to learn from spontaneous feedback received from others—be they enemies or friends. And sometimes we need to go looking for someone to help us. An important component in the process is the willingness to bare our soul to another person. Such trust is almost always a risky venture, since we can never know in advance how another will respond. What motivates us in thus exposing ourselves is the determination not to live in such potentially delusional isolation that we may never arrive at a fair assessment of our resources and liabilities and so are liable never to realize the gifts and possibilities that are ours. Others serve as a mirror to tell us what we are and who we are. And the big surprise, for most of us, is that the news is not bad. Part of the mystery of Christ's Church is the sacrament of the brother or sister who can be for us a channel of counsel and healing wisdom.[11] "Bear one another's burdens and so you will fulfill the law of Christ" (Gal 6:2).

It is only when we have arrived at an understanding of the complexities of human motivation that we begin to appreciate the extent to which many actions are determined by unconscious forces, such as insecurity, prejudice, ambition, and various forms of acquisitiveness. If we have learned any measure of compassion, we will want to act to ease our neighbor's burden and not merely to assuage our own appetite for self-glorification. To reach such a disinterested concern for another's welfare we need first to identify and then to neutralize whatever in our behavior is the result of self-will.

(d) Abandoning self-will: Divesting ourselves of self-will is a goal easily stated, yet it takes half a lifetime of effort even to make a beginning. Without thorough self-knowledge, we can never be sure that our effort is not merely a subtle expression of the very self-will we are striving to eliminate. For this reason, the task is usually left to other people. Family, friends, associates, superiors, and those who are supposed to take the lead from us will all join together in a massive conspiracy to frustrate our plans and projects. At least this is how it seems on our more paranoid days. It is interesting in reading biographies of the saints to note how often they are blocked by

the well-meaning interventions of small-minded and conventional wielders of power, subjected to scorn and humiliation and reviled by those who ought to know better. This is especially evident in the lives of founders and reformers of religious orders. Blessed Mary McKillop was hounded by certain bishops in colonial Australia for much of her life and eventually excommunicated; she has been beatified, they not. Anyone who speaks or acts against the institutional status quo can expect trouble—irrespective of whether their message is from God or from themselves.

Indifference, misunderstanding, passive aggression, and various degrees of harassment are unavoidable especially for those who try to live creatively. They are generated in others independent of our will and often of our deserts. If we resist the temptation to become professional victims, such mistreatment can be a potent means of purifying the subtle promptings of self-will in the ordering of our life. It is not enough, however, to be totally passive, waiting for someone to come along and persecute us. Once we have developed the capacity to discern the stirrings of self-will, we can refuse to cooperate with it. We are given a measure of freedom; we can say "No"!

Over the years, we can become quite good at withholding our consent. That is admirable, of course, but it can turn us into very negative people. Excessive caution and suspicion, combined with an element of rigidity, can rob our life of any sense of lightness and joy, isolate us from many of the harmless pleasures of life, and risk our being dismissed as eccentrics by those whom otherwise we may have been able to help. Just because most of the Ten Commandments begin "Thou shalt not" does not mean that religion is merely a matter of saying "No"!

Christianity, in particular, is principally a matter of learning to say "Yes!" Merely abandoning self-will condemns us to live in an affective desert until such time as the love of God becomes paramount in our awareness. For most of us, this is too hard. This is why a more excellent way is proposed to us; genuine, unselfish love is a sweeter and equally effective means of neutralizing disordered self-will, but it also needs to be worked at.

Saying "Yes!" to others is not only a marvelous means of being kind to them, it is also an effective means of blocking our self-will and ensuring that the good deeds we do are not being poisoned by a hidden agenda. It is one of the more attractive effects of the spiritual gift of meekness (Gal 5:23; see Mt 5:5). That is why, in the history of monasticism, obedience has always played such a strong role. It was not seen primarily as a means of establishing or enforcing a social order, but as a technique by which the monk could put self-will on hold while repair work was undertaken to remedy some of the ravages of sin. Obedience exists for the growth of virtue. It serves much the same purpose as a splint does for a broken arm. It holds the limb steady until the fracture mends.

Saint Benedict certainly sees obedience primarily as a means by which monks "leave behind the things that are their own and abandon their self-will."[12] Such submission is freely and trustfully chosen as a practical way of ensuring that behavior is not self-motivated and so has a better chance of being objectively good and consonant with God's will.

> They take the narrow road, of which the Lord said, "Narrow is the road that leads to life." They do not live by their own judgment, nor do they obey their own desires and pleasures, but they desire an abbot to have authority over them, to walk according to another's judgment and instructions, and to live in a community.[13]

Later in his Rule, Benedict will extend the idea of obedience to include "mutual obedience," recognizing that obedience to superiors alone can still leave plenty of scope for self-will.

The good of obedience is not only to be shown by all
to the abbot, but the brothers should be obedient to
one another in the same way, knowing that it is by this
obedience that they will go towards God.[14]

The motivation for this mutual deference is not merely
timidity, good manners, or compliance, but a real love for the
other.

Let the monks exercise this zeal by the most fervent
love, that is, let them anticipate one another in showing respect, let them tolerate their infirmities of body
and behavior with much patience, and let them give
themselves generously to mutual obedience. Let nobody do what he deems useful to himself but rather
what is so for another. Let them give themselves generously to a chaste love for their brothers.[15]

There are different levels of motivation for embracing the
relationship of obedience. Apart from its social utility, obedience
helps us to avoid subservience to our destructive or frivolous
inclinations, and it is a practical means of expressing respect
and love for those among whom we live. On a more theological level, obedience can be a way of associating ourselves
consciously with the self-emptying of Christ, obedient unto
death (Phil 2:8). "Without a doubt such as these imitate that
sentence of the Lord, 'I came not to do my own will, but the
will of the One who sent me.'"[16] When all else fails, obedience
links us with Christ. When practiced habitually, it generates a
conformity of will between ourselves and God which renders
us transparent, and opens up for us the world of contemplation.

(e) **Stripping off merits:** There is a danger in propagating a morality based on the imitation of Christ. This is certainly a wonderful ethical ideal but, in its completeness, is both unrealizable and unnecessary. We do not have to repeat the work of Jesus; it has already been accomplished by him on behalf of us. The phrase used in the Letter to the Hebrews "once and for all" is relevant here. "By [God's] will we have been made holy by the offering of the body of Jesus Christ once and for all" (Heb 10:10).[17]

What we need to realize is that we do not have to rely on our own meritorious achievements. God has given us a gift in Christ that enables us to transcend our innate and acquired limitations. What we cannot do, grace supplies.

> "Christ suffered for us leaving us an example that we might follow in his footsteps" (1 Pet 2:21). In Christ, dear friends, we do not merely have an example for ourselves to follow, but also an antidote against death; he not only encourages us to endure [hardship] but gives us grace so that we persevere. He not only forms us for battle but gives us strength to obtain the victory.[18]

At every stage of spiritual growth, we have to get rid of any sense that we are accomplishing anything. Achievement is so important to our self-esteem that we are reluctant to engage in any activity in which we do not have a reasonable hope of "success." The spiritual life is all back to front. We start off thinking how great we are, surprised at the good we can do, and delighted with the esteem in which others hold us. As we make a little progress, this sense of self-satisfaction diminishes. We become ever more aware of our limitations and liabilities, and there seem to be plenty of people around who are happy to tell us where we have gone wrong. More and more we rely on God's mercy. The more the reality of this seeps into our bones, the more we become in the eyes of others heralds of God's loving kindness. We become living gospels for others to see—walking, talking embodiments of the good news. This is because first we have received the message of mercy in our own lives and have made it our own. Mercy and merit cannot coexist; it is only when we are forced to abandon our claim to merit that our life is open to the inpouring of mercy. "My merit consists in the Lord showing mercy. I am not bereft of merit as long as he is not bereft of mercy."[19]

In such a state, our prayer changes. When we stand before God, it is not as the self-congratulatory Pharisee but as one conscious only of need. "O Lord, my poor soul is naked and cold and uncared for, it longs to be warmed by the heat of your love."[20] Before God, there is no necessity to cover up our deformity. We can simply be ourselves.

> Having cast off the garment of skins that you made for Adam to protect him from his shame and confusion, I show myself to you, naked, as you created me. Behold me, Lord, not as you have made me but as I have made myself, because I have fallen away from you.[21]

Our relationship with God activated in prayer is not intended to reinforce our delusions about our own virtue, but to bind us to God by bringing to our awareness a strong sense of our dependence and of God's loving dependability. The two of us fit together nicely: our need to be accepted as we are encounters God's ever-flowing, all-embracing love.

> Abyss calls out to abyss. Our mortality calls on the death of Christ the Lord as a source of example and of help; our suffering on his suffering, our patience on his.

(f) "A naked intent unto God": The third and highest level of renunciation described by Abba Paphnutius is that which accompanies the act of contemplation when we leave behind the cares and concerns of mundane existence and momentarily step out of space and time into the halls of eternity.

> When we have successfully expelled all vices we shall rise to the summit which is the third renunciation. Here with all the energy of our mind we transcend, and we despise as subject to vanity and soon to perish everything that is done in this world and especially what people possess, and the totality of things thought to be splendid. According to the word of the Apostle, we look not at things seen but at what is unseen, for what is seen is temporary; what is unseen is eternal.[22]

The intensity of the contemplative act is such that, while it endures, it engages and enthralls the total capacity of our being. Although the organism continues to function, awareness separates from it and disappears elsewhere, taking nothing with it. The spirit is nakedly intent upon God, to use the terminology of *The Cloud of Unknowing*.

> Be blind in this time and cut away all desire of knowing for it will more hinder than help you. It is enough that you feel yourself pleasantly stirred by something of which you have no knowledge except that in this stirring you have no particular thought of anything under God, and that your intent is nakedly directed to God.[23]

Divested of all the ordinary mental processes, the spirit is free to be clothed in God.

In this time your love is both chaste and perfect. In this time you both see your God and your love and nakedly feel him through being spiritually united to his love in the sovereign point of your spirit. [You experience God] as he is in himself but blindly as it must be here below, utterly despoiled of yourself and nakedly clothed in God's self as he is. Unclothed and not wrapped about by any of the feelings related to the senses (be they never so sweet or holy) for these must fall short in this life. But in purity of spirit, properly and perfectly, is God perceived and felt in himself as he is, far distant from any imagination or false opinion that must fall short in this life.[24]

The contemplative act anticipates the union of the human spirit with God that is the beatitude of heaven. This experience is possible only to the extent that the spirit has passed through a mini-death, leaving aside all that constitutes "life" here below. In other words, to experience the profundity of our relationship with God, we are in need of "purification" and detachment. This is the paradox of the Gospel. To attain the fulfillment of our destiny we must be prepared to give up everything, even life itself. We find life only by letting go of it; as long as we cling to it, we will lose everything. The clarity of the principle does not make it easier; most of us will begin to approach the necessary level of self-forgetfulness only in the latter stages of our lives—perhaps even in the last minutes. The words and example of Jesus leave us in no doubt: it is by the doorway of death that we enter eternal life. Conversely, it is our failure in trust and our efforts to avoid death and diminishment that constitute the most persistent incentive to sin. "Ah, who could have believed that crime consists less in making others die than in not dying oneself!"[25]

CHAPTER TWENTY-FIVE

Eternity

And when the sabbath had passed, Mary Magdalene, Mary the wife of James, and Salome brought aromatic herbs so that they could come and anoint him. And very early on the first day of the week, they came to the tomb at sunrise. And they were saying to one another, "Who will roll away the stone from the door of the tomb for us?" And looking up they saw that the stone had [already] been rolled away—and it was very big. And they entered the tomb and saw a young man seated on the right, with a white garment around him and they were astonished. And he said to them, "Do not be astonished; you seek Jesus the Nazarene who was crucified. He has risen. He is not here. See the place where they laid him. But go and tell his disciples and Peter: He goes ahead of you into Galilee; there you will see him, as he said to you." And they went out and fled from the tomb; they were trembling and not themselves. And they told nobody anything, because they were afraid.

MARK 16:1–8

Mark's version of the Good News ends abruptly. We are so carried along in the current of his narrative that we are hoping that the evangelist will bring the story to a satisfactory closure. Instead he leaves it hanging.[1] The tomb is empty; the young man announces the fact of the resurrection and promises that

Jesus will appear to them in Galilee; the women flee in terror, telling nobody what they had seen. Mark is making use of the technique of dramatic irony—since the reader already believes in the resurrection of Jesus. How could Mark know the women's story if they really "told nobody anything"?

In a certain sense, Mark's Gospel is saturated with the theme of resurrection—partly because the two terms used in Greek are commonplace words that can be used without religious connotations. Often they simply cover the ordinary meanings that we associate with the word "rise." They can also be used in the context of healing narratives, where Jesus raises the sufferer or bids the sick persons to rise. We can see in these cures, if we want to exercise a little pious imagination, examples of mini-resurrection, whereby those who are delivered from sickness are also freed from the power of death which had expressed itself through their infirmity. Levi too has a resurrection when he responds to Jesus' call (Mk 2:14). Jesus is roused from sleep to save the sinking boat (Mk 4:38) and experiences a sort of resurrection after his prayer in the garden and his calls on the disciples also to rise (Mk 14:42).

These are merely playful examples based on the ambiguity of the words used. There is, however, more solid evidence to ponder. The most remarkable statements of the theme of resurrection occur in the triple "passion prediction," the device used by the evangelist to structure the Galilean phase of his narrative. That Jesus predicted his future rejection and death at the hands of the authorities reveals the realism with which he assessed his own situation. He understood that the good news he proclaimed undermined the legitimacy of religious authority as it was then being exercised in his own nation, and that this would lead to condemnation. As early as Mark 3:6, at the end of the first series of controversies, we read the chilling sentence, "Going out, the Pharisees immediately took counsel with the Herodians against him, and how to destroy him."

Jesus is presented as solemnly predicting his death three times. Each time, however, there is a rider that is not always noticed:

- Mark 8:31: And after three days [the Son of Man] will rise again.
- Mark 9:31: And after three days [the Son of Man] will rise again.
- Mark 10:34: And after three days [the Son of Man] will rise again.

These were not only "passion predictions"; more amazingly they are presented by the evangelist as "resurrection predictions." Nor were they isolated incidents. He cautioned the three to reveal nothing of what they had witnessed on the mountain of the transfiguration "until the Son of Man will rise from the dead," a phrase which puzzled them considerably (Mk 9:9–10). After predicting the scattering of the disciples after his death, Jesus delivers an even more explicit promise: "After I have risen, I will go before you into Galilee" (Mk 14:28). The "good news" that the Gospel is designed to propagate is framed around an acceptance of the reality of Jesus' resurrection. It is a message of hope written for the Church in time of persecution, not to convince unbelievers.

The oldest account of the resurrection is given in 1 Corinthians 15:3–6. Already, by the time Paul is writing, it has been handed on as the core of Christian belief. Nowhere is the resurrection directly described—tradition offers merely the circumstantial evidence of the empty tomb supported by the testimony of those who had seen Jesus alive. Paul asserts that belief in the resurrection is the absolutely essential component of Christian faith. "If Christ were not risen then the message we preach is empty and your faith also is empty" (1 Cor 15:14).

The resurrection event did not take place in history, in the sense that it would have been possible to film a before-and-after sequence. The resurrection was Jesus' passing over from an existence in space and time into eternity. Jesus lives, but his being is not limited to one location in space and time. He is not absent from our world, but is no longer confined within it. In his humanity, Jesus exists in the sphere of God. The preferred way of speaking about this in the New Testament is to say that Jesus sits at God's right hand.[2] The bridge between time and eternity is open—any who wish to follow Jesus may cross it. Jesus is alive; he serves as a mediator between God and humanity (1 Tim 2:5), always making intercession on our behalf (Heb 7:25).

The Fourth Gospel tries to dramatize this mysterious moment of passing over by having Mary Magdalene catch Jesus after his "resurrection" but before his "ascension" (Jn 20:17). It is Acts 1:3 that specifies the interim period as being forty days after which Jesus "was lifted up and a cloud concealed him from their eyes" (Acts 1:9). Matthew and Luke record a number of post-resurrection appearances and then Jesus simply departed from them (Lk 24:51). In Matthew, he formally commissions the Eleven and promises to be with them every day until this age is complete (Mt 28:20).

It is the ongoing presence of Jesus, signaled in the Fourth Gospel by the verb "remain" that is interesting. Jesus departs yet remains. The only way to resolve such a contradiction is to conclude that there is question of two different modes of presence: one discernible by the senses, the other not. By our remaining in contact with his word through faith we are given access to eternal life.

In the context of this book, the resurrection is not only an event in the life of Jesus, it is a revelation of what is possible for humanity by God's gift. We were made for eternal life; the life and teaching of Jesus shows us the way—but that is not enough. We need also, as the Fourth Gospel reiterates, the "gift of the Spirit" to provide us with the energy to walk in the giant's footsteps. The death of Jesus has flung open the door, closing off the spiritual world with such violence that it can never be closed again. The moment of Jesus' baptism becomes permanent: the Spirit by which we also cry "Abba" continues to descend and the Father acknowledges us as the children whom he loves. Jesus has embraced solidarity with us in our sinful estrangement from God so that we may become sharers through the Spirit in the ecstasy of love by which he is one with the Father. The circle is complete.

For the moment we are landlocked in space and time, but this separation will not be permanent. Like a thief in the night, the hour will come in which we are summoned forth to our eternal destiny. If we have learned well the message of the Gospel, we will live our lives with our eyes fixed on eternity, not allowing ourselves to be weighed down by concern for what is transient and ephemeral. The "ethics" promulgated by the New Testament are designed for this single purpose. They are not primarily a charter for the perfect society on earth, but a map that will guide us to heaven. It is in the same context that the Second Vatican Council spoke about the Church. Chapter Seven of *Lumen Gentium* is grandly entitled: "The Eschatological Composition of the Pilgrim Church and its Union With the Heavenly Church."[3] There is an essential otherworldliness about the Church. What you see is not what you get. Through the energy of the Spirit, there is a hidden presence of Christ that goes beyond the pomp and circumstance of ecclesiastical ceremony, its social utility, or its external teaching function. This mystery is not inaccessible; it is something that can be experienced in faith; otherwise, admittedly, it is hard to demonstrate its reality. It is Christ in us, the hope of glory (Col 1:27). We are, as Jesus phrased it, "children of the resurrection" (Lk 20:36).

What this means baffles our mind and defies our imagination. It has not yet been revealed what we shall be (1 Jn 3:2): "Eye has not seen, nor ear heard, nor has it arisen in the human heart [to conceive] what God has prepared for those who love him" (1 Cor 2:9). It is hard to commit ourselves to something we cannot conceptualize. It is even harder to communicate what we believe to others when we cannot draw them a picture or explain it logically. I suppose that is why it is said that religion is caught and not taught. It makes no sense until you get inside it or, perhaps, until it gets inside you.

The way that this impinges on our experience is through a desire that seems permanently unsatisfied despite a lifetime's efforts to seek to gratify it. If it is true that we are made for God, then it is unsurprising that our hearts are restless until they find rest and completion in God. Desire was one of the main themes of Western spirituality during the first millennium or so.[4] The famous medieval scholar Jean Leclercq has typified the spirit of the monasticism that stemmed from the Rule of Saint Benedict in the title of his book, *The Love of Learning and the Desire for God*.[5] For ourselves, we will find it a useful exercise to sound our depths and to ask what is it that we most passionately seek.

The theological term "desire for God" can be replaced by "desire for heaven"; for what we feel is a yearning for the fullness of life and an end to the limitations, compromises, and struggles that characterize our present existence. Eternity has been defined as the complete and simultaneous possession of life, whereas our hold on life in this present mode of existence is fragmentary and impermanent. All our desires to acquire and accumulate stem from our insecurity about life itself. We want to do more than survive: we want to have life abundantly.

Many of us, nowadays, feel a little naive if we say in public that our Christian life is based on the hope of heaven. We sense that many think such a belief is childish and on a level with believing in Santa Claus. Popular images of clouds, white nighties, and harps scarcely help. Others regard looking forward to the "rewards" of heaven as being too mercenary and claim themselves as adherents of a more disinterested religion. Still others prefer a vague agnosticism, fearful lest any thought of the existence of heaven might conjure up the prospect of the existence of hell. So mostly we keep quiet about heaven. Few sermons are preached about it, and it scarcely merits a mention in catechesis. We are almost ashamed of our belief in heaven and so tend to concentrate on the more "reasonable" aspects of Christianity like morality, doing good to others, and social justice.

The resurrection of Jesus means that our resurrection is possible also. Jesus did not simply leave his humanity behind and return to the state in which he existed prior to the Incarnation. Jesus rose in his humanity. Our resurrection is, therefore, something for which it is not unreasonable to hope. The Nicene Creed, as it is recited at Mass, includes a profession of faith in the "resurrection of the dead." The "Apostles' Creed" is more explicit, "I believe...in the resurrection of the body and life everlasting." The resurrection for which we hope is not some thinned-out version of our present life; it is the bringing together into an intense and eternal instant every moment of life and fulfillment that has been imperfectly experienced here below. Heaven is infinitely richer that the half-life to which we are accustomed; the frontiers between self and others are fully open and there is no time and space to attenuate what we feel. If we really believe, we cannot help ourselves desiring eternal life with all the affective energy of our being.

If we desire that communion with God which is characteristic of heavenly existence, we have to live our earthly lives as citizens of heaven (Phil 3:20). Our desire is to become the guide to how we behave.

Since you have been coresurrected with Christ, seek
what is above, where Christ is seated at the right of
God. Fill your mind with what is above, not with things
here on earth. You are dead and your life is hidden
with Christ in God (Col 3:1–3).

The heart will linger in the place where its most cherished
possessions are to be found. Fundamentally, this is a spiritual
connection that is not reducible to any particular experience,
devotion, exercise, or activity—although it may subsist and
express itself in any of them. What Saint John calls the inner
anointing (1 Jn 2:27) trains us by a double-sided dynamism,
secretly attaching us to God and simultaneously detaching us
from the false self, as this is mirrored to us by an unbelieving
ambience. Saint John says that this anointing teaches us everything; this is not so much an imparting of theological information as a deep affective bonding that retrains our instincts and
gives us a nose to distinguish what is of God and what is not.

Mostly, the inward workings of grace are beyond our awareness. They may make an appearance on the surface of the mind
in the experience of conversion, for example, or vocation and
we can recognize their influence in the intense and profound
feelings that sometimes interrupt and sometimes permeate our
attempts to pray. There is often a profound Christocentric
component in this spiritual affectivity that is substantially distinct from pious enthusiasm, sentimentality, or even a clan-
destine erotic or homoerotic attachment to the person of Jesus.
It is a strong sense of affinity, connaturality, solidarity, being
with. A sense of finding oneself in the person of Jesus, but in a
manner that is different from the fervor experienced earlier in
our journey. It is calm, quiet, sober, self-forgetful, energizing,
compassionate, and effective. It is perhaps best described by
all those verbs that Saint Paul invented with the prefix *syn-*.[6]
Our ultimate union with God in the Spirit and with or through

the Second Person of the Trinity begins to be realized in the life of grace here below. The same meaning attaches to Paul's use of the phrase "in-Christ." There is a certain interpenetration of being that changes the quality of what we are and what we do. "I live, but it is not I that lives but Christ lives in me" (Gal 2:20). This is why quantitative judgments do not apply, and a cup of cold water given in mindfulness becomes sufficient payment to enter the Kingdom. In a participative sense, our actions too become theandric, as those of Jesus were. In what we are and in what we do, divinity and humanity overlap, coincide, work together for good. Our longing for heaven goes hand in hand with doing good here on earth.

We were originally formed in God's image and likeness. Deformed by sin though we are, we can allow ourselves to be reformed and transformed by being conformed to Christ. Thus Isaac of Stella encouraged his monks.

> Let this be for you the form of life, brothers, this is the true discipline of a holy way of life: to live *with Christ* by having your thought and desire [fixed] on the eternal homeland, and in this troublesome journey to refuse no task of charity *for Christ*. Follow the Lord Christ upwards towards the Father and by making time for meditation reduce, simplify, and unify [your life]. Follow Christ downwards to your brother, letting yourself be stretched by action, divided into many parts, and becoming all things to all people. Never consider anything associated with Christ to be of little value and hold nothing dear except for Christ's sake. Where Christ is one, thirst after one thing, make time for one thing. Where Christ is manifold, be willing to be of service to all.[7]

The hidden dynamism of God's action in our lives leaves
its imprint in a strong, interpersonal, hope-filled anticipation
of our definitive sharing in the resurrection of Jesus. We who
in our own small way have borne a portion of the sufferings
of Christ are called to be coheirs of his Kingdom, and to become, in the fullest possible sense, sharers in the divine nature. We are called to divinization, and the promise of God is
certain. If we were to fill our minds more often with this
thought, no doubt our journey would seem less wearisome.

Bernard of Clairvaux preached a strong devotion to heaven.
In one of his sermons, he includes a short lyrical acclamation
that compresses his theology into a few lines. Heaven is a place
where all that is good becomes so intensely present that whatever remains of past evil dries up and disappears. Heaven lacks
impermanence; it lasts forever. In heaven, the best of each of
the four seasons combines. Heaven has the intense simplicity
of the noonday sun; it is the ultimate solstice, lasting forever,
it is the coming together of apparent opposites: all the seasons
of life coexist in a single moment of being.

> *An Ode to Eternal Day*
> O true noon-day
> when warmth and light are at their peak
> and the sun at its zenith
> and no shadows fall;
> when stagnant waters dry up
> and their fetid odors disperse.
>
> O never-ending solstice
> when daylight lasts forever.

O noon-day light,
marked with the mildness of spring,
stamped with summer's bold beauty,
enriched with autumn's fruit—
and lest I seem to forget—
calm with winter's rest from toil.[8]

We are divinized to the extent that nothing of our humanity is denied, despised, or ignored, when nothing of what makes
us human is lost or left behind. Just as God's Son left behind
nothing of his divinity during his sojourn on earth, so we will
carry to eternal life everything in our lives that is genuinely
human. May the humanity of Jesus inspire us to accept our
own humanity in all its present ambiguity, so that through
him and with him and in him we may become, in a manner
that is beyond our imagination, full sharers in his divinity.

Notes

Preface

1. Although the term "divinization" is noticeably absent in contemporary religious discourse, it has a long history in Christian spirituality. Its importance can be judged by the fact that a recent reference volume devotes eighty-nine columns to the theme, tracing its development from the earliest times until the seventeenth century. See Charles Baumgartner, et. al., [ed.], *Dictionnaire de Spiritualité, Tome III* (Paris: Beauchesne, 1967) 1370–1459. The notion is central to the present work since it offers a unique theological perspective to the discussion of spirituality.

Introductory Note

1. A useful anthology of Cistercian texts has been compiled by Pauline Matarasso. *The Cistercian World: Monastic Writings of the Twelfth century* (Harmondsworth: Penguin Classics, 1993). Since 1970, several hundred books have been published by Cistercian Publications, Kalamazoo, Michigan.

Chapter One

1. This expression occurs in the late fifth-century Latin Creed *Quicumque*, wrongly attributed to Saint Athanasius. See [H. Denziger and] A. Schönmetzer, *Enchiridion symbolorum, definitionum et declarationum de rebus fidei et morum* [=DS] (Freiburg: Herder, 1973), #76. The formulation reflects the Greek "Formula of Union" drawn up by John of Antioch and

agreed to by Cyril of Alexandria in 433 and sanctioned by Pope Sixtus III (DS 272). It was later rephrased slightly and incorporated in the Creed of the Council of Chalcedon quoted at the head of this chapter (DS 301).

2. The term "condescension" is much used by Greek theology. Its basic meaning is the kindness or "philanthropy" of God in stooping down to our level; it does not imply a patronizing attitude towards humanity.

3. *Sermon for Epiphany* 1,1; SBOp 4, 293, 6–9.

4. This approach is found in many Fathers of the Church who have developed the Genesis theme of humanity as created in the image and likeness of God. Human dignity derives from our being compatible with God and our capacity, through grace, to be continually reformed to a higher level of likeness to God.

5. Origen of Alexandria, *Contra Celsum* 3, 28; PG 11, 956d.

6. "What use was the descent of the Son of God if the only one to ascend was the same Son of Man?" Isaac of Stella, *Sermons* 42.6; SChr 339, p. 40. The following text is difficult to render into inclusive language without losing some of its conciseness. "To the degree that God, the Son of God, emptied himself to become man, to that degree the Man, the son of man, is exalted so that he might become God." *Sermons* 28,12; SChr 207, p. 158.

7. The preposition is ἀντί; thus Exodus 21:24, Leviticus 24:20, Deuteronomy 19:21, cited in Matthew 5:38.

8. Isaac of Stella, *Sermons* 42,14–15; SChr 339, p. 49. I have simplified one sentence slightly and have made the language more inclusive.

9. John Paul II, *Incarnationis Mysterium*, 2 (29 November 1998).

10. As Friedrich Schleiermacher remarked in 1799, *On Religion: Speeches to Its Cultured Despisers,* translated by John Oman (San Francisco: Harper and Row, 1958), p. 31.

11. Martin Marty speaks of the churches as "agencies of boredom." "The Nature and Consequences of Social Conflict for Religious Groups," in Robert Lee and Martin E. Marty, *Religion and Social Conflict* (New York: Oxford University Press, 1964), p. 183. In Australia the 2001 National Church Life poll found

that 42 percent of respondents cited boredom as the reason why they did not go to church more often. Quoted in *The Age* (2 July 2002), News p. 8.

12. Thus Cyril of Alexandria: "Everything that comes about in Christ comes about on account of us" (*In Ioann* 12; PG 74, 628) and "Everything that comes about in Christ is for us" (*Thesaurus* 20; PG 75, 333).

13. This is expressed pithily in the Opening Prayer for the Seventh Sunday of the year: "Father, keep before us the wisdom and love you have revealed in your Son. Help us to be like him in word and deed."

14. [1:1], 1:11, 3:11, 5:7, 9:7, (12:6), 14:61, 15:39.

15. Adopting the more difficult variant of the Codex Bezae.

16. Aelred of Rievaulx suggests that Jesus' contemporaries may have despised him for his lack of glamor. "They saw him as a poor man, as one who fled the glory of the world rather than seeking it, as hungry, thirsty. So they despised him, thinking that he was...without the light of deity, just like other people." *Sermons* 26,27; CCM 2A, p. 216.

17. Thus Tertullian, *De resurrectione carnis* 8; PL 2, 852a. The whole passage reads as follows. "Let us see the particular relationship [of the flesh] in Christianity, and how greatly privileged this slight and sordid substance is with God. We could simply say that it is impossible for the soul to obtain salvation unless it comes to faith while it is still in the flesh. **The flesh is the hinge of salvation.** When the soul is bonded to God, it is by means of the flesh that it is so bonded. The flesh is washed so that the soul may be cleansed from stain; the flesh is anointed so that the soul may be consecrated; [with a cross] the flesh is signed so that the soul may be strengthened; the flesh is overshadowed by the imposition of hands so that the soul may be enlightened by the Spirit; the flesh is fed with the body and blood of Christ so that the soul may be fattened on God." See also Cyprian Vagaggini, *The Flesh: Instrument of Salvation* (New York: Alba House, 1969), pp. 76–79.

18. Thus Gregory Nazianzen, in his letter to Cledonius (PG 37, 181): Τὸ γὰρ ἀπρόσληπτον, ἀθεράπευτον. Under the form: *Quod*

non est assumptum, non est sanatum, this sentence became axiomatic in later Christology.

Chapter Two

1. J.-P. Sartre, *Being and Nothingness,* translated by Hazel E. Barnes (London: Methuen, 1957), pp. 47–70. The characteristic element in bad faith is that it is precisely because I know the truth and find it distasteful that I seek to conceal it from myself. As an example, Sartre discusses (pp. 55–56) the process of seduction whereby there is a concerted effort not to look beyond the facticity of each moment or each action. There is a refusal to attend to the meaning, direction, or finality of what is happening, even though this is perfectly obvious even to the most casual observer. The result is that a point of no return is reached before any decision is made. Afterwards any memory of complicity in the outcome is suppressed or repressed.

2. The Council of Carthage (A.D. 418) insisted that saints remain sinners. Contrary to the perfectionist tendencies of some African churches, the Council reaffirmed that the saints continue to rely on the mercy of God. "It pleased the assembly: Anyone who wants [to believe] that when we say in the Lord's Prayer 'forgive us our trespasses,' the saints say this out of humility and not in truth, *let them be anathema*. Who could bear someone lying at prayer, not to people but to the Lord himself? This is what is done by those who say with their lips that they want forgiveness while in their hearts they say that they have no trespasses to be forgiven" (Canon 8; DS 230). See also M. Casey, *A Guide to Living in the Truth: Saint Benedict's Teaching on Humility* (Liguori, Mo.: Liguori/Triumph, 2001), p. 182.

3. Matt Ridley, "The Honorary Animal," *Times Literary Supplement* No. 4863 (14 June 1996), p. 4.

4. Far from being a dualistic rejection of the material body in favor of a spiritual soul, this approach, which owes much to ancient monasticism, insists not only on the essential interrelatedness of body and soul, but on the necessity of beginning the active aspects of spiritual life at the level of the flesh. See Peter Brown, *The Body and Society: Men, Women and Sexual Renunciation*

in Early Christianity (London: Faber, 1988). "Life in the desert revealed, if anything, the inextricable interdependence of body and soul....The ebb and flow of sexual energy was consistently presented, by Evagrius and John Cassian, as a symptom that reflected, in the obscure but crucial frontier-zone between body and spirit, changes that happened deep in the soul....In the desert tradition, the body was allowed to become the discreet mentor of the proud soul....The rhythms of the body and, with the body, his concrete social relations, determined the life of the monk....Of all the lessons of the desert to a late antique thinker, what was most "'truly astonishing' was 'that the immortal spirit can be purified and refined by clay' [John Climacus]," (pp. 236–237). Brown notes that, according to the Desert Fathers, the reason for this was that the "body" was not the principal problem. "It was the human will, sensed by the monk as an impacted mass of willfullness lodged at the very bottom of his heart, and not the malleable 'clay' of the body itself, that stood 'like a brazen wall' between the monk and God" (p. 226). In the same sense, see Jean-Guy Nadeau, "Dichotomy or Union of Soul and Body? The Origins of the Ambivalence of Christianity to the Body," *Concilium* 2002/2; pp. 57–65. "Several of [the Church Fathers] expressed a scorn for the body, but once again this was precisely because of its intimate connection with the soul: whatever affects, pollutes, or purifies the body affects, pollutes, or purifies the soul. For the fathers, bodily experience retains a crucial importance for determining salvation" (p. 61). Also Robert H. von Thaden, Jr., "The Redemptive Role of the Body in Early Christian Ascetic Literature," *Cistercian Studies Quarterly* 38.2 (2003), pp. 191–210. Certain strands of Buddhism seem to advocate a radically more negative approach to the body. See Bhikku Khantipalo, *Bag of Bones: A Miscellany on the Body* (Kandy: Buddhist Publication Society, 1980).

5. "We read the texts of tradition through the filter of Cartesian dualism, which promotes a disenchanted, mechanical, and functional vision of the body 'devoid of any spiritual essence or expressive dimension.'" Nadeau, "Dichotomy or Union of Soul and Body," p. 58.

6. For Saint Augustine, the fact that the body reacts reflexively to sexual stimulation (whether welcome or unwelcome), independent of any act of the will is a sign that the rule of will over the flesh is precarious and incomplete. This working antipathy comes to a climax in death where "soul" and "body" are separated. *Literal Commentary on Genesis* 9, 9, 17; PL 34, 399; *The City of God* 14, 15; CChr 48, p. 437.

7. Augustine, *De nuptiis et concupiscentia*, 1, 25; PL 44, 430b.

8. Saint Augustine reminds us not to forget how we used to be so that we do not despair of those who are now as we were in the past. *On Psalm 50* 24; CChr 38, p. 615.

9. "I was an ambassador ordered abroad by some fragile coalition, a bearer of conflicting orders from the easy masters of a divided empire." W. D. Hamilton, *Narrow Roads of Gene Land*, quoted by Matt Ridley, "The Honorary Animal," *Times Literary Supplement* No. 4863 (14 June 1996), p. 3.

10. The Greek text contrasts ἐνδημοῦντες with ἐκδημοῦμεν both here and in verse 9 to indicate the diametrical opposition between being "in the body" and being "with the Lord" (apart from the body).

11. Thus interpreting the Genesis stories of our primal state also as evocations of a future and final blessedness. Scholars tell us that in such mythic compositions the imaginative description of origins, the *Urzeit* (the original state), was intended to reveal the shape of things to come, the *Endzeit*. It is interesting that in popular parlance the name "Paradise" is attributed to both.

12. The false facade is particularly prevalent among those who are supposed to be professionally good. This is why the moral collapse of the sanctimonious clergymen in such novels as Jane Austen's *Pride and Prejudice*, William Golding's *Rites of Passage,* and Somerset Maugham's *Rain* are cause for secret celebration. Every day millions scour the tabloid newspapers in the hope of discovering new evidence that other supposed paragons of virtue are not as good as they should be.

13. Thus Joachim Jeremias, *New Testament Theology, Volume One* (London: S.C.M. Press, 1971), pp. 147–148. Casuistry, which views the individual sin in isolation, and the idea of meritorious

works that compensate for sins devalue sin as rebellion against God and lead to the smug self-righteousness that is often described as "pharisaic."

14. I have written about this in *Toward God: The Ancient Wisdom of Western Prayer* (Liguori,Mo.: Liguori/Triumph, 1996) pp. 105–117.

Chapter Three

1. Pope John Paul II, *Reconciliatio et Paenitentia* (Post-Synodal Apostolic Exhortation of 2 December 1984), #16. "To speak of *social sin* means in the first place to recognize that, by virtue of a human solidarity which is as mysterious and intangible as it is real and concrete, each individual's sin in some way affects others. This is the other aspect of that solidarity which on the religious level is developed in the profound and magnificent mystery of the *Communion of Saints*, thanks to which it has been possible to say that 'every soul that rises above itself, raises up the world.' To this *law of ascent* there unfortunately corresponds the *law of descent*. Consequently one can speak of a *communion of sin*, whereby a soul that lowers itself through sin drags down with itself the Church and, in some way, the whole world. In other words, there is no sin, not even the most intimate and secret one, the most strictly individual one, that exclusively concerns the person committing it. With greater or less violence, with greater or less harm, every sin has repercussions on the entire ecclesial body and the whole human family."

2. "What would it mean for me to have eternal life if death were the lot of your people?" Thus Catherine of Siena (d. 1380), *The Dialogue* 13; translated by Suzanne Noffke, OP, in The Classics of Western Spirituality series (New York: Paulist Press, 1980), p. 49.

3. John 1:29. In both Greek and Latin, the verb used has two meanings, both of them true. Jesus bears the world's sin; he also removes it. This is an important text for the twelfth-century Cistercian theologian Isaac of Stella who expands it thus: *Agnus Dei qui tollit quae pertulit peccata mundi*, "the Lamb of God who removes the sins of the world which he carried" (Sermon

42.18; SChr 339, p. 52). The notion of redemption through solidarity is central for Isaac. See Leonard Gaggero, "Isaac of Stella and the Theology of Redemption," in COCR 22 (1960), pp. 21–36. This seems to be based on A. Piolanti, "*De nostra in Christo solidaritate praecipua Isaac de Stella testimonia,*" in *Euntes Docete* 2 (1949), pp. 349–369.

4. Translated by Derwas J. Chitty, *The Letters of St. Antony the Great* (Fairacres Publications 50; Oxford: SLG Press, 1975), p. 26.

5. Thus the Roman poet Terence (195–159 B.C.): *Homo sum— humani nil a me alienum puto* (in *Heauton timoroumenos,* 25). Pope Paul VI applied this saying to the Church as an explanation of its catholicity in a homily preached on Pentecost Sunday 1964. *Per celebrare* of 17 May 1964 translated in *The Pope Speaks* 10 (1964), p. 79.

6. Thus Saint Augustine, *On the Psalms* 29:2.1; CChr 38, p. 174.

7. "The cause of Christ's coming to baptism was to join humanity to God." Isaac of Stella, *Sermons* 48.12; SChr 339, p. 162.

8. This was why the Baptist speaks of a great inner change (*metánoia*), and Paul speaks of "a new creation" (2 Cor 5:17) and "newness of life" (Rom 6:4). First the old order must be terminated.

9. Christ's death is later described as a "baptism" (Mk 10:32, see Lk 12:50). Saint Paul, perhaps echoing a fragment of early liturgy, clearly links baptismal immersion with entombment: "We have been jointly buried with Christ through baptism into death" (Rom 6:4).

10. Mark has the graphic word "split" to describe what happened to the sky. Luke 3:21 and Matthew 3:16 have "open," and some manuscripts of Matthew add the words "to him [Jesus]." In these cases the opening of the sky enables downward traffic. In Acts 7:56, the movement is upwards. The sky opens and Stephen sees.

11. See 1 John 1:10.

Chapter Four

1. Baldwin of Forde: *Spiritual Tractates* VI (CFS 38; Kalamazoo, Mich.: Cistercian Publications, 1986), p. 169.

2. The method of doing this can be oblique: "...among the upper classes, extreme politeness is merely the most highly refined expression of one's scorn for others." Arturo Perez Reverte, *The Flanders Panel* (London: Harvill, 1997), p. 32.

Chapter Five

1. "There is no more manifest pointer to a heavenly origin than maintaining one's inborn likeness even in this region of unlikeness, than the glory of the celibate life being lived on earth by an exile, than one living as an angel in a body which is almost that of the beasts. These things derive from heavenly not from earthly possibility; they indicate that the soul which is capable of them is truly from heaven." Bernard of Clairvaux, *Sermons on the Song of Songs* 27, 6; SBOp 1, 185, 22–26.

2. Borrowing an image from the Platonising tradition, Saint Augustine and others spoke about this present life as existing in the "region of unlikeness," *regio dissimilitudinis*. Instead of acting out of God's likeness in which we were created, we choose alternative models and so lose the divine likeness and thus become deformed.

3. In Saint Athanasius' *Life of Antony*, the saint is tormented by bestial specters. "All at once the place was filled with the phantoms of lions, bears, leopards, bulls, and of serpents, asps, and scorpions and wolves" (8). "At night [the visitors] saw the mountain alive with wild beasts. They also saw [Antony] fighting as with visible foes, and praying against them....And it was truly remarkable that, alone as he was in such a wilderness, he was neither dismayed by the attacks of the demons, nor, with all the animals and creeping things there, did he fear their savageness. But as Scripture has it, he truly *trusted in the Lord like Mount Sion*, with a mind unshaken and unruffled. Thus the demons rather fled from him, and the wild beasts, as it is written, kept peace with him" (51). Translated by Robert B. Meyer, *St. Athanasius: The Life of Anthony* (ACW 10; New York: Newman Press, 1978), pp. 28, 64.

Chapter Six

1. Thus *The Testament of Reuben* 3:1–9a.

2. *The Rule of the Community* (or *The Manual of Discipline*) 3,13–4,26. Translated by Florentino García Martínez, *The Dead Sea Scrolls Translated: The Qumran Texts in English* (Leiden: Brill, 1994), pp. 6–7.

3. Gregory of Nyssa seems to have been of the opinion that the notion of all having two personal spirits was a part of the deposit of faith transmitted by the Fathers. See *The Life of Moses* Th II 45 SChr 1bis, p. 43–44.

4. For an explanation of this term and a rich description of the world to which it refers, see Jean Daniélou, *A History of Early Christian Doctrine; Volume One: The Theology of Jewish Christianity* (London: Darton, Longman and Todd, 1964).

5. Thus *Didache* 1,8; the *Letter of Barnabas* 18–20. Other texts of this period that seem familiar with this theme include the *Apostolic Constitutions*, the so-called Letters of Clement and *The Shepherd of Hermas*.

6. Thus Isaac of Stella, *Sermon* 43.8; SChr 339, p. 66. Here he identifies the vices with particular "demons." See also *Sermon* 38.6; SChr 207, p. 308.

7. The persistence of this theme, even in the popular imagination, can be seen from an episode of the comic strip "Li'l Abner" that appeared in *The International Herald Tribune* on 20 March 1972. The text runs thus: "When each child is born it is accompanied by **two elves**—a **rotten** elf and a **good guy** elf. Nobody can **see** them, but children can **hear** them!! For years they fight it out and then on his seventh birthday **one wins!!** And the world has a good guy or a **swine!!**"

8. *The Shepherd of Hermas*, Sixth Precept, 36; SChr 53, p. 172.

9. Origen, *In Num Hom* 6:3; SChr 29, pp. 125–126.

10. Origen, *In Iesu Nave* 15:5; SChr 71, p. 348.

11. Evagrius of Pontus, *Praktikos* 6; SChr 171, p. 508. An English translation preceded by an excellent introduction, both by John Eudes Bamberger, was published by Cistercian Publications in 1970.

12. *Praktikos* 6–14; SChr 171, pp. 506–535. Note that Evagrius, although he sometimes used "demon," preferred the term "thought." John Cassian, who expanded on Evagrius' scheme in Books V–XII of his *Institutes* and transmitted it to the Latin Church used not only "spirit" but also the term "vice." Usually vice is considered to be the opposite of virtue and as such is a habit. That is to say it is not so much the universal effect of human nature but the reprehensible residue of past actions or sins. Saint Gregory the Great externalized the eight vices further and spoke of the "seven deadly sins" (*Moralia* 31, 87). The next and longer section of Evagrius' work discusses strategies for dealing with the eight "thoughts," *Praktikos* 15–39; SChr 171, pp. 536–591.

13. "Avarice puts before us the prospect of a lengthy old age, the powerlessness of our hands [to work], the likelihood of famines, the illnesses to which we will be subject, the bitterness of poverty and the shame of having to receive what we need from others." *Praktikos* 9; SChr 171, p. 512.

14. The verb "to care" with negative connotations appear six times in one section of the Sermon on the Mount (Mt 6:25–34; there are three occurrences in Luke 12:22–26). There are other important texts such as the Mary and Martha episode (Lk 10:41), Saint Paul's discussion of celibacy (1 Cor 7:32–34). Two particularly significant texts are Luke 21:34: "Beware lest your hearts be weighed down by gluttony, drunkenness, and the cares of life" and 1 Peter 5:7: "Casting all your care upon [God] who is concerned about you."

15. *The Shepherd of Hermas*, 40, 2; SChr 53, p. 186. In a later section (42, 2; p. 191), Hermas explains why this is so. "The sad always do evil: firstly by saddening the Holy Spirit who is cheerful and who is given to us; secondly, they sadden the Holy Spirit by committing sin and by not coming near to God and giving praise. The prayer of the sad never has the power to rise up to God's altar…because sadness has taken its seat in their hearts."

16. *Praktikos* 11; SChr 171, p. 516.

17. *Praktikos* 38; SChr 171, p. 586.

18. S. Giora Shoham, *Society and the Absurd* (Oxford: Blackwell, 1974). See also M. Casey, art. "Acedia," in Michael Downey [ed.] *The New Dictionary of Catholic Spirituality* (Collegeville, Minn.: Michael Glazier, 1993), pp. 4–5.

19. *Praktikos* 13; SChr 171, p. 528.

20. See M. Casey, *A Guide to Living in the Truth*, pp. 1–2.

21. *Praktikos* 14; SChr 171, p. 534.

22. *Praktikos* 8; SChr 171, p. 510.

23. "What is called 'induction' is not confined to the lower levels of the brain and the nervous system. It also takes place in the cortex and is the physical basis of that ambivalence of sentiment which is so striking a feature of man's psychological life. Every positive begets its corresponding negative. The sight of something red is followed by a green after-image. The opposing muscle groups involved in any action automatically bring another one into play. And on a higher level, we find such things as a hatred that accompanies love, a derision begotten by respect and awe. Sister Jane and her fellow nuns had had religion and chastity drummed into them from childhood. By induction, these lessons had called into existence within the brain and its associated mind, a psychophysical center from which there emanated lessons in irreligion and obscenity. (Every collection of spiritual letters abounds in references to those frightful temptations against the faith and against chastity to which seekers after perfection are peculiarly subject. Good directors point out that such temptations are a normal and almost inevitable feature of the spiritual life and must not be permitted to cause undue distress.)" Aldous Huxley, *The Devils of Loudun* (Harmondsworth: Penguin, 1971), pp. 188–189.

24. *On Psalm 41* 18; CChr 38, p. 473.

25. "So it happens that even if he lifts himself up to pursue the highest realities, then suddenly driven by a slippery capacity for change he falls down into himself. He wishes to stand in contemplation, but he cannot. He tries to shape the path of his thought, but he is unmanned by the falls his weakness brings about." Gregory the Great, *Moralia* 8, 8; CChr 143, p. 386.

26. See M. Casey, *A Guide to Living in the Truth*, pp. 125–140.

Chapter Seven

1. In the Deuteronomic history (2 Kings 4:9), Elijah is reverently described by the Shunammite woman as "the holy man-of-God." In Sirach 45:6, Aaron is described as "a holy man like [Moses]." In the apocryphal Fourth Book of Maccabees, composed about the time of Jesus or later, Eleazar (7:4) and the seven martyred youths (14:7) are eulogized as all-holy (πανάγιος). There are also those described in Job, in the Psalms and elsewhere as "the holy ones," but these beings are probably "the sons of God," the members of the heavenly court. We would probably call them "angels."

2. Apart from the present text = Luke 4:34, this predication is found only at Luke 1:35, Acts 3:7, 4:27, 4:30, and John 6:69, 1 John 2:20, Revelation 3:7. Note, however, that the members of the Christian community are frequently referred to as "the saints" and in 1 Peter 3:5, the term is applied to Sara and other women of sacred history.

3. The word translated as "power," ἐξουσία, could equally be rendered "authority," since, throughout the Gospel, Mark exploits the double meaning of the word; in the present instance, the violent physical aspect is more important than its legal status.

Chapter Eight

1. John Cassian, *Conferences* 2.2; SChr 42, p. 113. See Columba Stewart, *Cassian the Monk*, p. 44: "Cassian knew that obsession with 'perfect' monastic observance can lead to despair and abandonment of the monastic life, or to anger (a most fatal passion) or to a judgmental stance towards others."

2. Thus Isaac of Stella, *Sermons* 48, 9–11; SChr 339, pp. 160–162. "Sad to say, nearly all evil acts grow on good things. Virtues nourish vices and when these grow up a little, the virtues are weakened and absorbed by them. This is why, my dear friends, there is a need for frequent caution; we must be circumspect. All events, whether good or bad, are preceded by causes which bring them about, matrices which prepare and nourish the manner of their development. There are certain

warning signs when they are about to happen....Nothing occurs without a reason. Nothing is confused. Nothing is sudden. Sometimes all that brings about these things is hidden from all poor mortals, sometimes everything is clear to all, and sometimes it is clear to some and hidden from others."

3. Brian Keenan, who was kidnapped in Lebanon and held captive for more than four years, recounts the sad history of a young Maronite who was forced by his family to kill his sister who had become pregnant to a Muslim. So split off did his action become that the murderer himself was convinced that his sister had been slain by Muslims and progressively worked himself up into a frenzy of revenge, with ultimately tragic consequences. See *An Evil Cradling* (London: Vintage, 1993), pp. 136–137.

4. "The only ones who do not fall into unlawful acts are those who sometimes restrain themselves in matters that are lawful." Gregory the Great, *Moral Exposition on the Book of Job* 5, 11, 17; CChr 143, p. 230.

5. For clarification on this point see Karl Rahner, "The Theological Concept of Concupiscentia," in *Theological Investigations: Volume One, God, Christ, Mary and Grace* (London: Darton, Longman & Todd, 1974), pp. 347–382. See also J. P. Kenny, "The Problem of Concupiscence: A Recent Theory of Professor Karl Rahner," *The Australasian Catholic Record* 29 (1952), pp. 290–304 and 30 (1953), pp. 23–32.

6. For a dense but worthwhile consideration on this point, see Rahner, "Concupiscentia," pp. 360–369. "In the concrete man of the present order, free personal decision and self-determination are not capable of perfectly and exhaustively determining the operative subject throughout the whole extent of his real being....In the course of its self-determination, the person undergoes the resistance of the nature given prior to freedom, and never wholly succeeds in making all that man is into all that he comprehends himself to be in the core of his person. There is much in man which always remains in concrete fact somehow impersonal: impenetrable and unilluminated for his existential decision; merely endured and not freely acted out. It is this dualism

between person and nature, insofar as it arises from the dualism of matter and spirit and not from man's finitude, the dualism of essence and existence and the real distinction of his powers given with it, that we call concupiscence in the theological sense....Concupiscence consists essentially in the fact that man in this regime does not overcome even by his free decision the dualism between what he is as nature prior to his existential decision and what he becomes as person by this decision" (pp. 368–369).

7. "Carnal concupiscence is not only the punishment for Adam's sin of disobedience, but a defect which makes a person disobedient to his higher aspirations and the command of God." J. Patout Burns, *The Development of Augustine's Doctine of Operative Grace* (Paris: Études Augustiniennes, 1980), p. 106. "This reality can be properly grasped when concupiscence is seen as the dynamism of man's self-assertion against the supernatural. Only thus is concupiscence revealed as it is in the present economy of salvation. It is the rebelliousness of man under sin against his 'supernatural' orientation and his infinite destiny. It is then a negative 'existential' which prevents man's self-realization in terms of his natural-supernatural fulfillment. The comprehensiveness of concupiscence which stems from the revolt against the supernatural order has also natural consequences which display the negative character of concupiscence in the whole field of human nature and not just in sensuality....It cannot be treated as a fixed objective entity. It is a fluctuating movement which is constantly being thwarted by the tendency of the will to the good and the realization of this tendency through grace." Leo Scheffczyk, art. "Concupiscence," in *Sacramentum Mundi: An Encyclopedia of Theology* (London: Search Press, 1968); Vol. 1, p. 404.

8. Scheffczyk, "Concupiscence," p. 405.

9. Baldwin of Forde: *Spiritual Tractates* VI, trans. Bell, p. 169. See Nadeau, "Dichotomy or Union of Soul and Body" p. 58: "We have to talk of a dichotomy between salvation and pleasure, particularly sexual pleasure, and not a dichotomy between soul and body." This is not necessarily at odds with the position

taken by Aristotle and Saint Thomas Aquinas that pleasure is the sign of a virtuous action. At this point, however, a discussion of the issue would take us too far afield for our present purposes.

10. Bernard of Clairvaux, *Sentences* 3.2; SBOp 6b.62.1–3.

11. DS 1515.

12. This is a fine sentiment expressed by Gervase Crouchback in a letter to his son in Evelyn Waugh's *Unconditional Surrender* (Harmondsworth: Penguin 1964), p. 17. It is a principle that underlies a lot of Catholic moral theology: malevolence is as much expressed in small crimes as in large; the difference is due to external opportunity and not to a lesser culpability. The Sermon on the Mount makes the same point. See Matthew 5:21–47.

13. *On the Song of Songs* 11:2; SBOp 1.55.12–19.

14. *Mors animae oblivio. Sentences* 2.19; SBOp 6b.29.16–18.

15. See M. Casey, *Sacred Reading: The Ancient Art of Lectio Divina* (Liguori, Mo.: Liguori/Triumph, 1995).

16. William of Saint-Thierry, *Golden Epistle* 122; SChr 223, p. 240.

17. Arnulph of Boheries, *The Mirror of Monks* 4; PL 184, 1178a.

Chapter Nine

1. This can be confirmed by paging through a modern edition of the Bible where poetic passages are distinguished typographically from prose. Metaphorical or nonlogical elements appear in every book of the Scriptures—and cause unceasing trouble to those who wish to translate them or explain them to literal-minded congregations since, as W. H. Auden once remarked, poetry is precisely that part of a text that *cannot* be translated.

2. The moral interpretation given to the parable in Mark 4:13–20 is secondary and should not be allowed to overshadow the primary meaning of the parable, which is a celebration of a bounteous harvest, despite the obstacles encountered.

3. This is clear in the Greek text of Mark, although it is not usually reflected in English translations. One seed falls on the road, one on the rocks, and one among briars, the rest fall on good soil and bring forth fruit abundantly. The secondary and presumably later passage in Mark 4:13–20 has changed the

singulars to plurals. Luke 8:5–7 has maintained Mark's usage and even strengthened it by using "one...another...another." Matthew has all categories of seed in the plural as also, in early Christian literature, the Gospel of Thomas 9, and First Clement 24:5. On the other hand, Justin has all singulars (*Dialogues* 125.1–2).

4. This is the theme of the "messianic secret" publicized by Wilhelm Wrede (1859–1906) and subsequently much discussed by expositors of this Gospel. See his book *The Messianic Secret* (Cambridge: James Clark, 1971).

5. Thus Matthew 6:25, Luke 10:41, 1 Peter 5:7. The Greek concept is not consistently rendered as "care" in the different translations. Some versions, such as the New Revised Standard Version seem to use the term "care" only in the positive senses of being careful or caring.

Chapter Ten

1. John Cassian, *Conferences* 9.19; SChr 54, pp. 57–58.

2. Bernard of Clairvaux, *Letter* 136 to Pope Eugene III; SBOp 7.332.4–8.

3. *L'Osservatore Romano (Weekly Edition in English)* 37 (546), 14 September 1978, p. 8.

4. Gregory the Great *Dialogues* 3, 14, 12; SChr 260, p. 312.

5. Gregory the Great *Moral Exposition on the Book of Job* 23, 43; PL 76, 227–228.

6. Bernard of Clairvaux, *Sermon on Psalm 90* 4.4; SBOp 4.400–401.

7. Bernard of Clairvaux, *Sermons on Psalm 90* 2, 1–2; SBOp 4.389–390.

8. Bernard of Clairvaux, *Sermons on the Song of Songs* 17, 2; SBOp 1, 99, 14–21.

9. Translated from Julian of Norwich, *Revelation 13* (Ch. 39); Edmund Colledge and James Walsh [ed.], *A Book of Showings to the Anchoress Julian of Norwich* (Toronto: Pontifical Institute of Mediaeval Studies, 1978), pp. 447–448.

10. Translated from Julian of Norwich, *Revelation 14* (Chapter 61), pp. 602–603.

11. Translated from Julian of Norwich, *Revelation 14* (Chapter 48), pp. 501–502.

12. Augustine of Hippo, *On Psalm 36* 2, 11; CChr 38, p. 354. See also 48, 10 (p. 561): "Be prudent, therefore, imitate the ant. As scripture says [Proverbs 6:6, 30:25] gather in summertime so that you may not be hungry in the winter." Also *Sermons* 38, 6; PL 38, 238b: "It is now summer; collect what will be useful for you during the winter."

Chapter Eleven

1. "The dominant view in Mark's Gospel is that Jesus' majesty breaks through already in his earthly ministry, in his authoritative teaching (1:22), and in his exorcisms and healings (1:27, 41; 3:10; 5:1–20; and so on)." Rudolf Schnackenberg, *Jesus in the Gospels: A Biblical Christology* (Louisville: Westminster John Knox Press, 1995), p. 57.

2. Although the narrative seems to have been interrupted by private consultations with the Twelve (Mk 4:10).

3. Isaac of Stella, *Sermons* 15, 8–9; SChr 130, p. 288.

4. Gregory the Great, *Dialogues* II, 8, 2-3; SChr 260, pp. 160-162. Visiting St. Benedict's monastery at Subiaco in the early 1970s, I was assured that I was seeing the raven's lineal descendants (alas, since deceased).

5. Gregory the Great comments, "The virtue of patience never exists when all is well. The one who is genuinely patient is the one who is crushed by adversities and yet never deviates from the directness of hope." *Moralia in Iob* 11, 47; CChr 143A, pp. 612–613.

6. Bernard of Clairvaux, *Parables* 1, 6; SBOp 6b, 265,15–17, based on Psalm 107:26.

7. Augustine of Hippo, *Sermons* 38, 10; PL 38, 240d.

8. Isaac of Stella, *Sermons* 13, 12; SChr 130, p. 268.

9. "The greatest sign of Antony's recovery of the state of Adam was not his taut body. In his very last years, this state was revealed more frequently in the quintessentially fourth-century gift of sociability. He came to radiate such magnetic charm, and openness to all, that any stranger who came upon him, surrounded

by crowds of disciples, visiting monks and lay pilgrims, would know at once, in that dense press of black-garbed figures, which one was the great Antony. He was instantly recognizable as someone whose heart had achieved total transparency to others." Peter Brown, *The Body and Society*, pp. 225–226.

Chapter Twelve

1. Bernard of Clairvaux, *Sentences* 3, 114; SBOp 6b, 204–205.
2. Bernard of Clairvaux, *Sermones varii: in Epiphania* 7; SBOp 6a, 27, 9–20.
3. Bernard of Clairvaux, *On Conversion* 31; SBOp 4, 107–108. The idea of a threefold peace is developed further in *De Diversis* 98; SBOp 6a, 364–365.
4. See M. Casey, "The Virtue of Patience in Western Monastic Tradition," CSQ 21 (1986), pp. 3–23. Reprinted in *The Undivided Heart*, pp. 95–120.
5. As might be expected, the idea of persevering under hardship is frequent in New Testament exhortations. The noun ὑπομονή and its cognate verb used in this sense may be found in the following texts, which together provide a profound overview of this essential quality of discipleship. See Mark 13:13 = Matthew 10:22 = 24:13, Romans 5:3–4, 8:24–25, 12:12, 15:4–5; 1 Corinthians 13:7; 2 Corinthians 1:6, 6:4; 12:12; Colossians 1:11; 1 Thessalonians 1:3; 2 Thessalonians 1:4, 3:5, 1 Timothy 6:11; 2 Timothy 2:10, 2:12; Titus 2:2; Hebrews 10:32, 10:36, 12:1–3, 12:7; James 1:3–4, 1:12, 5:11; 1 Peter 2:20; 2 Peter 1:6; Revelation 1:9, 2:2–3, 2:19, 3:10, 13:10, 14:12. See also the sermon of Saint Augustine "On Restraint and Endurance," *Sermons* 38; PL 38, 233–241.
6. See C. H. Talbot [ed.] *Sermones inediti B. Aelredi Abbatis Rievallensis* (Rome: Editiones Cistercienses, 1952): [No. 20] "Sermo Beate Mariae," pp. 136–144. I have given a brief commentary on this text in *A Guide to Living in the Truth*, pp.114–117.
7. This is a free rendering of a brilliant text of Bernard in Epi 1:2; SBOp 4, 292, 21–22. *Ecce pax non promissa sed missa, non dilatata sed data, non prophetata sed praesentata.*

Chapter Thirteen

1. The full title is *The Virgin spanking the Infant Jesus before three witnesses: André Breton, Paul Eluard and the artist.*

2. *The Infancy Gospel of Thomas* 5:1-3. See M. R. James, *The Apocryphal New Testament* (Oxford: Clarendon Press, 1924), p. 60. In the omitted section, those who complained to Joseph about such arbitrary vengeance are struck blind. A Hereford carol (*The Bitter Withy Carol*) sings of a similar incident which leads up to the penultimate verse: "And Mary mild fetched home her child, / and laid him across her knee, / and with a handful of withy (willow) twigs / she gave him slashes three." See James Fenton, "Giving Offense," *The New York Review of Books* (16 December 1999), pp. 18–23.

3. This is the point that Origen makes in his commentary on Saint Luke's Gospel. "They found him sitting among the teachers, or rather not merely sitting, but seeking knowledge from them and listening" (Hom 18; PG 12, 1818b). "He was a boy learning, not a teacher," as Aelred of Rievaulx notes: *quasi puer discens, non docens. De Iesu puero duodenni* 1, 3; SChr 60, p. 52, 14–15. The same conclusion is reached by Raymond E. Brown, *The Birth of the Messiah: A Commentary on the Infancy Narratives in Matthew and Luke* (London: Geoffrey Chapman, 1977), pp. 474–475.

4. Again in this text we note Mark's linkage of teaching (wisdom) and miracles (powerful deeds).

5. The first part of this citation seems like a proverb, appropriate in a society where sons typically learned their fathers' trades and then continued on in the family business. It was understood that apprentice could learn only gradually what his master had practiced for years. See Matthew 10:24.

Chapter Fourteen

1. In documents emanating from the Vatican there has been a noticeable shift in emphasis in the way the phrase "signs of the times" is interpreted. Originally, about the time of the Council, it had an optimistic connotation and meant the positive indications

of new growth everywhere to be perceived. More latterly, perhaps under the influence of a species of neoapocalypticism, it tends to refer to contemporary manifestations of things best avoided.

2. The example of the billionaire Howard Hughes' bizarre attempts to exclude germs should be a warning to us. Trying to exclude that part of reality which we reject leads progressively to the exclusion of all reality. The final result is madness.

3. Translation in Most Rev. Dr. Healy, *The Life and Writings of St. Patrick* (Melbourne: William P. Linehan, 1905), p. 708.

4. Augustine of Hippo, *Confessions* 9, 8, 18. "Would anything avail against this hidden disease except your healing power, O Lord, that always keeps watch over us?...What did you do, O God? By what means did you effect a cure? How did you restore health? Did you not, by your secret providence, produce from another soul a hard and sharp reproof that served as a scalpel to cut away such rottenness with a single stroke....Just as friends can lead us astray by flattery, so our enemies often correct us by their accusations....You, O Lord, are the ruler of heavenly and earthly spheres; ordering the tumultuous flow of the centuries you divert the course of the torrent for your own purposes, and thus use the sickness of one soul as a means of curing another...."

5. Ignatius of Antioch, *Letter to the Romans* 4, 6, 7; SChr 10, pp. 130, 132–136.

Chapter Fifteen

1. *Conferences* 1.22; SChr 42, p. 107.

2. *Nudus nudum Christum sequi*: this theme will be discussed in a later chapter.

3. Günther Bornkamm, *Jesus of Nazareth* (translated by Irene and Fraser McLuskey with James M. Robinson; New York, Harper & Row, 1960), pp. 57–60. The passage reads in context: "There is nothing in contemporary Judaism which corresponds to the immediacy with which he teaches....What the Gospels report on numerous individual occasions about Jesus' attitude to and influence on the different people he encounters is important in

this context....Every one of the scenes described in the Gospels reveals Jesus' astounding sovereignty in dealing with situations according to the people he encounters....The passages in the Gospels which deal with Jesus' perception and penetrating insight ought to be assembled without fear that this would be merely a sentimental undertaking. In reality, we are here concerned with a most characteristic trait in the historical Jesus, one which is quite accurately confirmed by the nature of his preaching. The Gospels call this patent immediacy of Jesus' sovereign powers his 'authority.'"

Chapter Sixteen

1. Bernard of Clairvaux, *Sermons on the Song of Songs* 26, 1–2; SBOp 1, 69–70. The text is based on Song of Songs 1:4 and Psalm 120:6, both of which mention the "tents of Kedar." Following the interpretation offered by Jerome, the Hebrew word *Kedar* is understood to mean "darkness." See *Liber interpretationis hebraicorum nominum* under "Cedar": CChr 72, p. 63.
2. Augustine of Hippo, *On Psalm 138* 21; CChr 40, p. 2006.
3. Augustine of Hippo, *On Psalm 106* 14; Chr 40, p. 1581.
4. Augustine of Hippo, *On Psalm 50* 24; CChr 38, p. 615.
5. Augustine of Hippo, *On Psalm 99* 13; CChr 39, p. 1402.
6. Augustine of Hippo, *On Psalm 99* 12; CChr 39, p. 1401.

Chapter Seventeen

1. *Deus cuius ineffabile Verbum, angelo nuntiante, virgo immaculata suscepit et domus divinitatis effecta Sancti Spiritus luce repleatur, quaesumus ut nos, eius exemplo, voluntati tuae humiliter adhaerere valeamus.*
2. Karl Rahner defines human beings in terms of their being able to receive the gratuitous revelation of God. See *Hearers of the Word* (New York: Herder and Herder, 1969).
3. *Sermons for the First Sunday after Epiphany* 1, 2; SBOp 4, 315, 14–17.

Chapter Eighteen

1. "The spirituality of the future will not be supported or at any rate will be much less supported by a sociologically Christian homogeneity of its situation; it will have to live much more clearly out of a solitary immediate experience of God and his Spirit in the individual....That is why the modern spirituality of the Christian involves courage for solitary decision contrary to public opinion....It has already been pointed out that the Christian of the future will be a mystic or he will not exist at all. If by mysticism we mean, not singular parapsychological phenomena, but a genuine experience of God emerging from the very heart of our existence, this statement is very true and its truth and importance will become increasingly clearer in the spirituality of the future." "The Spirituality of the Church of the Future," in *Theological Investigations: Volume XX: Concern for the Church*, translated by Edward Quinn (London: Darton, Longman & Todd, 1981), pp. 148–149.

2. Bernard of Clairvaux, *On Grace and Free Choice* 15; SBOp 3, 177, 4–15. "What is to be said of those who are sometimes snatched away by the ecstasy of contemplation, and who are thus able to experience something of the sweetness of heavenly joy?...They, like Mary, have chosen the better part and it shall not be taken away from them. Those who, in the present, hold onto what is not to be taken from them certainly experience what is future. And what is future is happiness, and since happiness and unhappiness cannot coexist, it can be said that when the Spirit allows them to enjoy such happiness, then they enjoy the "freedom which is blessedness" [proper to heaven], even though this is a partial experience, very deficient relative to the full experience and also most rare."

3. Bernard of Clairvaux, *Advent Sermons* 3,3; SBOp 4, 177, 6–16.

4. Beatrice of Nazareth, *The Seven Modes of Love*, Sixth Mode. Translated by M. Casey in *Tjurunga* 50 (1996), p. 78 (lines 347–353).

5. Gertrude of Helfta, *Exercises* 2, 84–85; SChr 127, p. 98. See M. Casey, "Consecrated Chastity: Reflections on a Text of

Gertrude of Helfta," reprinted in *The Undivided Heart* (Peter-sham, Mass.: St. Bede's Publications, 1994), pp. 122–134.

6. Bernard of Clairvaux, *The Steps of Humility and Pride* 18–19, SBOp 3, 30–31.

7. The theme of dread was well treated in Thomas Merton's final finished book, *The Climate of Monastic Prayer* (Cistercian Studies Series 1; Spencer: Cistercian Publications, 1969). This volume was subsequently republished by both Herder and Doubleday under the title *Contemplative Prayer*.

8. Gregory the Great, *Gospel Homilies* 37, 1; PL 76, 1275a.

9. Francis Thompson, *The Hound of Heaven*. The author answers his own objection in the concluding verses of the poem, putting into the mouth of God the following words: "All which I took from thee I did but take, / not for thy harms, / But just that thou might'st seek it in My arms. / All which thy child's mistake / Fancies as lost, I have stored for thee at home: / Rise, clasp My hand, and come."

10. Gregory the Great, *Gospel Homilies* 25, 2; PL 76, 1191a.

11. Gregory the Great, *Gospel Homilies* 11, 2; PL 76, 1118a.

12. Bernard of Clairvaux, *Sermons on the Song of Songs* 85, 13; SBOp 2, 315–316. This was the last sermon in the series that Bernard completed. He died before he finished dictating Sermon 86.

13. Bernard of Clairvaux, *Sermons on the Song of Songs* 69, 1; SBOp 2, 202, 11–12.

14. Bernard of Clairvaux, *Sermons on the Song of Songs* 85, 13; SBOp 2, 316, 8.

15. See M. Casey, *Toward God*, Chapter 14; pp. 160–171. Also, "The Deconstruction of Prayer," *Tjurunga* 51 (1996), pp. 91–102.

16. Translated from Phyllis Hodgson [ed.], *The Cloud of Unknowing and the Book of Privy Counselling* (The Early English Text Society; London: Oxford University Press, 1944), Chapter 34; p. 70.

17. *The Cloud of Unknowing*, Chapter 68; pp. 121–122.

18. Julian of Norwich, *A Book of Showings*, Revelation 14; Chapter 41; pp. 464–465.

19. Bernard of Clairvaux, *Sermons on the Song of Songs* 74, 7; SBOp 2, 243, 28–30.
20. Bernard of Clairvaux, *Sermons on the Song of Songs* 49, 4; SBOp 2, 75, 14–18. Notice that the word translated here as holiness is *iustitia*. Only sometimes in medieval texts is this term appropriately translated by the English equivalent "justice."
21. Isaac of Stella, *Sermons* 4, 10; SChr 130, p. 136.
22. Bernard of Clairvaux, *Sermons on the Song of Songs* 74,5–6; SBOp 2, 242–243.
23. Beatrice of Nazareth, *Seven Modes*, Sixth mode; p. 79 (lines 384–392).

Chapter Nineteen

1. Bernard of Clairvaux, *Sermon for Palm Sunday* 1.1; SBOp 5, 43, 10–13.
2. This is much less than the mention of vast crowds that we note in the other Gospels: Matthew 21:8, 9; Luke 19:37, John 12:12, 17, 18. Matthew says that the whole city was shaken as by an earthquake (Mt 21:10), with everyone wanting to know who Jesus was. John has the Pharisees grumbling, "The [whole] world has gone off after him" (Mt 12:19). With each retelling of the story the crowd gets bigger and their enthusiasm greater, with Luke's Jesus telling his opponents, "If [the disciples] kept quiet, the stones would cry out."
3. *An Essay on Criticism*, line 525.
4. See 1 Samuel 21:1–6; Matthew and Luke omit the reference to Abiathar. In Matthew 23:35 there is a confusion of two Zechariahs. The Zechariah murdered in the narrative of 2 Chronicles 24:20-22 was not the son of Barachiah (Zech 1:1).
5. Elisabeth Kübler-Ross, *On Death and Dying* (New York: Macmillan, 1969), p. 39.
6. Kübler-Ross, *On Death and Dying*, p. 50.

Chapter Twenty

1. See Diane Vaughan, *Uncoupling: How and Why Relationships Come Apart* (London: Methuen, 1987).

2. Bernard of Clairvaux, *Various Sermons* 104, 2; SBOp 6a, 375, 11–15.

3. I devoted a chapter to this in *Toward God*, pp. 134–146. See also *A Guide to Living in the Truth*, pp. 125-140. On this topic see also André Louf, *Grace Can Do More: Spiritual Accompaniment and Spiritual Growth* (Cistercian Studies Series #195; Kalamazoo, Mich.: Cistercian Publications, 2002).

4. Bernard of Clairvaux, *Various Sermons* 40, 6; SBOp 6a, 239–240. In a parallel passage in *Sermons on the Song of Songs* 16, 8; SBOp 1, 94, 11–12, he says that confession must be humble, pure or simple and faith-filled.

5. Bernard of Clairvaux, *Various Sermons* 40, 6; SBOp 6a, 240, 6–12.

6. Bernard of Clairvaux, *Various Sermons* 40, 7; SBOp 6a, 241, 15–16.

7. Helinand of Froidmont, *Fifth Sermon for Palm Sunday*, PL 212, 582B.

Chapter Twenty-One

1. "Nothing equal to the description of Jesus' distress is found in any Jewish or Christian accounts of martyrdom, nor is there anything like it in the announcements of the Passion (the only exception is Luke 12:50). Jesus is portrayed here as one whose suffering is real, and we would completely misunderstand the passage were we to consider Jesus as a Stoic standing aloof from all human suffering and ultimately not affected by it." Eduard Schweizer, *The Good News According to Mark*, translated by Donald H. Madvig (London: S.P.C.K., 1971), p. 311. See also Pierre Benoît, *The Passion and Resurrection of Jesus Christ*, translated by Benet Weatherhead (London: Darton, Longman and Todd, 1969), p. 195: "We should not be afraid to admit Jesus' distress and we certainly should not make his sufferings out to be merely apparent, as though he did not really suffer because he knew what the outcome would be. We must not empty this mystery of its substance by toning it down. Jesus, the Son of God, lived as a man in the fullest sense of the word, and willingly experienced the full tragedy of human death."

2. John of Forde, *Sermons on the Song of Songs* 10:2; CCM 17, pp. 95–96.
3. See, for instance, Birger Gerhardsson, *The Testing of God's Son (Matt 4:11 & Par): An Analysis of an Early Christian Midrash* (Coniectanea Biblica 2; Lund: CWK Gleerup, 1966).
4. Augustine of Hippo, *On Psalm 29* 2, 1; CChr 38, p. 174.

Chapter Twenty-Two

1. Here and elsewhere I am relying on the data collected in *The Compact Oxford English Dictionary* (Oxford: University Press, 1971). Similar developments were occurring in other European languages during the same period.
2. For a definitive philosophic treatment of development see Bernard J. F. Lonergan, *Insight: A Study of Human Understanding* (London: Longmans, Green & Co, 1958), pp. 451–458.
3. See Ian Ker, *John Henry Newman: A Biography* (Oxford: University Press, 1988), pp. 298–318. Interestingly the chapters describing this period in Newman's life are entitled "Crisis" and "Development."
4. See Bernard J. F. Lonergan, *Method in Theology* (London: Darton, Longman & Todd, 1972), pp. 130–132.
5. In a parable that describes the soul's journey towards God, Bernard highlights what we have all experienced: prayer is most difficult when we need it most. "At the onset of such a violent and unforeseen attack from their enemies, they all staggered and reeled like drunkards and all their skill was gone....For a long time a search was made for prayer. So great was the upheaval that it was found only with great difficulty." Bernard of Clairvaux, *Parables* 1, 6; SBOp 6b, 265, 15–22.
6. I have discussed this in "The Deconstruction of Prayer," *Tjurunga* 51 (1996), pp. 91–102.

Chapter Twenty-Three

1. John of Forde, *Sermons on the Song of Songs* 53,7; CCM 17, p. 376.
2. Translated from Julian of Norwich, *A Book of Showings*, Revelation 8, Chapter 16; pp. 358–359.

3. "The cross means rejection and shame as well as suffering." Dietrich Bonhoeffer, *The Cost of Discipleship* (London: SCM Press, 1964), p. 78.

4. The sundering of the temple curtain was considered significant enough to be recorded by all three Synoptic evangelists: Mark 15:38 = Matthew 27:51 = Luke 23:45. Matthew makes it part of a wider cataclysm. In Hebrews 10:20 the curtain hiding the inner mystery is seen as Jesus' flesh; if some symbolism was perceived in the event, it may have been thought to illustrate that the humanity of Jesus no longer concealed his inner mystery; it could break forth. A similar meaning is possible for John 19:30 where the phrase usually translated "he gave up his spirit" can also be rendered in the sense of "he gave out his spirit" in the sense of handing it on; the verb "used" is linked to the noun "tradition."

Chapter Twenty-Four

1. This is one of the themes which Thomas Merton explored in *Inner Experience: Some Notes on Contemplation*, a work, the author insisted, that was never to be published as a book. Happily, this embargo was circumvented. Most of it was serialized in *Cistercian Studies Quarterly* 18 (1983), pp. 3–15, 121–134, 201–216, 289–300; 19 (1984), 62–78, 139–150, 267–282, 336–345. I have discussed this in "Merton's Notes on 'Inner Experience': Twenty Years Afterwards," in *The Undivided Heart: The Western Monastic Approach to Contemplation* (Petersham, Mass.: St. Bede's Publications, 1994), pp. 190–217.

2. Jerome, *Letters* 58, 2; PL 22; 580.

3. As we have seen in Chapter Two, Peter Brown in *The Body and Society* insists on the exact opposite. Ascetical practice is not the rejection of the body but a matter of taking seriously its power to disrupt our personal life if its impulses are not subject to discernment and restraint.

4. The proceedings of a multidisciplinary, multireligious conference held at the Union Theological Seminary in April 1993 demonstrate the breadth of expertise interested in this phenomenon. See Vincent L. Wimbush and Richard Valantasis [ed.] *Asceti-*

cism (New York: Oxford University Press, 1998). The volume is over six hundred pages in length and includes contributions from more than forty authors distinguished in their fields.

5. Aelred of Rievaulx, *Sermon on the "Burdens" of Isaiah (De Oneribus)*, 27; PL 195, 472c.
6. John Cassian, *Conferences* 3, 6; SChr 42, p. 145.
7. Gregory the Great, *Gospel Homilies* 32, 2; PL 76, 1233b.
8. Bernard of Clairvaux, *Sentences* 3.94; SBOp 152.2–8.
9. Gregory the Great, *Gospel Homilies* 32, 2; PL 76, 1233b.
10. *The Interior House*, 14; PL 189, 520c. *The Interior House* is a Cistercian treatise of spiritual anthropology, originating in the late twelfth-century.
11. I have written about different aspects of this in *Toward God*, pp. 133–146, "A Story to Tell," and *A Guide to Living in the Truth*, pp. 125–140, "Radical Self-Honesty."
12. Rule of Saint Benedict (= RB) 5, 7.
13. RB 5, 12.
14. RB 71, 1–2.
15. RB 72, 3–8.
16. RB 5, 12. See also RB 7, 32. On all this see M. Casey, *A Guide to Living in the Truth*, pp. 89–105: "Doing God's Will."
17. The word used is *ephapax*; it occurs in the same sense at Hebrew 7:27 and 9:12; a slightly less intensive form is found three times in Hebrews 9:26–28.
18. Isaac of Stella, *Sermons* 15, 13; SChr 130, p. 290.
19. *Meum proinde meritum, miseratio Domini.* Bernard of Clairvaux, *Sermons on the Song of Songs* 61, 4; SBOp 2, 151, 7–8.
20. William of Saint-Thierry, *On Contemplating God* 12; SChr 61bisp. 112, lines 45–46.
21. William of Saint-Thierry, *Meditative Prayers* 12; PL 180, 233d.
22. John Cassian, *Conferences* 3, 10; SChr 42, p. 154.
23. Translated from Phyllis Hodgson [ed.], *The Cloud of Unknowing and the Book of Privy Counselling* (The Early English Text Society; London: Oxford University Press, 1944), Chapter 24, p. 70.
24. *The Book of Privy Counselling*, Hodgson [ed.], p. 169.

25. Albert Camus, *The Fall*, translated by Justin O'Brien (Harmondsworth: Penguin, 1963), p. 83.

Chapter Twenty-Five

1. In the most important manuscripts, the original Gospel ended at 16:8. This was found so unsatisfactory that in the second century two alternative endings were devised and added. They are considered canonical, but not original.

2. This may take its origin from Jesus' reply to the high priest, "You will see the Son of Man sitting at the right of the Power": Mark 14:62 = Matthew 26:64 = Luke 22:69. The theme is attested in all the major streams of New Testament thought except in the Johannine literature. See Mark 16:19; Acts 2:32, 5:31, 7:55–56; Romans 8:34; Ephesians 1:20; Colossians 3:1; Hebrews 1:3, 8:1, 10:12, 12:2; 1 Peter 3:22.

3. *De indole eschatoligica Ecclesiae peregrinantis eiusque unione cum Ecclesia coelesti.* The most commonly used English translation of the documents has dumbed this down to "The Pilgrim Church."

4. See M. Casey, "Desire and Desires in Western Tradition," in *Desire: To Have or Not to Have* (Canberra: The Humanita Foundation, Occasional Papers No. 2, 2000), pp. 3–31. "Spiritual Desire in the Gospel Homilies of Saint Gregory the Great," CSQ 16 (1981), pp. 297–314. *Athirst for God: Spiritual Desire in Bernard of Clairvaux's Sermons on the Song of Songs* (CSS 77; Kalamazoo, Mich.: Cistercian Publications, 1977).

5. Second Edition, London: S.P.C.K., 1978.

6. The most convenient summary of this usage is Walter Grundmann, *art.* σύνμετά in Gerhard Kittel e.a. [ed.] *Theological Dictionary of the New Testament* (Grand Rapids, Mich.: Eerdmans, 1971), vol. VII, pp. 781–792. Fourteen compound verbs are listed on pp. 786–787.

7. Isaac of Stella, *Sermons* 12, 6; SChr 130, p. 254.

8. Bernard of Clairvaux, *Sermons on the Song of Songs* 33, 6; SBOp 1, 237, 21–25.

Index of Biblical Texts

Index of Authors

Aelred of Rievaulx, 131, 134, 317, 334, 343
Antony of Egypt, 31, 322, 323–324
Apostolic Constitutions, 324
Arnulph of Boheries, 85, 330
Athanasius of Alexandria, 315, 323–324
Augustine of Hippo, 15, 60, 75, 107, 114–115, 126–127, 147, 153, 168, 187–189, 235, 248, 320, 322, 323, 332, 333, 335, 336, 341
Auden, W. H., 330
Austen, Jane, 320

Baldwin of Forde, 78, 323, 330
Baumgartner, Charles, 315
Beatrice of Nazareth, 201, 206, 219, 338, 339
Benedict of Nursia, 124, 297–298, 308, 343
Benoît, Pierre, 341
Bernard of Clairvaux, 3, 35, 82, 83, 106, 109–111, 132–133, 177–178, 198, 205, 207, 209–210, 215, 217–219, 246–247, 290, 312–313, 323, 330, 331, 332, 333, 334, 336, 337–338, 339, 340, 341–342, 343, 344, 345
Bonhoeffer, Dietrich, 342
Bornkamm, Günther, 162, 336
Brown, Peter, 318, 333, 343
Brown, Raymond E., 334
Browning, Robert, 104
Burns, J. Patout, 329

Camus, Albert, 344
Casey, M., 318, 326, 327, 330, 333, 338, 339, 343, 344–345
Cassian, John, 73, 105, 165, 288–289, 325, 327, 331, 343, 344
Catherine of Siena, 321
Churchill, Winston, 139
Claudel, Paul, 107
Cloud of Unknowing, 21, 212–13, 301–302, 320, 344
Council of Trent, 75, 79
Cyril of Alexandria, 315, 317

Daniélou, Jean, 324
Darwin, Charles, 262
Denziger, H., 315
Didache, 324
Dorotheos of Gaza, 147

Evagrius of Pontus, 54, 55–59, 325, 326

Faed Fiada, 151
Fenton, James, 334

Gaggero, Leonard, 322
Galen, 20
Gerhardsson, Birger, 340
Gertrude the Great, 207, 338
Goldng, William, 320
Gospel of Thomas, 331
Gregory the Great, 108–109, 208–209, 289–290, 325, 327, 328, 331, 332, 338, 343, 344
Gregory Nazianzen, 318
Gregory of Nyssa, 324
Grundmann, Walter, 345